An Historical Survey
of
SOUTHERN SHEDS

Barnstaple Junction engine shed and turntable.
British Rail

An Historical Survey
of
SOUTHERN SHEDS

by
Chris Hawkins and George Reeve

OPC

Oxford Publishing Co

First published 1979
Reprinted 2001

ISBN 0 86093 020 3

Published by Oxford Publishing Co

an imprint of Ian Allan Publishing Ltd,
Hersham, Surrey KT12 4RG.
Printed by Ian Allan Printing Ltd,
Hersham, Surrey KT12 4RG.

Code: 0107/A

Acknowledgements

Assistance in a book of this kind comes from dozens of people in various forms and at
different times. All contributions major and minor were essential and invaluable and
accordingly we would like to acknowledge these people for their help.

We would particularly like to thank Stephen Townroe for allowing us the benefit of his
detailed knowledge and kind advice, Reg Randell of British Rail, Ted 'Smokey' Crawforth
and Dick Riley for their interest and help and Beverly Cook for the many hours spent
typing the manuscript.

We would also like to thank for their help, assistance and encouragement: Bluebell
Railway Company; staff of the British Museum Map Room, in particular George Meredew
and Douglas Brookman; British Rail staff at Bricklayers Arms, Hither Green, Slade Green,
Southampton, Stewarts Lane and Torrington; British Transport Docks Board, Southamp-
ton; Decca Radio and T.V. Ltd., Devon County Library; Dorset County Library; IPC
Printers Ltd., Kent County Library; Merchant Navy Preservation Society; National Rail-
way Museum, York; Linda Miller; Dave Newman, British Rail; Ivo Peters; Photographers
at Birkbeck College, Malcolm Hobbs, Ed Cory and Andy Hilton; staff of the Public
Records Office; Public Relations Officers of Southern Region and Western Region British
Rail; South Eastern Steam Centre; Railway Correspondence and Travel Society, who we
acknowledge for the use of the 1947 allocation list; C.D. Read, British Rail; staff of the
University of London Senate House Map Room and Library, particularly Ross Wollard;
Swanage Railway Society; staff of the Tate Library, Brixton, Chris Unwin; Derek Virtue.

Contents

Introduction

The 'Southern Sheds' of this book are those locomotive depots operated by the Southern Railway during its existence from 1923 to 1947. They underwent considerable change between the grouping of 1923 and nationalization in 1947 and many depots in existence at the beginning had disappeared within a few years. New ones were built during the period while others closed or changed in status. Most sites that at some time were in recognised use as 'sheds' or 'depots' have been included in this book. A completely definitive list is not available for the whole period but there is little doubt that virtually all places deserving such a title have been noted in this account.

The sheds are listed as they were at the end of the Southern's existence in 1947. For the sake of continuity, where depots were straightforward replacements or reconstructions, details of the early buildings have also been included. Other sheds closed between 1923 and 1947 are listed in a separate section.

The authors have set out to give a detailed picture of these sheds, their origins and histories, with details of construction, layout and the type of duties and locomotives they were responsible for. The histories complement scale plans of the depots and their adjacent areas. These have all been verified and, in the main, depict the sheds in Southern Railway days. Most of the diagrams are based on second and third edition O.S. maps, mainly from the period 1890-1920, brought up to date using British Railways line surveys, photographs, written descriptions, various other published plans, and actual site measurements and surveys by the authors. Where possible, period photographs of the buildings have also been obtained.

The sheds concerned were never all in use simultaneously and in addition codes and status also varied throughout the period. The sheds therefore appear in alphabetical order rather than in operating divisions, etc.

Southern Railway Engine Sheds 1947

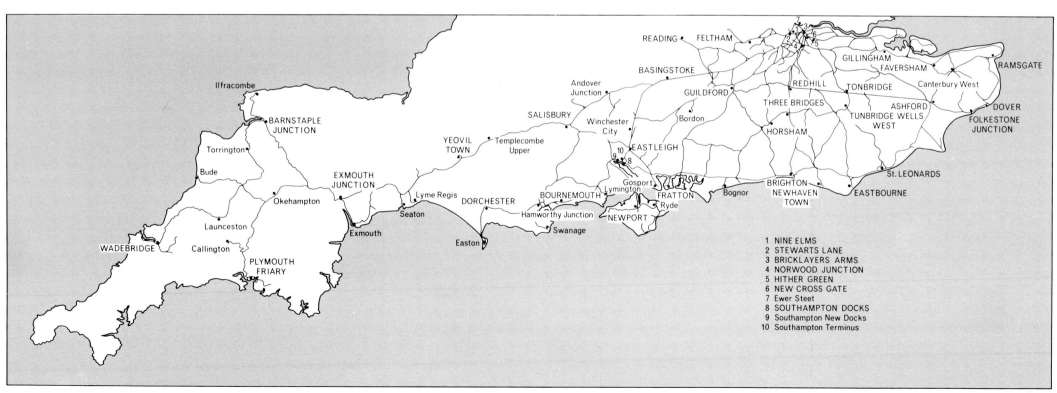

1 NINE ELMS
2 STEWARTS LANE
3 BRICKLAYERS ARMS
4 NORWOOD JUNCTION
5 HITHER GREEN
6 NEW CROSS GATE
7 Ewer Steet
8 SOUTHAMPTON DOCKS
9 Southampton New Docks
10 Southampton Terminus

In the Southern Railway organization the running of locomotives in service, together with the engine crews and maintenance staff, were contained within a separate Locomotive Running Department. It was composed of a variety of Locomotive Depots or Running Sheds, the terms being interchangeable. Roughly, they fell into three main groups:—

(i) the premier depots, so rated because of numbers of staff and/or locomotives allocated and importance of the traffic worked. Each of these were under the control of a Locomotive Running Shed Superintendent, and were Ashford, Bricklayers Arms, Eastleigh, Exmouth Junction, Nine Elms and Stewarts Lane;

(ii) moderately important depots under the control of Locomotive Foremen, a leftover title from the earliest days of the railway, belieing their high qualifications and status. BR later altered the title to 'Shedmaster';

(iii) small sheds where a few locos were stabled and several men usually living locally signed on and off duty. Repairs and washouts were carried out at the parent depot, which was also responsible for paperwork, etc.

Much has already been published on the actual working of a steam locomotive depot, books by a number of authors fully describing the servicing and repair work carried out. Devotion and skill at the 'loco' was commonplace but no amount of romanticising can disguise the fact that much of the work was hard, unpleasant and dirty. The eventual extinction of the steam shed is perhaps significant testimony of this. Nevertheless, much affection remains for the unique atmosphere and 'feel' of the engine shed, amongst railwaymen and enthusiasts alike, and although this book relates only to the Southern we hope it will find a welcome amongst enthusiasts, modellers and railwaymen in general as well as those particularly interested in the Southern Railway.

The Southern Railway divided naturally into major divisions derived from its three main constituent companies, the London and South Western Railway, the London Brighton and South Coast Railway and the South Eastern and Chatham Railway. Generally speaking, a certain family resemblance in building style, etc. could be detected amongst the engine sheds of each individual company.

The LSWR had gone in for large, well-equipped depots at strategic points and had in the years up to 1923 carried out a number of major new projects. New secondary sheds, for instance, had been built at Andover and Basingstoke just after the turn of the century, and new hydraulic coaling apparatus had been installed at a number of locations. A new shed was built at Eastleigh and a large new depot had been constructed at Salisbury, a key point on the West of England main line. It was provided with modern lighting, a high capacity coal stage and the rare 'luxury' of an enginemen's dormitory. By the time the grouping took place, another carefully planned and laid out depot was nearing completion at Feltham, and further plans had been approved for a modern replacement to the decrepit shed at Exmouth Junction. This eleventh-hour provision of new large sheds with well-equipped workshops was an attempt to remedy a situation found on all three constituent companies. Workshop facilities at sheds were only elementary prior to 1923, for the reason that most of them were not far from the main workshops at Eastleigh, Ashford and Brighton — locos could either run light to the works or parts be sent for attention. While this policy had some advantages, it meant engines were often out of service for weeks instead of days, and the beginnings of a change of policy can be seen in the planning of Exmouth Junction and Feltham. Improved repair shops were subsequently provided at most new Southern sheds.

To the east, and something of a contrast, was the LBSCR system. This was a smaller railway and its policy towards the accommodation of its engines and staff could hardly, perhaps, be described as progressive. The depots were generally small, often with cramped and awkward layouts. Lack of large-scale rebuilding often meant that important depots had expanded into unsuitable, constricted sites leaving little scope for expansion and improvement. There was little possibility of grand scale clearances and rebuilding on the lines of Salisbury or Exmouth Junction. Brighton was typical of this situation, squeezed into a fork in the lines north of the station, with every square inch of space occupied.

The main London depots were little luckier; New Cross Gate was a rambling, confused collection of buildings and the Battersea Park roundhouses were built against and under adjacent viaducts. Eastbourne was a praiseworthy exception, however, being an excellently laid out shed, with good facilities and room for expansion. If suitable alternative sites had existed on the system perhaps the story may have been repeated. Roundhouses seemed to find greater favour on the 'Brighton' than on its two main neighbours; it shared such a building at Fratton with the LSWR and three were in use at Battersea Park. A semi-circular open building had also been built at Horsham very similar in design to the second depot at Eastbourne. Coaling, even at major depots like Brighton and St. Leonards tended to be carried out from wagons using a small crane.

The story of the SECR provided a foretaste of what was to take place on the Southern in the coming years. Two constituent companies, the South Eastern Railway and the London Chatham and Dover Railway had amalgamated in 1899 and since then a number of developments had occurred in the motive power department. Duplicated sheds in many towns had been closed down and maintenance concentrated at the more suitable depot, as at Ashford and Dover, while new sheds had also been constructed. To improve services in and out of London, new depots were built at Orpington and Slade Green enabling the closure of much older unsuitable buildings at places like Deptford and Woolwich. Slade Green was a huge depot on the outskirts of London with 10 roads, and turntables installed at each end of a through building, but Orpington was a much smaller, more conventional two road shed. After the initial burst of closures and new building at the turn of the century, however, little development seems to have taken place and the twenty or so main depots on the system remained much the same until the Southern was founded in 1923.

The Southern, on taking over this somewhat mixed bag in 1923, embarked on a praiseworthy attempt, up until the outbreak of war that is, to bring about some measure of modernization in its motive power department. Over thirty closures took place within the first ten years, partly because of electrification but mainly as part of a continuing rationalization process. This was principally to be seen in the south of England around London where electrification was concentrated and the web of often duplicated routes was most open to economies in operating procedure. The management inherited the nearly completed ferro-concrete buildings at Feltham and decided to continue with the construction of the LSWR's proposed new depot, of similar design, at Exmouth Junction. Several large new sheds followed in the 1920s and early 1930s, broadly similar concrete buildings replacing antiquated ones at Dover and Ashford.

Two completely new sheds primarily intended to facilitate freight workings to and from nearby yards were constructed at Hither Green and Norwood Junction, both enabling

SER shed at Ashford, 1928.   *H.C. Casserley*

Dorchester in 1938.   *S.C. Townroe*

considerable operating economies to be made.

Improvements, vast in scope and in some cases resulting in virtually completely new sheds, were carried out at other locations throughout the system. The depots at Bricklayers Arms and Stewarts Lane were transformed out of all recognition and Bournemouth was drastically altered to improve turnround and maintenance facilities. The track layout and services at Redhill and Reading underwent considerable improvement.

In addition to all this, lesser alterations were being made all over the system. Few steam locomotive sheds in Britain kept their original roofs throughout their existence and those on the Southern were no exception. Because of the nature of the machines housed beneath them they were highly susceptible to damage, corrosion or fire and many shed roofs on the Southern were life-expired and decrepit.

The asbestos sheeting which was to become the standard roofing material seems first to have been installed, on any large scale that is, at Bricklayers Arms in the 1930s. The programme was interrupted in 1939 but BR continued to install the roofs, the asbestos sheeting being supported on a steel framework. St. Leonards, Faversham and Tonbridge all received roofs after the war, with brick gables, but the more common all-asbestos version appeared at a number of other sites, such as Tunbridge Wells West and Guildford.

Water softening apparatus was provided at a number of sites by the Southern and this was a considerable advantage at many depots. Several had existed on the pre-Grouping companies but under the Southern this useful item of equipment became virtually standard, at a number of stations as well as the more important sheds.

A few of the smaller, more remote sheds also benefited under the Southern. A brand new structure arose at Ryde, on the Isle of Wight, utilising redundant LBSCR electrification gantries, and brand new sheds appeared at Ilfracombe, Seaton and Exmouth, although the first two were probably reluctant rebuilds necessary after station expansion. Generally speaking, however, small country depots remained untouched.

Perhaps the most significant engineering development, however, of the Southern era was the extensive electrification programmes carried out between the Grouping and the outbreak of World War II. The Southern enthusiastically continued the schemes of the LBSCR and the LSWR and the third rail system spread rapidly throughout London and the south leading to the closure of numerous sheds in the area, both large and small. Strawberry Hill and Slade Green, both major depots, were converted to EMU maintenance (and are still in use today) and smaller sheds at Epsom, Littlehampton, Cannon Street, Maidstone, Leatherhead, Purley and Orpington among others were closed. Some of these had been open barely twenty years. Electrification did have an important adverse effect on the locomotive depots however — the staff and management in the 'thirties confidently expected complete coverage of the system with third rail, and the drawbacks and shortcomings at many of the depots would not have to be endured for long. This had the effect of starving investment in repairs and equipment at many sheds and despite the advances made by new building at many locations it was obvious by 1935 that many depots cried out for modernization. This drove the Running Department to acquire redundant Works machinery, earning itself the nickname 'The Cinderella Department'!

The war called an abrupt halt to any further electrification developments, the Southern finding itself in the front line of the Battle of Britain, with many installations, including engine sheds, suffering damage. Even fairly small sheds at Canterbury West and Tunbridge Wells West sustained bomb damage while larger sheds received direct hits during the indiscriminate bombing of towns and cities. Plymouth Friary, Bricklayers Arms, Nine

Bomb damage at Nine Elms, 1940.   *S.C. Townroe*

methods were relatively crude at some of the larger sheds. Normal servicing procedures such as washing out were not made any easier and workshop facilities were still poor. Turntables were often small and in need of replacement — this made the balancing of locomotives difficult and the task of turning them more time-consuming and wearisome than it needed to be.

Much of the damage sustained during the war was never made good, as for instance at Nine Elms and Eastbourne, but despite the money shortage and the uncertainty prior to nationalization, some advances began to be made. Although pre-war schemes to re-construct Bournemouth shed inside the Branksome triangle and to replace Nine Elms were never revived, the run-down of the old sheds at New Cross Gate continued and power operated 70 ft. turntables began appearing at strategic points on the network. The Southern had attempted at least a measure of recovery in the last months of its existence.

Nationalization did not at first affect the 'Southern Sheds' of this book, the majority of those taken over by British Railways surviving in a gradually deteriorating condition until the mass closures of the 1960s. Some received the standard asbestos roofs and attempts were made to improve servicing with replacement turntables and other items of equipment. Alterations were made to Fratton and Exmouth Junction as part of the great oil-firing débâcle of 1946-47 but operating and working conditions remained generally grim, helping to ensure that the steam locomotive depot eventually passed into oblivion. Money for modernization of the sheds, essential if steam operation was to be maintained at the same level of efficiency as other forms of traction, was particularly hard to come by after the announcement of the Modernization Plan of 1955. It became virtually non-existent after 1960.

Gradual dieselisation throughout the 1950s, the steady loss of freight work and line closures led to the run-down of many sheds, while large electrification projects like the Kent Coast scheme turned the closure trickle of the 1950s into a torrent in the 1960s. Formerly prestigious depots like Ramsgate, Dover and Bricklayers Arms were closed early in the decade or converted for other use, Gillingham and Faversham lost their engines and the new depot at Ashford, by this time decrepit and dangerous, followed soon after.

The increasing pace of dieselisation eliminated steam from the Central section during the next two or three years, sheds like Horsham and Brighton closing completely, with the West Country depots, transferred to the Western Region some years previously, succumbing soon after.

The truncated SW section out of Waterloo remained the last stronghold of steam in the south of England and sheds like Bournemouth, Salisbury and Nine Elms probably became the most visited and photographed 'Southern Sheds' ever. The last half dozen survivors finally closed, little changed since the war, in 1967 and a type of building synonymous with the steam railway for well over a hundred years and beloved of enthusiasts had all but disappeared entirely.

Chris Hawkins
George Reeve

Elms and Stewarts Lane all suffered extensive damage in this way. Eastbourne received particularly heavy damage while Exmouth Junction was actually machine-gunned from the air! Some of the more vulnerable depots in Kent and Sussex were virtually transferred, men, engines and equipment, to more secure inland sites like Ashford and Guildford. Keeping depots functioning 24 hours a day with bombing, the blackout and staff short of food and sleep was a tremendous task. Superintendents and foremen at the worst-hit sheds were later awarded the British Empire Medal.

By the time nationalization came in 1947 the sheds of the Southern Railway must have had a somewhat ragged look about them. Although some great advances had been made, shortage of money and the outbreak of the war had meant that many overdue modifications had not been carried out. Many shed buildings were ill-lit and shabbily kept, decent facilities for crews and shed staff were often non-existent and any kind of modern aid to ash disposal was rare. Curiously, the Factories Act of 1937, which made staff amenities mandatory, contained a clause excluding engine sheds from its provisions. Coaling

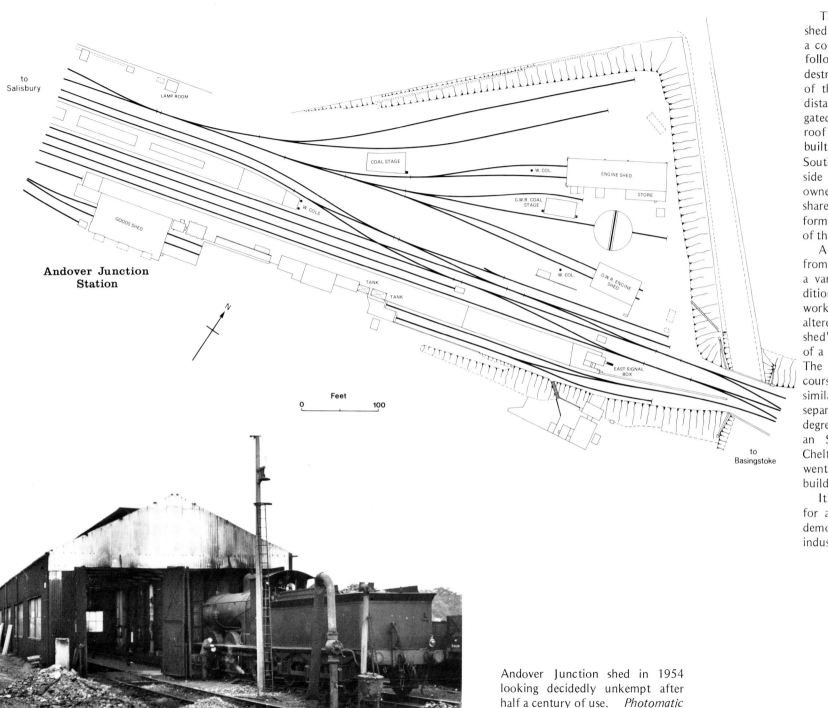

to
Salisbury

LAMP ROOM

COAL STAGE

W. COL.

ENGINE SHED

STORE

W. COLS

G.W.R. COAL
STAGE

GOODS SHED

**Andover Junction
Station**

N

W. COL.

G.W.R. ENGINE
SHED

TANK

TANK

Feet

0   100

EAST SIGNAL
BOX

to
Basingstoke

Andover Junction shed in 1954
looking decidedly unkempt after
half a century of use.   *Photomatic*

The construction of this small two road
shed was authorised by the LSWR in 1903 at
a cost of £2,550 and was completed in the
following year. It replaced a smaller building
destroyed by fire in 1899, sited in the fork
of the main and Southampton lines some
distance to the east. Constructed in corrugated iron on steel framing, with a pitched
roof in similar material, the new shed was
built alongside the former Midland and
South Western Junction shed at the north
side of the station. The 50 ft. turntable,
owned by the MSWJR, was subsequently
shared by the LSW. A separate coaling platform was provided in the south western part
of the yard.

A handful of engines were outstationed
from Eastleigh, the parent depot, for working
a variety of turns to Southampton, in addition to local shunting and pick-up freight
work. This arrangement remained little
altered through the sixty or so years of the
shed's existence, apart from the substitution
of a BR 2-6-2T for an M7 in the mid-'fifties.
The most interesting feature at Andover of
course was the close proximity of two very
similar sheds, the GWR and SR, running as
separate units even into BR days. Some
degree of unified working occurred, however,
an SR 'U' 2-6-0 regularly working to
Cheltenham after 1948. The ex-GWR shed
went out of use in 1958 with the ex-SR
building closing in 1962.

It is believed that the buildings survived
for a few years, but they have now been
demolished and the site given over to
industrial development.

Andover Junction
1930

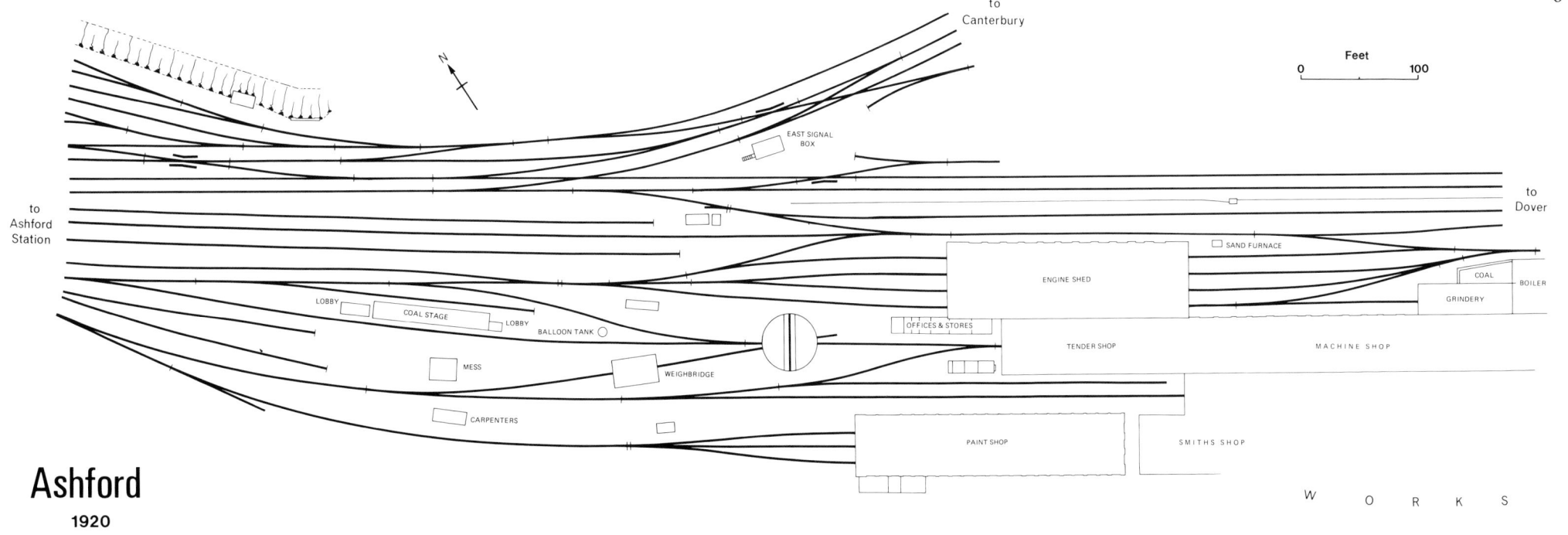

to
Canterbury

to
Dover

to
Ashford
Station

EAST SIGNAL
BOX

SAND FURNACE

ENGINE SHED

COAL

BOILER

GRINDERY

LOBBY

COAL STAGE

LOBBY

BALLOON TANK

OFFICES & STORES

TENDER SHOP

MACHINE SHOP

MESS

WEIGHBRIDGE

CARPENTERS

PAINT SHOP

SMITHS SHOP

W   O   R   K   S

Ashford
1920

Feet
0   100

The Southern Railway built a large modern depot at Ashford in the early 'thirties to replace an ex-SER building inconveniently sited alongside the works. This earlier structure dated from the first days of the South Eastern at Ashford and was built in brick with a slated pitched roof.

After 1899 the small LCDR shed in the town was closed and its duties transferred to Ashford SER depot. Estimates were obtained in that year for 'a new engine shed' in the works presumably to accommodate the extra locomotives, but no contract was let and the original building was retained, although a tender shop was later built alongside.

Situated at one of the principal junctions of the SECR, the depot was responsible for a variety of duties, passenger and freight, all over Kent and the adjoining counties, as well as shunting in and around the works. These were powered by an allocation of around fifty engines, 'C' and 'O1' 0-6-0s, 'H' tanks, and 4-4-0 passenger types. Engines were also provided for the sub sheds at Canterbury West, Maidstone and Sandgate, the latter closing before the Grouping.

A new depot to replace the cramped building in the works was recommended in 1927 at a cost of over £81,000, to provide not only improved servicing and repair facilities but to enable various improvements in the works yard. The new ten-road shed opened in 1931, built in concrete with a northlight pattern roof, and assumed all the duties and varied locomotives of its predecessor. A covered coal stage was provided on the north side and a 65 ft. turntable was installed in the yard.

Despite damage by German bombs on several occasions during the war, the depot survived to become an important Southern Region shed, and during the 'fifties various BR standard locos arrived to augment the fleet of ex-SECR and SR engines. The sub sheds at Maidstone East and West had been closed before the war and the surviving sub shed, Canterbury West, closed in the early 'fifties, although locos continued to be supplied for assorted pilot duties at these places. For a brief period in 1961 engines were supplied to a temporary servicing depot at Margate.

The Kent Coast and other electrification projects, with dieselisation and closures throughout the county led to a gradual run down of the shed and in 1963 it closed to steam, the crumbling roof later being partially removed. Diesels were serviced at the shed for a few years but even this ceased in 1968. It is now the home of the South Eastern Steam Centre and many of the facilities, although awaiting restoration, may be inspected.

The original shed at Ashford adjacent to the works in 1901.
Collection of W. Palmer

Ashford

1945

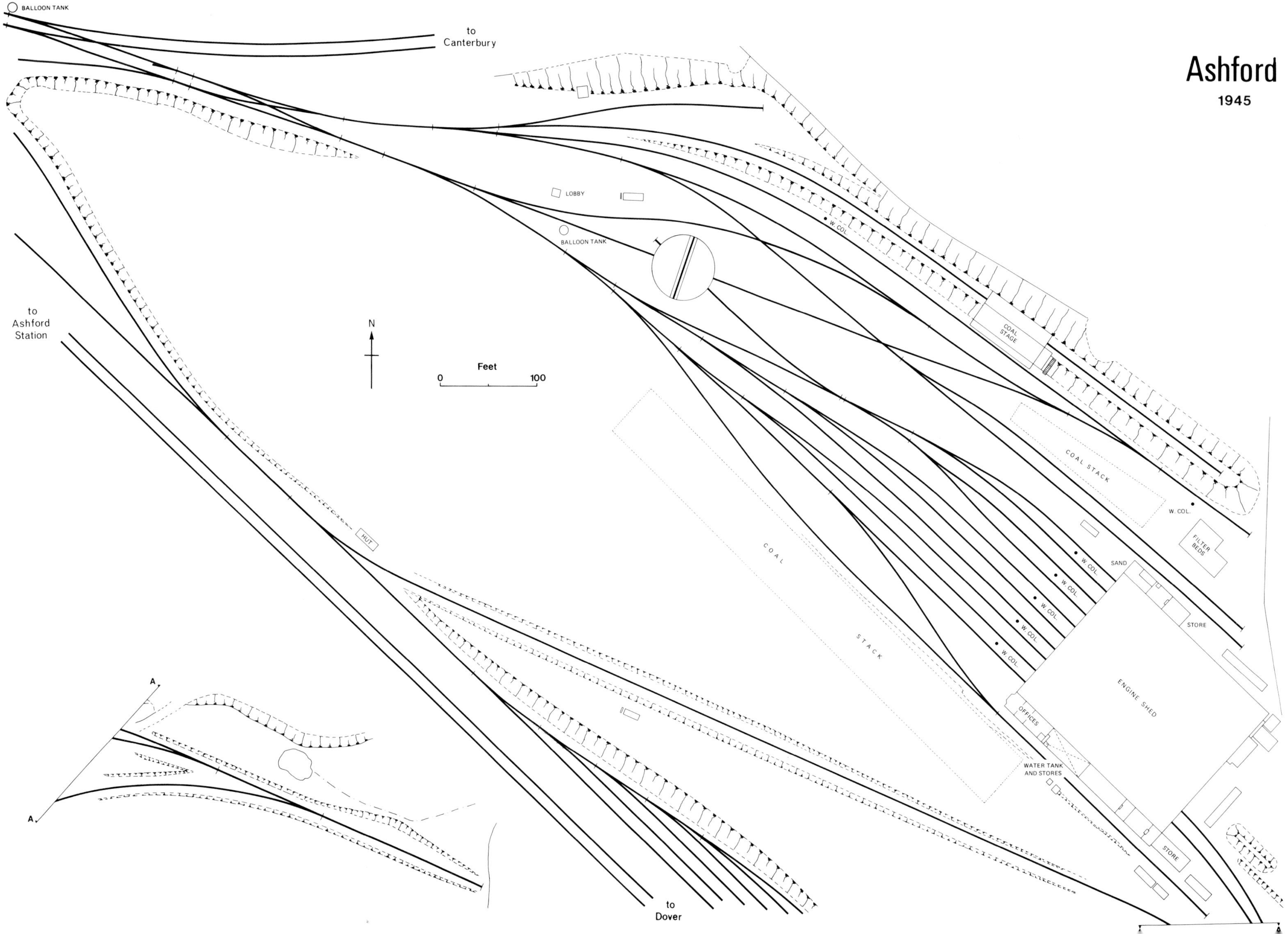

BALLOON TANK

to
Canterbury

to
Ashford
Station

LOBBY

BALLOON TANK

W. COL.

N

Feet

0   100

HUT

COAL STACK

COAL

STACK

W. COL.

W. COL.

SAND

W. COL.

W. COL.

W. COL.

COAL
STAGE

COAL STACK

FILTER
BEDS

STORE

ENGINE SHED

OFFICES

WATER TANK
AND STORES

STORE

A

A

to
Dover

Front Elevation

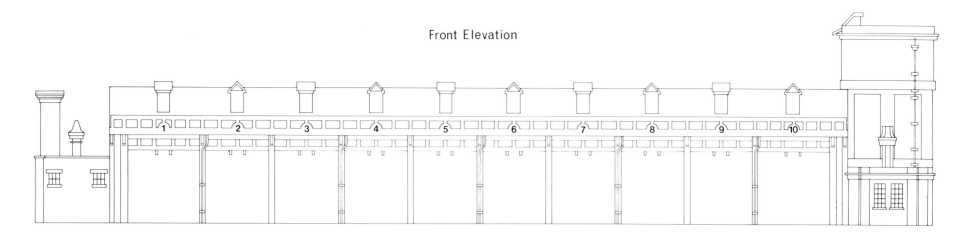

The shed in 1939.

Lens of Sutton

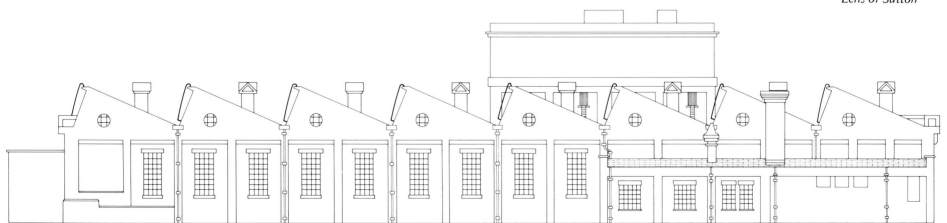

Side Elevation

The new shed, as originally constructed

9

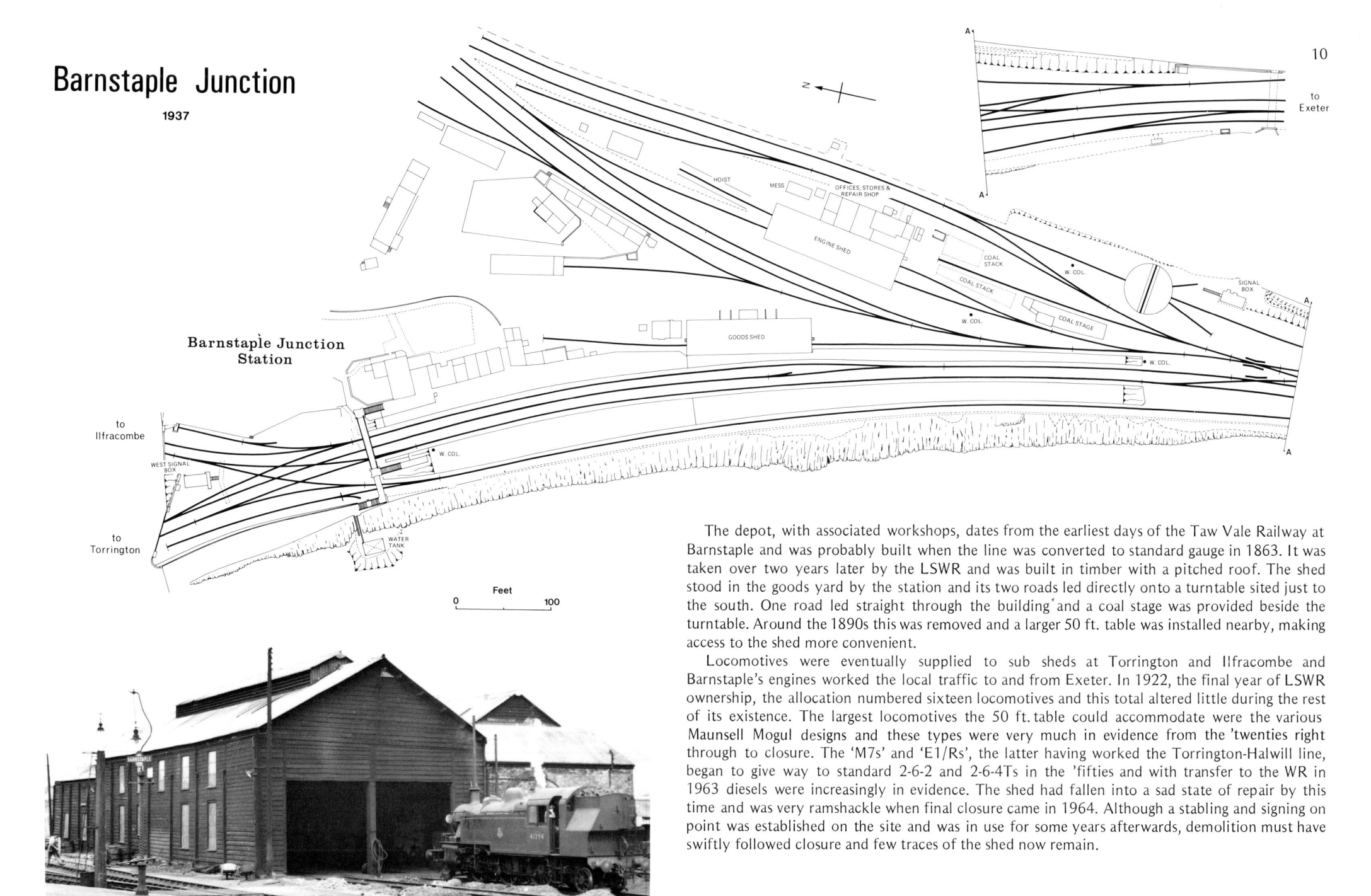

Barnstaple Junction

1937

to Exeter

HOIST

MESS

OFFICES, STORES & REPAIR SHOP

ENGINE SHED

COAL STACK

COAL STACK

W. COL.

W. COL.

COAL STAGE

SIGNAL BOX

Barnstaple Junction Station

GOODS SHED

W. COL.

W. COL.

to Ilfracombe

WEST SIGNAL BOX

W. COL.

to Torrington

WATER TANK

Feet

0   100

The depot, with associated workshops, dates from the earliest days of the Taw Vale Railway at Barnstaple and was probably built when the line was converted to standard gauge in 1863. It was taken over two years later by the LSWR and was built in timber with a pitched roof. The shed stood in the goods yard by the station and its two roads led directly onto a turntable sited just to the south. One road led straight through the building and a coal stage was provided beside the turntable. Around the 1890s this was removed and a larger 50 ft. table was installed nearby, making access to the shed more convenient.

Locomotives were eventually supplied to sub sheds at Torrington and Ilfracombe and Barnstaple's engines worked the local traffic to and from Exeter. In 1922, the final year of LSWR ownership, the allocation numbered sixteen locomotives and this total altered little during the rest of its existence. The largest locomotives the 50 ft. table could accommodate were the various Maunsell Mogul designs and these types were very much in evidence from the 'twenties right through to closure. The 'M7s' and 'E1/Rs', the latter having worked the Torrington-Halwill line, began to give way to standard 2-6-2 and 2-6-4Ts in the 'fifties and with transfer to the WR in 1963 diesels were increasingly in evidence. The shed had fallen into a sad state of repair by this time and was very ramshackle when final closure came in 1964. Although a stabling and signing on point was established on the site and was in use for some years afterwards, demolition must have swiftly followed closure and few traces of the shed now remain.

The shed in 1957.   *Ken Fairey*

50 ft. turntable with coal stage and
ramshackle shed in the background.
R.C. Riley

Top Right
Virtually roofless in 1964.
J. Aston

The shed in Southern days.
British Rail

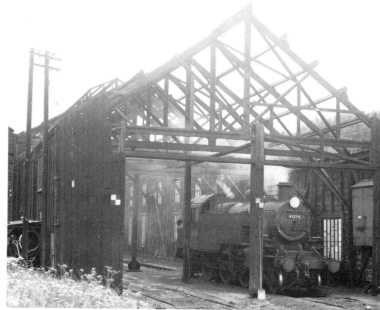

Opened by the LSWR in 1905 as part of a general station area improvement scheme, the shed was sited to the west of Basingstoke station. It was a three road single-ended building constructed in brick with a slated pitched roof. A 55 ft. turntable sited at the north side of the shed was replaced in 1943 by a larger 70 ft. table further down the yard, the twin coal stages giving way to a canopied stage at the same time.

The depot originated as a servicing point on a busy freight junction and its own allocation of around twenty engines was responsible for various secondary duties, shunting, as well as semi-fast trains to Waterloo and Salisbury. The shed was notable for having a spare loco in steam at all times, similar to the more well-known LNER arrangement at Grantham. An Adams 'Highflyer' 4-4-0 was the usual stand-by in the 'twenties and 'thirties to rescue cripples on the main line. The shed also covered work on the erstwhile Basingstoke-Alton branch and the staff helped in the film 'Oh! Mr. Porter', part of which was shot on the old line.

The nearby ex-GWR shed closed in 1950 and visiting locomotives were subsequently serviced at Basingstoke which remained something of a steam outpost well into the 1960s, BR standard 4-6-0s and 2-6-0s being the usual engines by that time. The shed was officially regarded as a stabling point during the last few years of its existence, although it remained as busy as ever. Finally closing with the end of steam in 1967, it was completely demolished two years later.

Basingstoke

1946

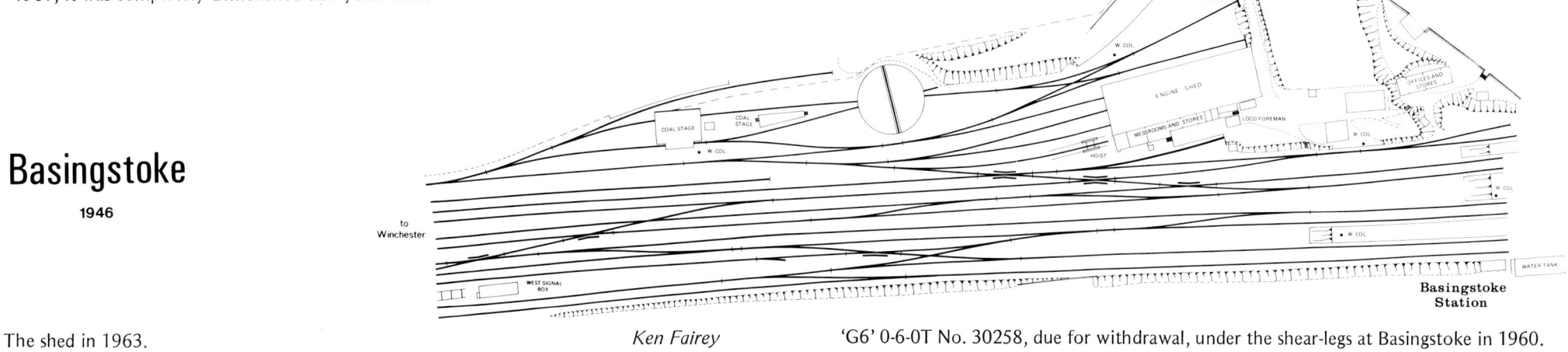

The shed in 1963.

Ken Fairey

'G6' 0-6-0T No. 30258, due for withdrawal, under the shear-legs at Basingstoke in 1960.
E. Crawforth

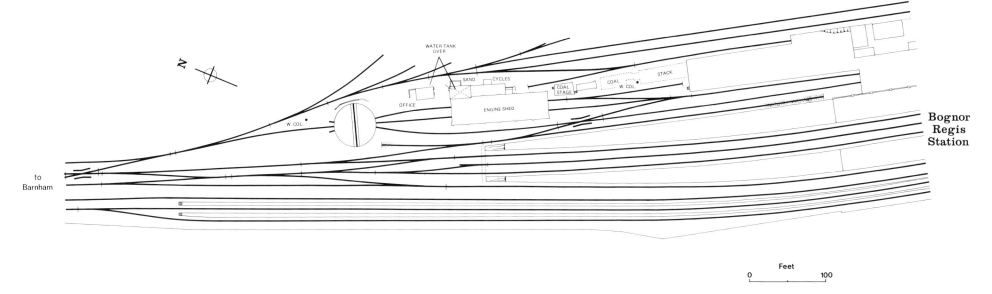

WATER TANK OVER

SAND   CYCLES

OFFICE

COAL STAGE

COAL W. COL.

STACK

ENGINE SHED

W. COL.

**Bognor
Regis
Station**

to
Barnham

Feet
0   100

Bognor

1939

Bognor shed in 1935.

W.A. Camwell

The original shed at Bognor was a small two road wooden building dating from the opening of the new branch in the 1860s, but this was replaced by a new depot opened by the LBSCR in 1903. The later building was constructed in brick and was of the through type with a slated transverse pitched roof. The two roads led on to a 55 ft. turntable and when first opened the depot was sub to Horsham. It was the home of a number of Brighton Atlantics for many years and the total allocation averaged around fifteen to twenty locomotives, a high number which resulted in its eventual independence from the parent depot in the 1920s. Some new office accommodation was acquired around the same time, replacing an old van previously used for the purpose!

The 'Portsmouth No. 2' electrification project inaugurated in July 1938 led to the closure of the sub shed at Littlehampton and the loss of steam passenger duties much reduced the importance of Bognor shed. It reverted to a sub of Horsham in 1941 and declined still further with dieselisation after the war. It finally closed in 1953, but visiting engines continued to use the yard until 1958 when it was taken over by the Traffic Department. The shed building itself had been largely demolished in 1956 and now only the east wall with its offices remains.

13

The dilapidated shed in 1938.
W.A. Camwell

This small LSWR shed opened when the line was completed in 1905, and was a typical end-of-line engine shed, a single road terminal building with a nearby water tower. It was built in corrugated iron on steel framework with a pitched roof and offices and stores adjoining the entrance. It was later enlarged and a coal stage and additional siding provided. A turntable was proposed on the opening of the line but was never installed, although a site was prepared, a few yards to the west of the signal box.

The shed does not even appear on a LSWR shed list of 1922 but the facilities were required for visiting locos handling military traffic. In addition the branch engine, usually an 'M7' 0-4-4T, was housed between trips. However, the shed survived though apparently little-used, until 1951 when it was finally abandoned and shortly afterwards demolished. Although the siding and water tower remained for a number of years, probably until the branch closed completely in 1966, no trace now exists of the shed.

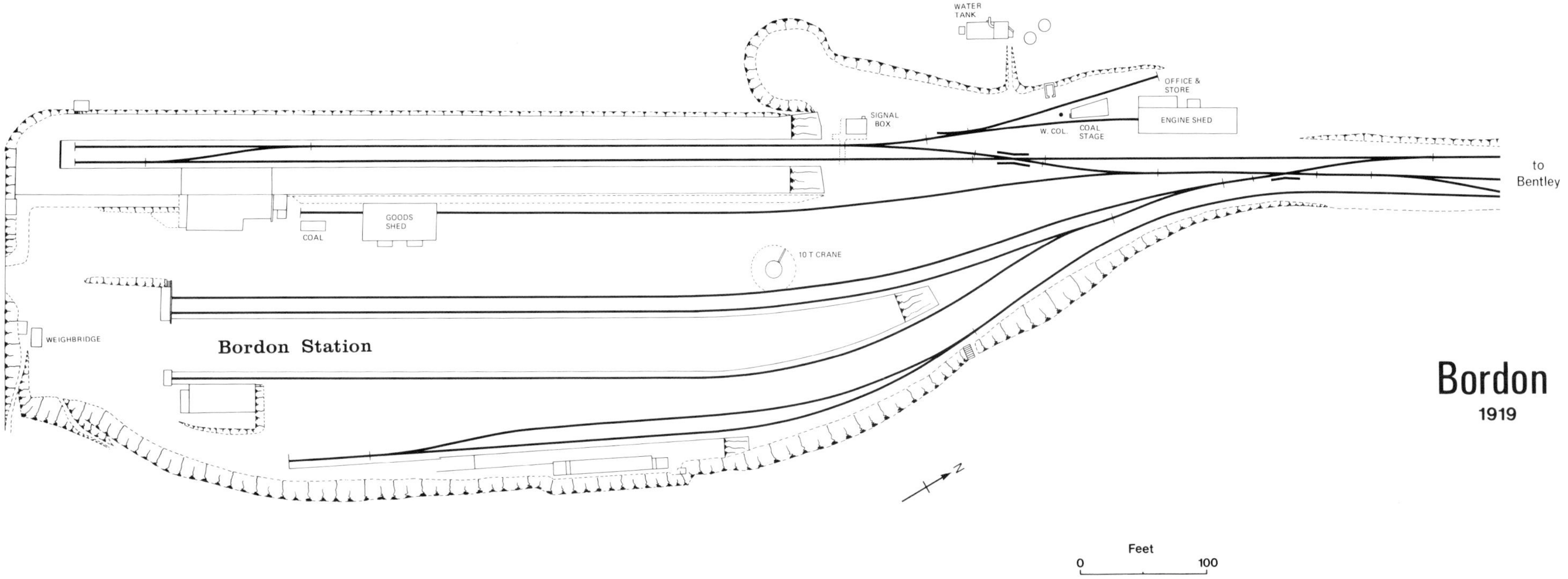

WATER TANK

SIGNAL BOX

OFFICE & STORE

W. COL.

COAL STAGE

ENGINE SHED

to Bentley

COAL

GOODS SHED

10 T CRANE

WEIGHBRIDGE

Bordon Station

Bordon
1919

Feet
0   100

The depot at Bournemouth dated from the mid-1930s when the Southern completely remodelled the old LSWR shed. It stood on slightly raised ground just to the west of the station and although a great improvement on the original shed, it continued to suffer from a somewhat cramped site.

The railway arrived rather late in Bournemouth and the first locomotive building dates from the opening of the station by the LSWR in 1885. Eventually two shed buildings were in use, separated by a 50 ft. turntable and a coal platform, the larger more westerly shed being the later building authorised in 1887. It was at this time that the first proposals to move the depot out to Bournemouth West were discussed, and in 1908 approval was actually granted to construct a large new depot inside the Branksome triangle, an idea still being put forward just prior to the outbreak of the Second World War!

By 1923 the depot, built in brick with a pitched slated roof, despite its cramped awkward site, housed nearly forty locomotives of all types, including express engines for the Waterloo workings, and was responsible for sub sheds at Swanage and Hamworthy Junction. The small three road shed had disappeared by this time, but the allocation rose under the Southern, a batch of 'King Arthurs' arriving in 1925 and at times, in the 'thirties, nearly fifty engines were dealt with at the depot. Shortly before the grouping the LSWR had extended three roads at the rear of the shed and in 1926 the Branksome triangle proposal surfaced once again, only to be eventually abandoned after a number of years in favour of improving the existing shed. A new 50 ton hoist had been approved in 1926 and general improvement work began in 1936. A larger 65 ft. turntable was installed, the shed was extended and extra pits were constructed in a rearranged yard. The old coal platform was demolished and an electric crane provided. Alterations were complete when the water softener was brought into use in 1938. A new roof, in asbestos on steel framing, was added by BR after the war.

After the war and throughout the rest of its history Bournemouth continued as an important depot with a number of express engines, culminating in the Bulleid Pacifics, among its allocation and many BR standard locomotives were shedded there in the later days. Hamworthy Junction closed in 1954 but was replaced as a sub shed when Dorchester was down-graded the following year. The depot lasted in its 1938 condition virtually unchanged till the end of steam, its remaining express locos producing some notable 'last flings' shortly before closure in July 1967, but the site was shortly afterwards cleared and few traces of the buildings and yard now remain.

A 1959 view with BR steel and asbestos roof, water softener, etc.

John Meredith

Bournemouth
1947

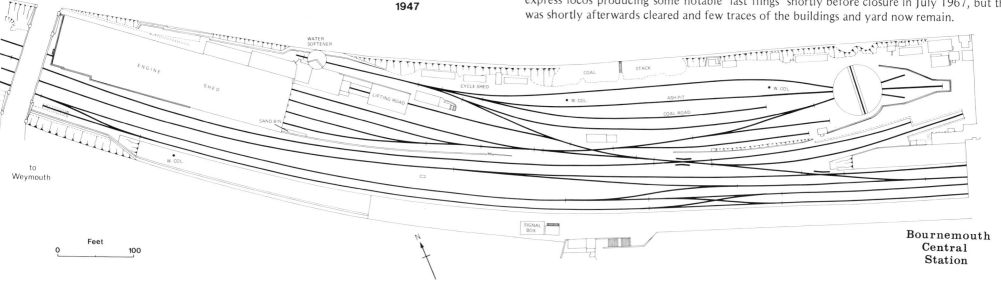

to Weymouth

Feet
0   100

Bournemouth
Central
Station

15

Bricklayers Arms
1947

This was the principal shed of the SER and the use of the site for locomotive purposes dates from the 1840s when Bricklayers Arms was briefly a passenger terminus. Sited at the end of a spur, the first depot opened in 1844 and was successively enlarged to include a number of separate buildings, and soon became by far the largest depot on the system, providing engines for numerous freight turns as well as passenger services from Charing Cross and Cannon Street. The depot was responsible for sub sheds at both these stations as well as Deptford and Woolwich, and had around 150 locos on allocation in 1898. After the amalgamation with the LCD, the 'Brick', in spite of a larger allocation, was placed second to Stewarts Lane in the SECR list. The more glamorous trains worked by the Battersea rivals helped to sustain this 'inferiority' in the ensuing years.

Bricklayers Arms saw great changes after the Grouping, losing the last of its original sub sheds at Cannon Street but retaining the increasingly important servicing depot at Ewer Street in Southwark. Located within one of the largest goods depots on the Southern Railway much of its work continued to be freight naulage. In the 1930s a series of improvements were carried out at the depot; a large repair shop was constructed in 1934 and under a £76,000 scheme approved in 1936, the 'old' shed was rebuilt with a steel and asbestos roof, with a water softener and larger turntable also to be provided. All this would eventually enable complete closure of the crumbling New Cross Gate sheds and

make Bricklayers Arms the principal maintenance base of south east London. The repair shop, equipped with wheel drop, overhead cranes, wheel lathes, etc. was able to undertake repair work on the largest locos, which none of the other London depots could do and as time went on engines were sent there from depots far afield. The scheme was incomplete in 1939 when it was interrupted by the outbreak of war, but the depot that eventually passed into BR ownership comprised large modern servicing and repair sheds, a water softener and 65 ft. turntable.

The depot suffered severe damage during the war and it was not found possible to close New Cross Gate until 1949. Bricklayers Arms allocation by this time numbered around 100 locomotives but it declined with electrification and increasing dieselisation throughout the 'fifties, culminating in the Kent Coast scheme of 1959. The shed's varied freight and passenger turns were severely restricted after 1960 and a year later only a handful of main line duties were left for the surviving Bulleid Pacifics and 'N' class Moguls. The rambling depot eventually closed in 1962 and its last sixteen or so steam locos were dispersed amongst other sheds, the buildings being partly demolished. Although the site is now given over to freight facilities, the turntable and repair shop leading off it are intact and apparently still in use.

The 'Old' shed in pre-grouping days.

Lens of Sutton

Top Right
A similar view taken in 1955 shows Southern and later BR steel and asbestos roofing styles.

S.C. Nash

'Schools' class No. 30935 *Sevenoaks* alongside the coaling plant on 14th March 1959.

P.J. Kelley

Brighton

1934

to
Hove

to
London

Brighton
Station

COAL STACK
COAL STAGE
HUT
CRANES
ASHES
W. COL
STORES
OFFICES
MESS
W. COL
WHEEL DROP
HUT
WEST SIGNAL BOX
WEIGH HOUSE
ENGINE SHED
WATER SOFTENER
WATER TANK
CARRIAGE CLEANING

N

Feet
0   100

This was a large building dating from the early days of the LBSCR at Brighton and moved to its site just to the north of the station in the fork of the Worthing and Haywards Heath lines in 1861. The large brick built shed had fourteen roads, each with a separate arched entrance under a slated roof of several pitches. A large carriage shed was sited alongside and a huge water tank was provided. Later a large water softening plant was also installed and an engine hoist with shelter stood in the middle of the yard. It was one of the most important LBSC sheds but occupied a cramped and awkward site — photographs taken on Sunday mornings show the shed and yard packed with locomotives. Prominent in the 1920s were the ex-LBSCR 'Atlantics' and 'Baltics' and SR 'King Arthurs'.

The electrification of the main line from London in 1932 reduced the importance of the shed but many passenger services and all freight remained steam hauled even after the coastal lines were electrified. The shed had over eighty locomotives in the mid-thirties and still had around sixty in 1951, 2-6-0s and 4-4-0s as well as numerous tank engines. Newhaven, although officially a sub shed retained a separate allocation for much of its existence.

Two major alterations took place at the depot, widely separated in time. A large turntable replaced the old 40 ft. table in 1909 and in 1938 most of the slated roof gave way to asbestos sheeting, a northlight pattern design replacing the original pitches, the arched entrances disappearing at the same time.

Steam working declined throughout the 'fifties due to loss of traffic and dieselisation and the shed eventually closed in 1964, its few remaining engines going to Bournemouth and Guildford. The facilities remained intact for a year or so, and locos were still arriving at the shed in late 1965, but in the summer of the following year the buildings were finally demolished. The site is now occupied by a National Carriers Ltd. depot.

The coal and ash roads in 1963.
Ken Fairey

The shed in 1954, with wheel drop
and hoist in foreground.

Photomatic

Top right
The depot with old roof in 1927.

H.C. Casserley

The shed and yard in 1961.

I. Shorter

Bude

1959

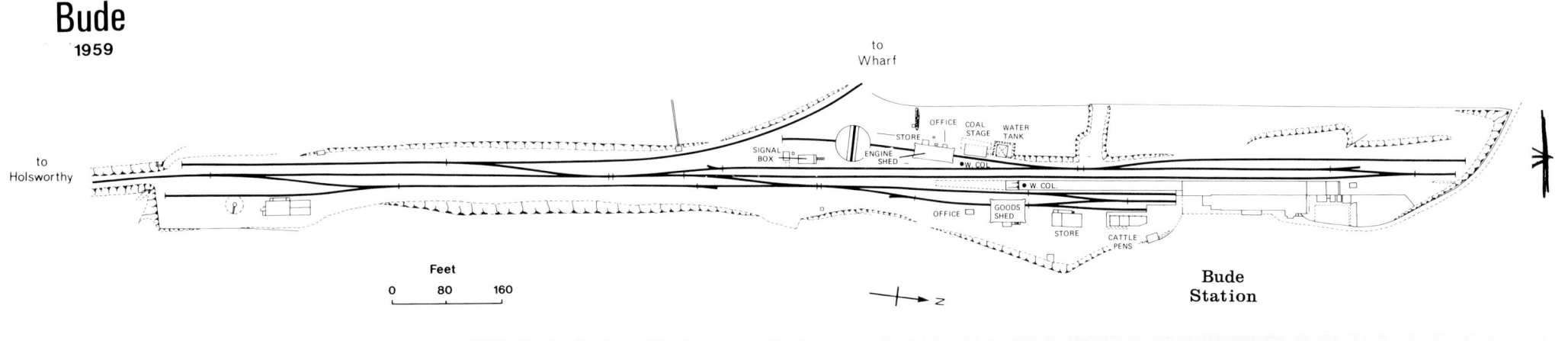

to
Wharf

to
Holsworthy

STORE · OFFICE · COAL STAGE · WATER TANK

SIGNAL BOX · ENGINE SHED · W. COL.

W. COL.

OFFICE · GOODS SHED · STORE · CATTLE PENS

Bude Station

Feet

0   80   160

The shed opened when the LSWR-promoted line was completed in 1898, the small shed previously built at the original Holsworthy terminus being abandoned around the same time. A single road through building, the shed at Bude was of brick construction with a pitched roof. There was a 50 ft. turntable at the rear of the building and a coal stage and water tank in front.

It was one of a number of sheds sub to Exmouth Junction and the engines supplied were used on the line to Halwill Junction. Beattie well-tanks were regular engines in the earliest days gradually giving way to M7s and other LSWR classes. After 1925 Moguls often put in an appearance at the shed, being joined by Ivatt and standard tanks under BR. The shed was transferred to the WR in 1962 but closed in September 1964 when diesel traction was introduced, and stood disused for a few years, even after closure of the line in 1966. The whole site has now been cleared.

SR Mogul No. 31836 at Bude in August 1963.
OPC Collection

Callington

1952

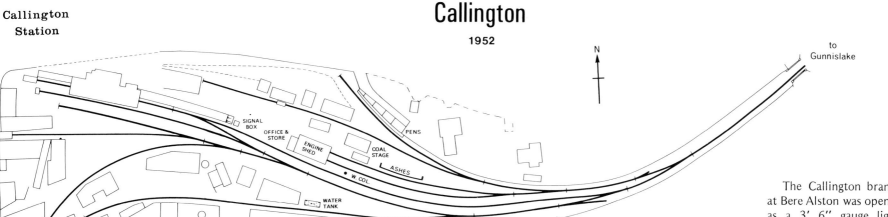

to
Gunnislake

SIGNAL BOX

OFFICE & STORE

ENGINE SHED

PENS

COAL STAGE

ASHES

W. COL.

WATER TANK

N

Feet

0   200

The shed in 1936.
Photomatic

The Callington branch through Calstock at Bere Alston was opened in 1872 originally as a 3' 6" gauge light railway and was bought by the Plymouth Devonport and South Western Junction Railway in 1894. The PDSWJR converted the line to standard gauge in 1908 and built the shed around the same time. Actually sited to the north of the town at Kelly Bray the shed was a single ended building constructed in corrugated sheeting on a timber frame, supported by a dwarf brick wall. It replaced a similar narrow gauge shed on the same site. The two roads were covered by a pitched roof again in corrugated sheeting. When the LSWR came to operate the line Callington became a sub shed of Plymouth Friary, but the ex-PDSWJ 0-6-2T locos worked the branch traffic for many years. It was usual to stable an engine inside the shed and another outside leaving a road free for coal wagons, a coal stage subsequently being added.

Grouping had little effect on the small depot, Friary continuing to be the parent shed, but ex-SW 0-4-4T classes became increasingly in evidence. Ivatt tanks appeared after nationalization and within six years the ex-PDSWJ locos were rarely seen, the regular allocation being an 'O2' and a '2MT' tank. The shed spent its final years as part of the Western Region of BR, sub to Friary at first but towards the end locos were supplied by Exmouth Junction. Closure came in September 1964 and the shed was afterwards demolished.

21

Callington shed on 20th April 1962.
P.J. Kelley

The shed and signal box in 1936.   *W.A. Camwell*

R1' tank at the shed in 1952. The Whitstable branch is on the left.   *E. Crawforth*

The SER opened its Canterbury station in 1846 and a small brick built shed was constructed in the same year. Sited on a connecting spur to the Canterbury and Whitstable Railway, the single ended building was also provided with a small turntable and water tank, with sand furnace at the rear. The turntable was later removed and the shed itself was subsequently rebuilt, being converted to a through shed approached this time from the main line.

The depot was sub to Ashford and housed the handful of tanks working the Whitstable line, taken over in 1853. Three or four 'R' class tanks, which were also used for general shunting duties, became the normal allocation after 1890 and on the formation of the SECR in 1899 the station and shed were renamed 'Canterbury West'. The small ex-LCD shed at Canterbury East probably went out of use at this time.

The shed remained in its SECR condition under the Southern but its duties gradually declined and by the end of the Second World War only three locos were normally in use. Despite some bomb damage, British Railways kept the shed open for several more years, even after complete closure of the Canterbury and Whitstable in 1953, but with only one loco remaining it was eventually closed in March 1955, and later demolished.

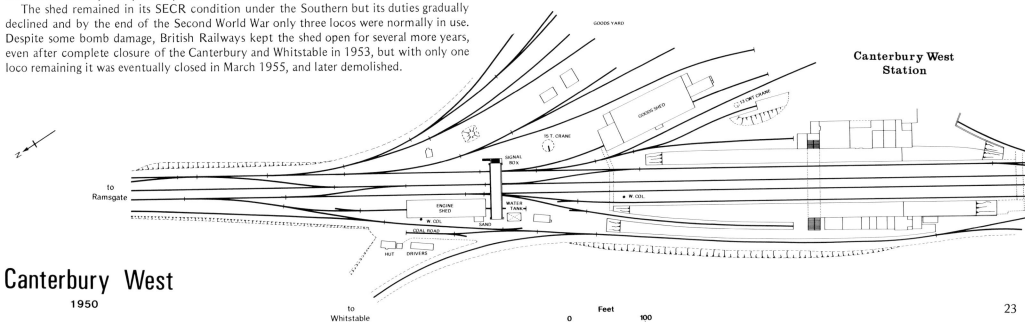

Canterbury West Station

Canterbury West

1950

to Ramsgate

to Whitstable

GOODS YARD

GOODS SHED

13 CWT CRANE

15 T. CRANE

SIGNAL BOX

ENGINE SHED

WATER TANK

W. COL.

SAND

COAL ROAD

HUT   DRIVERS

W. COL.

Feet
0   100

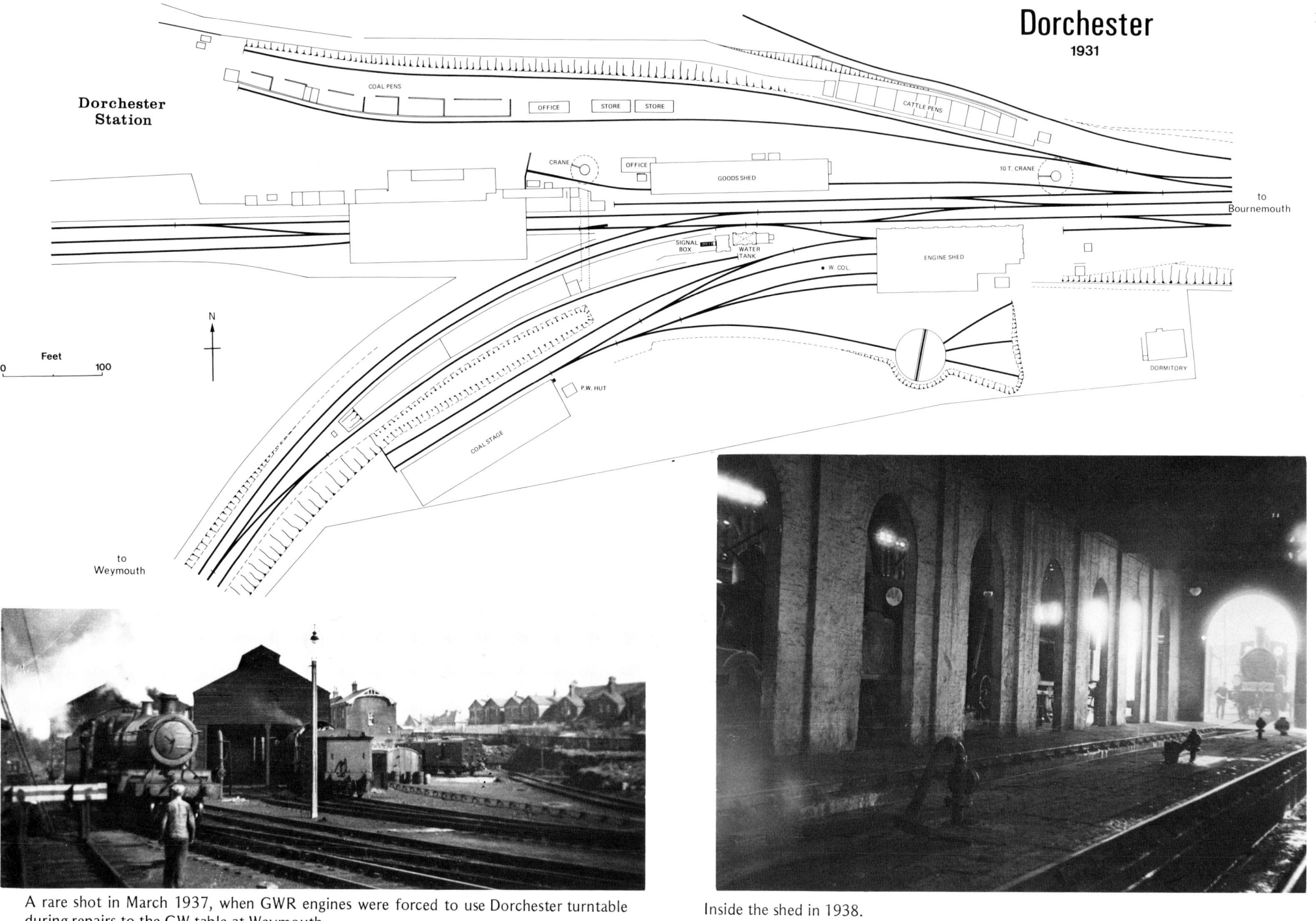

Dorchester
1931

Dorchester Station

COAL PENS

OFFICE   STORE   STORE

CATTLE PENS

CRANE

OFFICE   GOODS SHED

10 T. CRANE

to Bournemouth

SIGNAL BOX   WATER TANK

W. COL.

ENGINE SHED

N

Feet
0   100

P.W. HUT

COAL STAGE

DORMITORY

to Weymouth

A rare shot in March 1937, when GWR engines were forced to use Dorchester turntable during repairs to the GW table at Weymouth.

Inside the shed in 1938.

S.C. Townroe

Dorchester in 1937. The separate stages of construction can be appreciated in this photograph.

W.A. Camwell

The shed here, at the south side of the station, dates from the opening of the main line by the Southampton and Dorchester company in 1847. The line was worked from the first by the LSWR and the original two road shed was built in brick with a pitched slated roof. It was later doubled in size, probably in connection with the opening of the route to Weymouth via the GWR in 1857 when an additional two roads were added, covered by a separate pitched roof. A coal platform and turntable were provided at the far end of the yard. This was later replaced by a 50 ft. table sited at the south side of the shed.

The shed's major duties were passenger trains between Weymouth and Bournemouth but before the 1914-18 war Dorchester locos and men worked through trains to London via Wimborne. The allocation rarely exceeded twenty locos and for much of the time 'T9' 4-4-0s and '02' 0-4-4 tanks were the most numerous types. As a terminal depot on the SR main line the staff handled all classes of traffic, however, including banking duties, often required at short notice. In 1938 when some of the 'Lord Nelson' class were fitted with speed recorders, it was Dorchester men who managed to exceed 'the ton' on up expresses through Wool! A sub shed had been opened at Weymouth by the station but it was very small and only required a pair of tank engines. An unusual feature at Dorchester was the method of access to and from the running lines, locos entering the shed directly

from the down main line, a set of points actually inside the shed being operated from the station signal box. This was something of an inconvenience and meant that effectively the shed only possessed three roads.

One of the last acts of the LSWR was to recommend the transfer of soon-to-be redundant Exmouth Junction 65 ft. turntable to Dorchester, but this move never actually took place. This was to cause problems in later years when Weymouth table was out of action, Dorchester being unable to turn any loco larger than a 2-6-0. In 1935 the possibility was discussed of moving the depot to Templecombe but this idea was abandoned in the following year in favour of a move to Weymouth. The actual move did not take place but engines regularly used Weymouth GWR shed, the ex-LSW sub shed eventually being demolished in 1939. A second sub shed at Easton closed in 1952.

Dorchester declined after this and the remaining duties were much reduced in 1954, leaving only five engines, and even these were removed the following year, the shed becoming sub to Bournemouth. It closed in July 1957 and demolition, already partially carried out, began immediately afterwards. The whole site has now been cleared and little trace remains of the shed.

A line up of locomotives at Dover in 1950.

John Meredith

A distant view of the shed and coal stage, with No. 34070 *Manston*.

R.F. Orpwood

This was a modern Southern Railway shed approved in 1924 at a cost of £190,000. Opened in 1928 as part of a large reconstruction programme in the town, it replaced a former LCDR depot at Priory and was built on partly reclaimed land south of the old Town station. It was a six road shed constructed in concrete with a northlight pattern roof, one road running the full length of the building. A 65 ft. turntable was installed and a coaling ramp stood at the south side of the shed. A wheel drop formed part of the repair facilities and in 1930 a 10,000 gallon water softener was added at the west end of the yard.

Dover was responsible for main line freight and passenger work and from the first the allocation numbered around fifty locomotives. The first of the 'Schools' class spent some time there in 1930 but lesser 4-4-0s, 0-6-0s and tank engines were more usual during the 'thirties. The depot was virtually closed during the war, because of shelling from the French coast, and its work transferred to Ashford. After 1945 Bulleid Pacifics began to appear and in the 'fifties these were followed by the various BR standard classes. The depot maintained several tanks for a sub shed at Folkestone

Junction and shortly before electrification main line passenger services, including boat trains were being powered by Pacifics, BR class '5s' and 'Schools', but engines off the famous *Golden Arrow*, although serviced at Dover, were supplied by Stewarts Lane. Increasing electrification and subsequent dieselisation led to closure along with the sub shed at Folkestone in 1961, the depot being demolished shortly afterwards. Goods sidings now occupy the site.

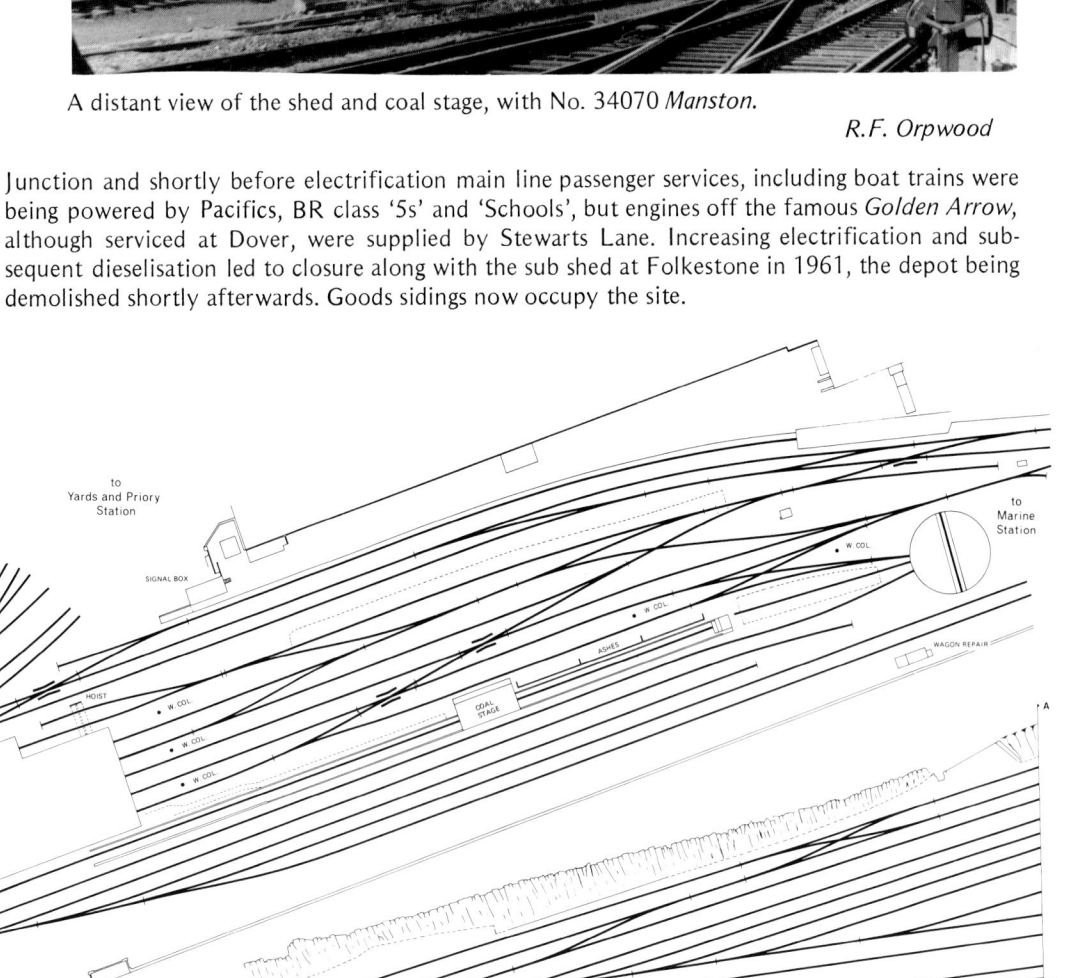

Dover
1947

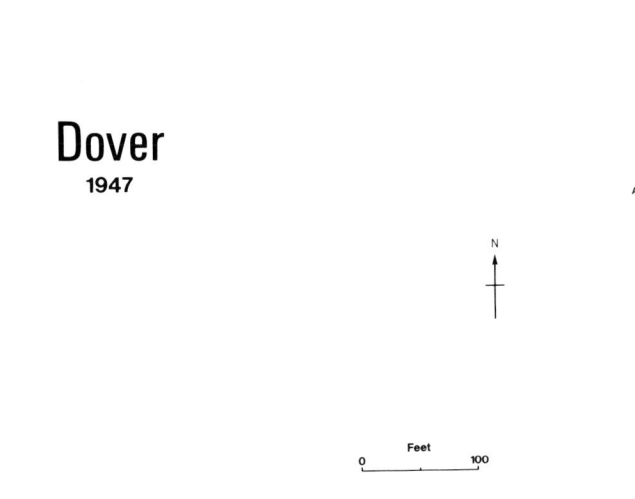

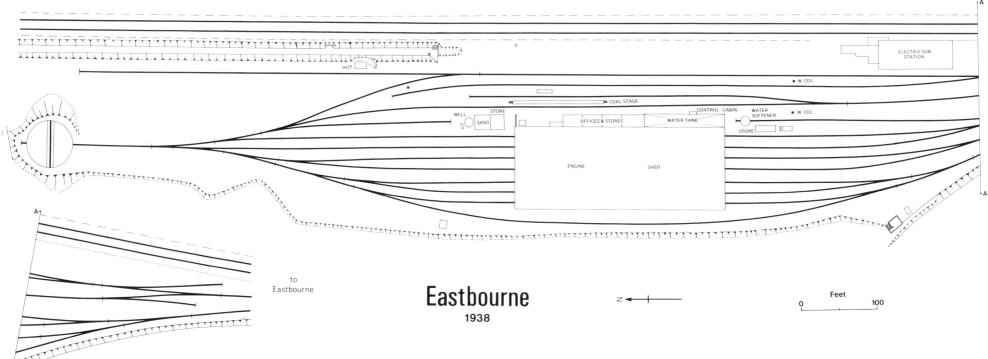

Polegate

to Eastbourne

Eastbourne
1938

Feet
0   100

The 'shed' around 1950 showing obvious signs of bomb damage.

Lens of Sutton

The shed at Eastbourne was built on land originally purchased by the LBSCR for a new carriage and wagon works and replaced a depot of the semi-roundhouse type sited by the station. This in its turn had replaced a two road straight shed built in the station yard. Constructed in brick with a northlight pattern roof, it opened in 1911 and was connected to the station yard by a special track, with engine movements controlled from a sub cabin within the shed. The depot was of the through type and had seven roads leading onto a 60 ft. turntable at the northern end of the yard. Early contract drawings of 1906 show a coaling ramp on the eastern side of the shed but later amendments resulted in a coal stage with crane eventually being provided. The most modern and well designed of the LBSC's engine sheds, the allocation just before the First World War included several 4-4-0s and two Atlantics among about forty tank and tender locos. 'Schools' and 'King Arthurs' were notable in SR days.

Apart from the installation and subsequent explosion of an experimental pulverised fuel plant in the early years the shed continued under Southern ownership much the same as it had in Brighton days, but after electrification in 1935 its duties were greatly reduced. Several bombing raids during the war left the shed virtually roofless and by the early 'fifties it housed only a handful of engines for local freight and shunting. It closed as an independent depot in 1952 and became little more than a stabling and turning point. A notable feature, however, during these last years was the often quite large number of withdrawn locos stored at the shed, awaiting scrapping at Ashford. It seems not to have officially closed, however, until 1968, though of course steam would have already been absent for several years. It was demolished in 1969.

The major LSWR locomotive depot in the Southampton area was originally Northam shed near Terminus station but around the turn of the century it was decided to construct a large new depot out at Eastleigh, an important junction. The new shed opened in 1903, sited in a fork south of the old Bishopstoke station, and replaced a small two road shed there.

The new depot was extremely large, having fifteen roads, including a repair bay. It was built in brick and the roof, consisting of several pitches, was slated and glazed. A coaling ramp was built with four roads leading on to a 55 ft. turntable. Although one of the key depots on the system, it was never equipped with a larger turntable or modern coaling plant, although a triangle was added for the larger locos. A coaling plant had in fact been planned in the 1930s but unsatisfactory experience at other sheds with breakage and dust nuisance led to its cancellation.

From the first Eastleigh was one of the foremost depots of the LSWR and it later became one of the most important sheds on the Southern network, usually having an allocation of 100-120 locomotives. It was placed at a strategic point on the system working all kinds of trains over many of the ex-LSWR lines and into GWR territory, especially with traffic from the Docks. In the heyday of ocean liner traffic, Eastleigh had 24 sets of men

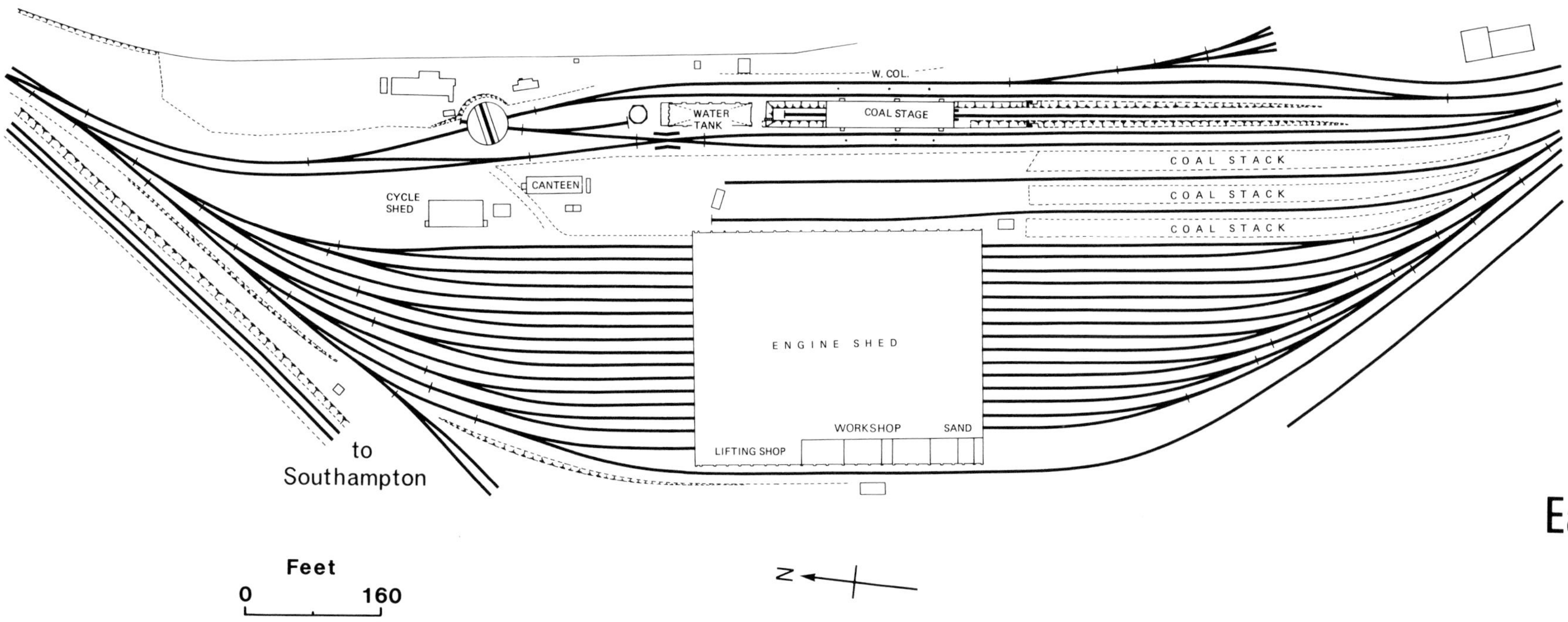

A general view of the shed in 1962.　　J. Scrace

Eastleigh

1958

Feet

0　160

to Southampton

purely to deal with the boat trains. Apart from the numerous freight and passenger turns it was responsible for sub sheds at Winchester City, Andover Junction, Lymington, Southampton Terminus and, as late as the 'forties, Southampton Docks. Regular duties also included running-in trips for engines outshopped from the nearby works.

After 1946 Eastleigh had all sixteen 'Lord Nelson' class locomotives and early developments in 1957 with petrol block trains from Fawley were handled by Eastleigh men using '9F' 2-10-0s.

The Southern carried out a number of improvements at Eastleigh and as well as the provision of a 20,000 gallon water softener in 1930, in 1938 built new offices for the foremen and clerks. In 1940 the offices were destroyed by bombing and thereafter the dormitory under the large water tank was converted into offices, classrooms, etc. The depot later played an important part in the Allied invasion of France in 1944-45 being on a vital junction. The depot began a slow decline after 1948 the roof being partially repaired with corrugated sheeting by BR in the 'fifties, and the coal ramp giving way to a steam crane in 1964.

Towards the end the allocation comprised mainly Bulleid Pacifics and the various standard types, although in the last months the numbers of withdrawn locomotives often rivalled those actually in use. It was one of the last major steam centres in the south of England and closed on the final day of steam operation in July 1967. Demolition began shortly afterwards and a diesel depot now occupies part of the site.

The shed, water tank and repair shops in BR days.

OPC Collection

Easton
1947

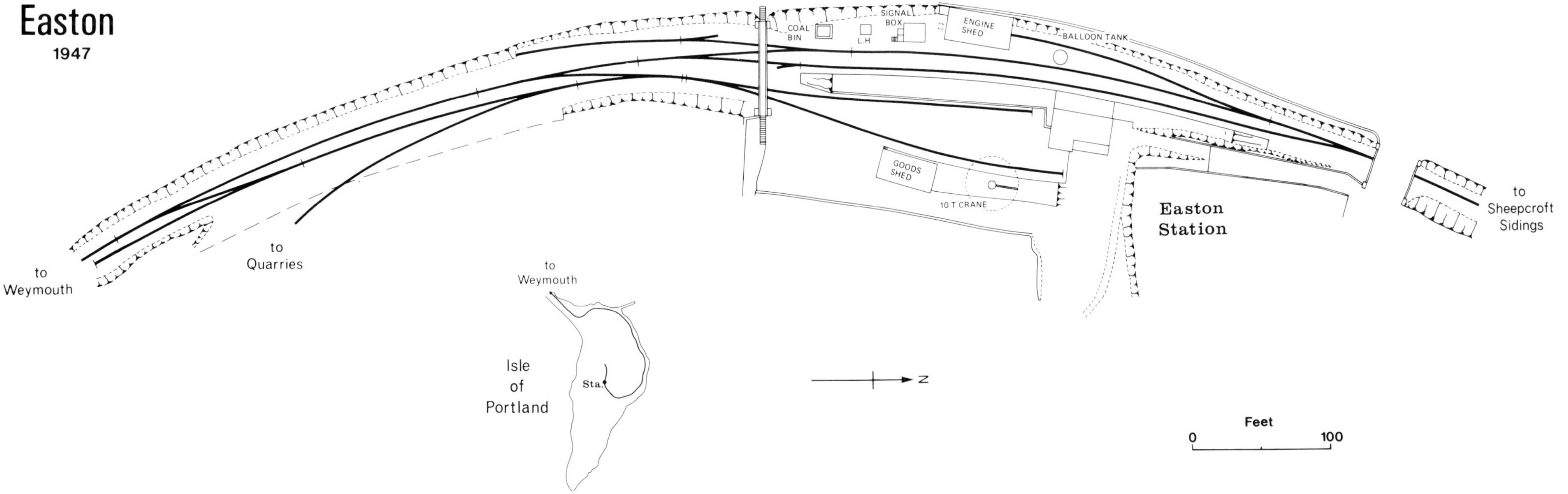

COAL
BIN

SIGNAL
BOX

L.H

ENGINE
SHED

BALLOON TANK

GOODS
SHED

10 T CRANE

**Easton
Station**

to
Weymouth

to
Quarries

to
Weymouth

to
Sheepcroft
Sidings

Isle
of
Portland

Sta.

Z

Feet

0   100

The line around the edge of Portland to Easton was built and owned by the Easton & Church Hope Railway and was completed in 1900. From the commencement of the passenger service two years later, however, the working of the line was the joint responsibility of the LSWR and the GWR and the SW completed the shed in 1904. It replaced a former E & CHR shed sited further down the line.

It was a single road terminus shed, built in the local Portland stone and had a pitched slated roof. The small shed housed the branch engine, usually a Dorchester 0-4-4T outstationed at Weymouth, although under the Southern it seems to have merited little more status than an engine siding after 1925.

It continued in use after the demolition of Weymouth SW shed in 1939 but only survived four years under British Railways ownership. Pannier Tanks would have replaced the 'O2s' but the shed officially closed with the end of the passenger service in 1952 and was shortly afterwards demolished. The whole station site has now been redeveloped.

Arrival from Weymouth alongside the stone built shed.

Lens of Sutton

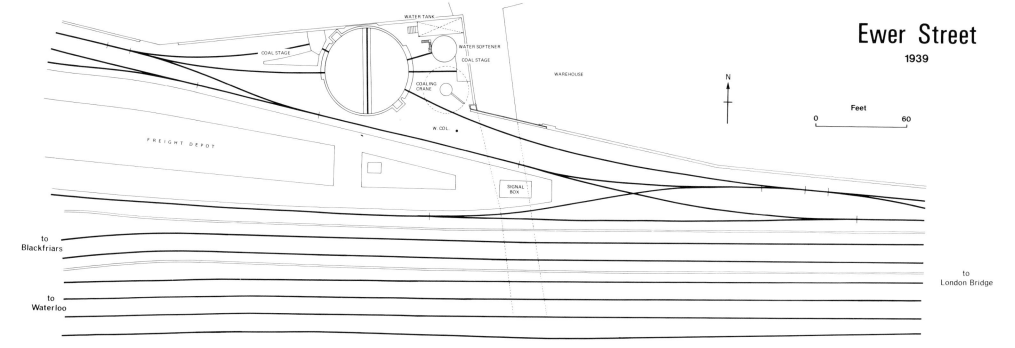

WATER TANK

COAL STAGE

WATER SOFTENER

COAL STAGE

COALING CRANE

WAREHOUSE

N

Feet
0   60

FREIGHT DEPOT

W. COL.

SIGNAL BOX

to Blackfriars

to Waterloo

to London Bridge

A wartime view of No. 901 *Winchester* at Ewer Street.

S.C. Townroe

The exact year of construction of Ewer Street depot is not clear but the most likely date would seem to be 1899, the first year of operation by the SECR, although the depot was actually planned by the South Eastern. There was no actual shed building but full servicing facilities — a 55 ft. turntable, coal stage and water tank were provided. It was sited alongside the continental freight depot and serviced engines working into Cannon Street and Charing Cross stations.

The importance of the depot increased after the electrification of 1926, when Cannon Street shed closed and servicing of remaining steam locomotives was concentrated at Ewer Street, avoiding light running to Bricklayers Arms. The Southern introduced several improvements at the depot including a water softener, approved in 1934 at a cost of £2,400, and a new water column to enable engines to coal and take water on adjacent roads. The depot was sub to Bricklayers Arms and remained in use until 1961 when it was finally made redundant by the Kent Coast electrification scheme. All trace of the depot has now disappeared and the site partially given over to the stabling of electric multiple units.

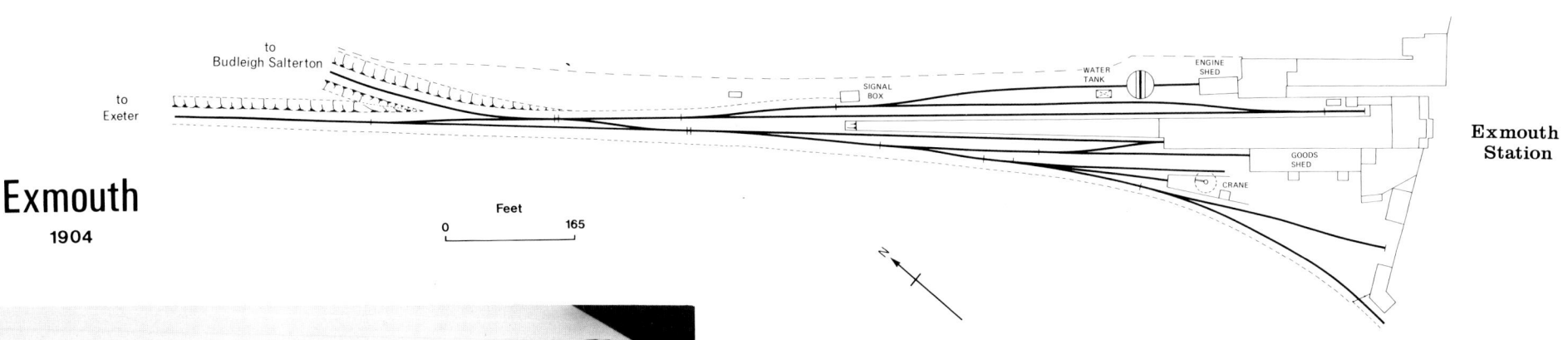

Exmouth

1904

Feet

0 — 165

to Budleigh Salterton

to Exeter

WATER TANK

SIGNAL BOX

ENGINE SHED

GOODS SHED

CRANE

Exmouth Station

N

The original shed at Exmouth probably dates from the opening of the Exeter and Exmouth Railway line in 1861, worked from the first by the LSWR and absorbed in 1866. The shed was a one road, single ended building, possibly wooden with a pitched roof, and a 42 ft. turntable was installed directly outside. A water tank and extra pit were provided in the yard. Main repairs to the five engines allocated were carried out at the parent depot, Exmouth Junction, and Adams or Beattie tanks were the regular locos up until the 1900s, working the lines to Sidmouth Junction via Budleigh Salterton as well as to Exeter.

Plans for a new shed were approved by the Southern in 1927 at a cost of £2200; the turntable was removed and a plain shed in concrete blocks, surmounted by a new water tank with offices at the side was constructed on virtually the same site. The new shed remained sub to Exmouth Junction and 'O2' and 'M7' 0-4-4 tanks were the usual engines provided until modern 2-6-2s arrived in 1952. The shed gradually went out of use with line closures and dieselisation under BR and eventually closed in November 1963. It has since been demolished.

Pair of Southern tanks at the new shed in 1952.

W.A.Camwell

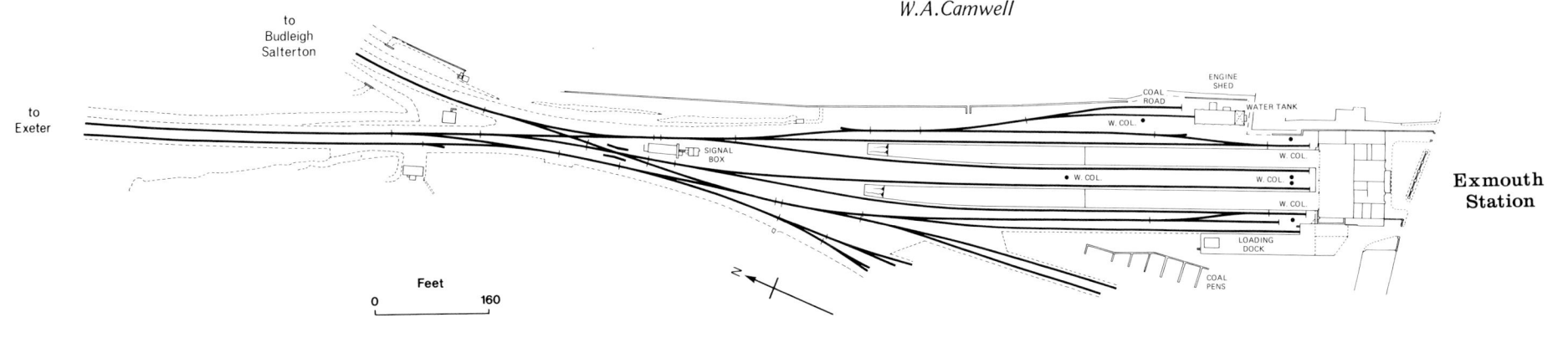

to Budleigh Salterton

to Exeter

ENGINE SHED

COAL ROAD

WATER TANK

SIGNAL BOX

W. COL.

W. COL.

W. COL.

W. COL.

W. COL.

LOADING DOCK

COAL PENS

Exmouth Station

N

Feet

0 — 160

Exmouth Junction

1905

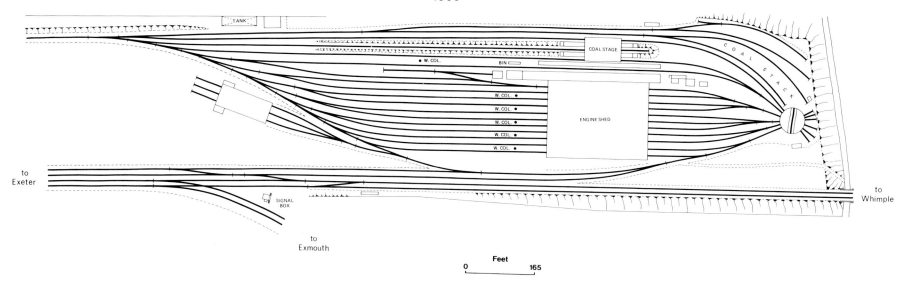

One of the last acts of the LSW board was to authorise in 1922 the construction of a brand new depot at Exmouth Junction. The first shed was opened in 1887 and had replaced a smaller three road shed sited by Exeter Queen Street station. The new depot was a large through shed with eleven roads leading onto a 65 ft. turntable. It was built in corrugated iron on steel framing and had a pitched slated roof with a coaling ramp provided on the north side of the yard. The original shed however, at Queen Street, remained open for servicing locomotives, and although the buildings had been demolished by 1904 the turntable and coal stage were not finally removed until 1930.

Exmouth Junction was one of the principal sheds of the LSWR and was responsible for all kinds of main line freight and passenger turns, as well as meeting the requirements of the meandering LSWR secondary lines in the West Country. One of the features of the depot was the large number of sub sheds and in the early years these included Okehampton, Bude, Seaton and Sidmouth. The allocation in 1922 numbered over eighty locomotives but this figure excluded the several outstationed engines.

By the 1920s, the shed had fallen into disrepair and shortly before grouping the decision was taken to construct a replacement depot. Work on the new shed was carried out mainly by the Southern and brick and concrete were chosen as the building materials. Work began in 1923 but not all the buildings and facilities were ready until 1929, probably because of the need to continue the servicing and repairing of locos while reconstruction was in progress. The new depot was built slightly to the east and differed from its predecessor in several important respects. It was single ended and had thirteen roads, covered by a northlight pattern roof. A ferro-concrete coaling plant replaced the former ramp and at one time the turntable was to have been replaced. The old 65 ft. table was to have

The original LSW shed in 1925.

H.C. Casserley

Two views of the shed in the summer of 1964.

Ken Fairey

been transferred to Dorchester but this never took place and it seems probable that the original table was incorporated, on a new site, into the rebuilt depot.

The allocation increased under the Southern and in the 'thirties usually numbered around 110 locomotives; 2-6-0s, 4-4-0s, 4-6-0s and a host of other types for working the varied duties. Thirty of the ubiquitous 'N' 2-6-0s, more than a third of the class, were allocated at one time. Exmouth Junction received some of the first Bulleid Pacifics and in 1947 a 70 ft. turntable was installed for the new locomotives. It was around this time that Exmouth Junction, along with Fratton, was to be converted to oil firing. A number of engines were converted but the project was eventually abandoned.

The shed was by far the largest Southern Region steam shed in the west, but of course with loss of traffic its allocation gradually declined and the sub sheds which at various times included Bude, Exmouth, Lyme Regis, Okehampton, Seaton, Callington and Launceston were closed one by one. The depot was incorporated into the Western Region in 1962 but was closed to steam three years later, remaining open for a short while to service diesels. The turntable was demolished in 1966 and the shed itself closed in March the following year. The depot lingered in a derelict condition for some years and the buildings and coal hopper were finally demolished in 1970.

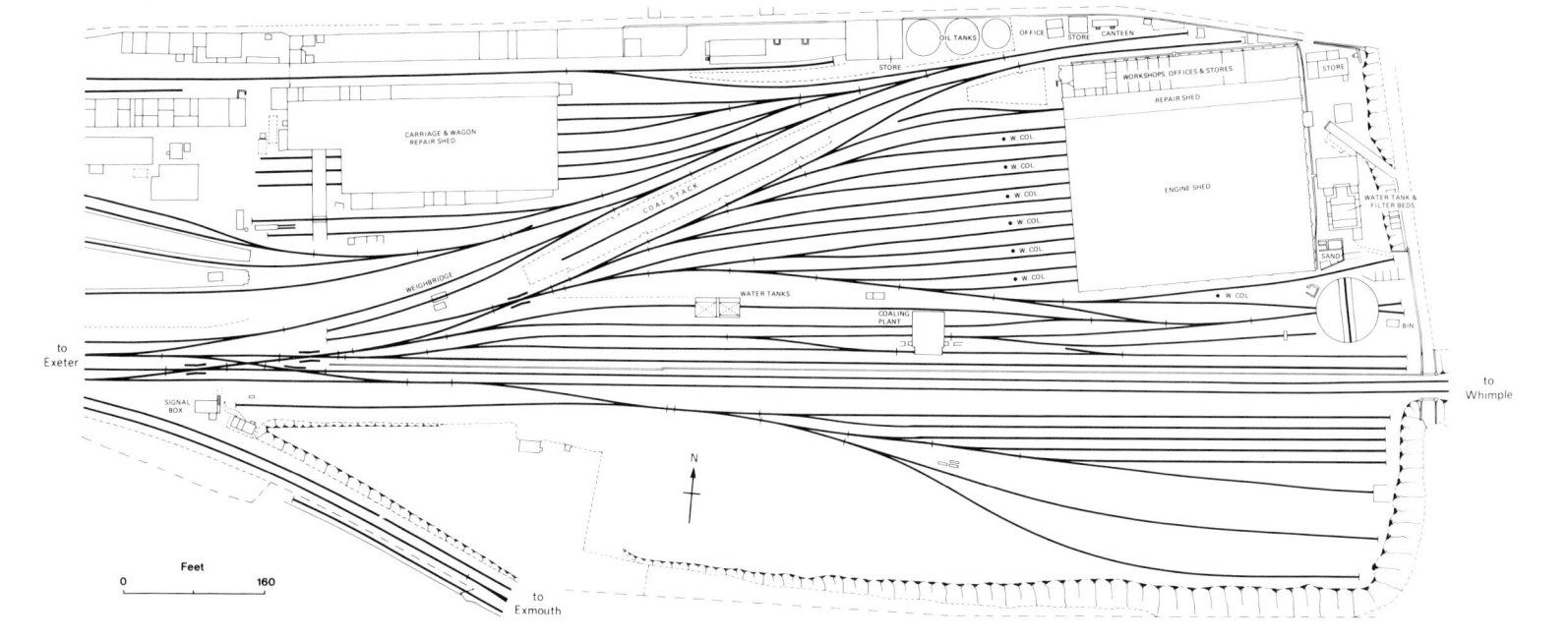

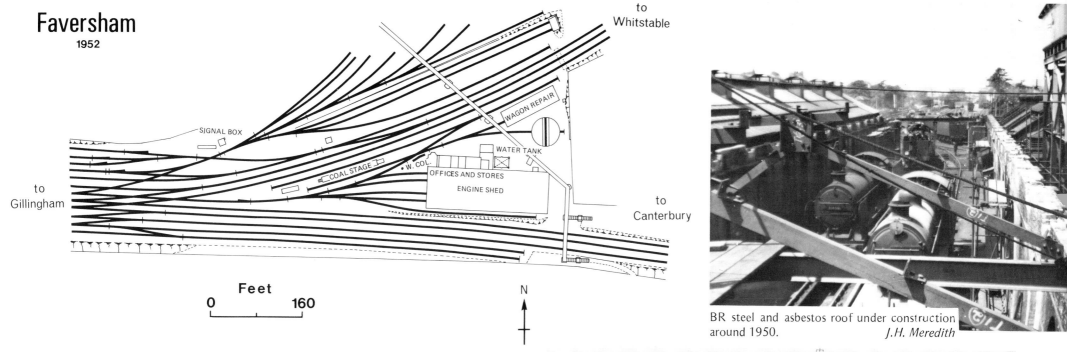

Faversham
1952

SIGNAL BOX

to Whitstable

WAGON REPAIR

WATER TANK

COAL STAGE

W. COL.

OFFICES AND STORES

ENGINE SHED

to Gillingham

to Canterbury

Feet

0   160

N

BR steel and asbestos roof under construction around 1950.   *J.H. Meredith*

The LCDR reached Faversham from Strood in 1858 and opened the sections on to Whitstable and Canterbury two years later. A map of 1868 shows a small two road building labelled 'engine shed' to the west of the station and this building perhaps dates from 1858, while the larger depot in the fork to the east dates from the extension of the line in 1860. The smaller shed had fallen completely out of use by the 1890s. The larger shed was a two road single ended building, in brick with a slated pitched roof, and a turntable and coaling stage with canopy provided. Offices were later added on the northern side and around the turn of the century the shed was doubled in size, with an extra two roads under a separate pitch and new offices provided, again on the northern side. A larger 50 ft. turntable was also installed.

Faversham was an important junction on the old LCD lines and the company's successor, the SECR and later the SR, maintained around thirty locos at the shed, mainly tank and freight types but including a number of 4-4-0s for passenger work. Gillingham ex-LCD shed was not very far away and the two depots worked closely together, engines often being freely interchanged. In the early years of the SECR this arrangement would also have applied to locomotives stationed at Strood ex-SER shed.

The Southern officially made the shed sub to Gillingham but it always maintained a considerable degree of independence, and this situation continued after 1948. However, with the introduction of the Kent Coast electrification project in 1959, this separate allocation was completely withdrawn and the shed converted to service diesel locomotives. The original half of the building, re-roofed in asbestos in 1935, was demolished and the remaining two road portion, itself re-roofed in the 'fifties, altered, although the turntable was not finally removed until 1966. The depot does not now appear to be used for locomotive purposes but the building is still standing in good condition.

Successive roofs at Faversham.   *H. C. Casserley and Photomatic*

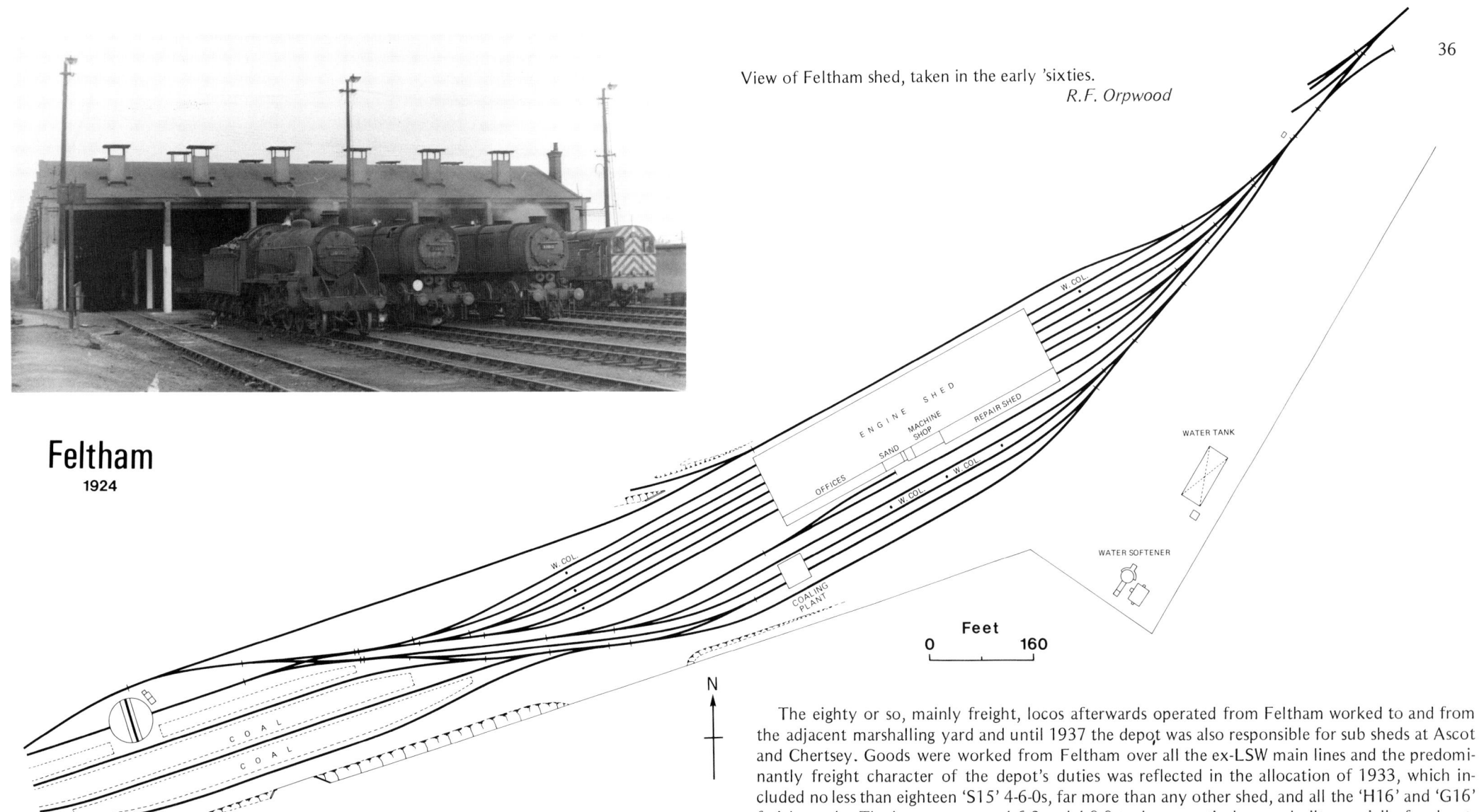

View of Feltham shed, taken in the early 'sixties.

R.F. Orpwood

Feltham

1924

ENGINE SHED

OFFICES

SAND

MACHINE SHOP

REPAIR SHED

W. COL.

W. COL.

W. COL.

WATER TANK

WATER SOFTENER

COALING PLANT

C O A L

C O A L

N

Feet

0   160

The eighty or so, mainly freight, locos afterwards operated from Feltham worked to and from the adjacent marshalling yard and until 1937 the depot was also responsible for sub sheds at Ascot and Chertsey. Goods were worked from Feltham over all the ex-LSW main lines and the predominantly freight character of the depot's duties was reflected in the allocation of 1933, which included no less than eighteen 'S15' 4-6-0s, far more than any other shed, and all the 'H16' and 'G16' freight tanks. The last two types, 4-6-2 and 4-8-0 tanks respectively were built especially for shunting in the new yards and for working the resultant transfer freights across London.

Apart from alterations to the coaling plant in 1930, enabling larger 20 ton wagons to be used, the Southern saw little need for improvements at Feltham and the depot remained much in its original condition throughout the war and during subsequent British Railways ownership. The first diesel shunters arrived in 1954 and BR standard locos began to appear around the same time. Towards the end all manner of engines were being used by the shed, BR 2-6-0s and 4-6-0s, 2-6-4 tanks and light pacifics as well as the inevitable 'S15' 4-6-0s. The yards saw less and less use in the 'sixties, however, and the duties of the depot were correspondingly reduced. The shed eventually closed with the end of steam in 1967 and although at one time a diesel depot was to be built nearby this never fully materialised and the whole marshalling yard/depot complex has now been demolished.

Dates vary regarding the exact opening of Feltham, obviously because of the gradual way in which the depot was brought into operation. It was part of a large scheme, the main part being a new hump marshalling yard, and involved the run-down and closure of an older shed at nearby Strawberry Hill. Nearly sixty engines, with all the associated staff, had to be transferred and the task obviously could not be accomplished overnight. Feltham was certainly planned and largely built by the LSWR, but it does not appear to have become fully operational until shortly after the grouping, the 65 ft. turntable and mechanical coaling plant not being approved until October 1922. The plant was similar in principal to the one at Nine Elms but at 200 tons was only half the capacity, though at £7,850 was over three quarters the cost! The shed, with associated repair shop, was built in pre-cast concrete and had a northlight pattern roof. A 50 ton overhead crane was installed in the repair shop.

Folkestone Junction
1958

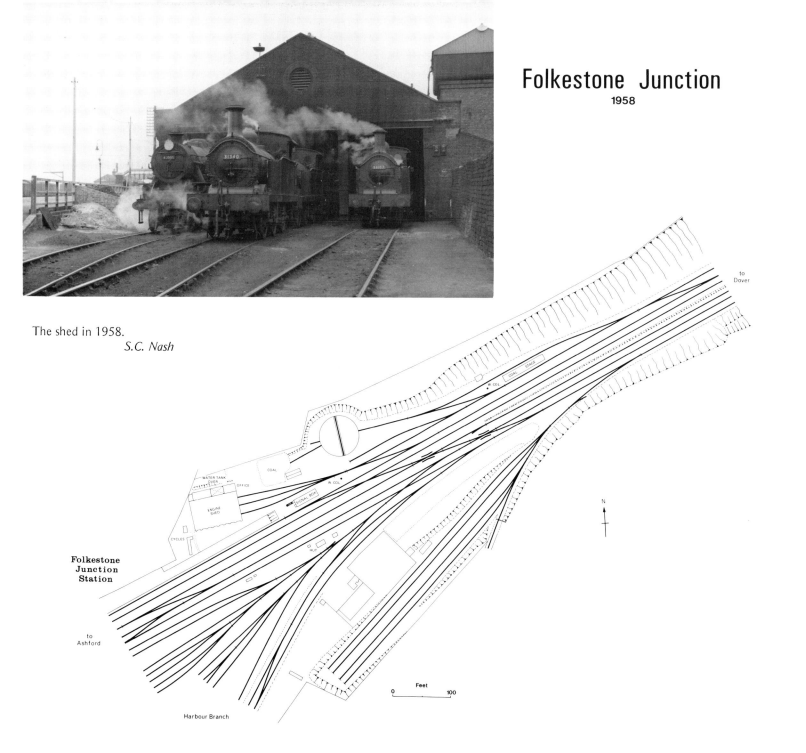

The shed in 1958.

S.C. Nash

Folkestone Junction Station

to Ashford

Harbour Branch

WATER TANK
DOVER
OFFICE
COAL
W COL
SIGNAL BOX
ENGINE SHED
CYCLES
HUT
W COL
COAL STAGE
to Dover

N

Feet
0   100

The SECR board authorised the construction of a new shed at Folkestone in 1899 to replace a much smaller ex-SER shed. The new depot, known as Folkestone Junction, was to house six locomotives instead of the previous two and with tank and coal stage would cost £4,510. The new shed opened shortly afterwards sited on the north side of the junction with the Harbour branch and was a three road single ended building in brick with a slated pitched roof. A coal stage was provided at the far end of the yard.

From the first the allocation consisted of half a dozen or so tanks for working the Harbour line and initially there was no turntable at the shed, but by 1918 a 65 ft. table had been constructed for larger visiting locomotives, particularly those working the boat trains. Under the SECR the small shed had its own separate coding but later in Southern days it became sub to the main depot at Dover. Folkestone still retained a large measure of independence however, particularly after 1940 and the allocation for many years consisted mainly of 'R1' 0-6-0Ts. This would have altered drastically if trials on the Harbour incline in the early 'thirties with 'W' 2-6-4Ts and 'Z' 0-8-0Ts had been successful, but the 'R1's continued in use for many years, eventually being replaced by ex-GWR 0-6-0PTs in 1959. The pannier tanks had only a short reign at the shed, however, as dieselisation and later electrification led to closure of the depot in 1961. The building was used to stable diesel locomotives for a few years but it has now been demolished.

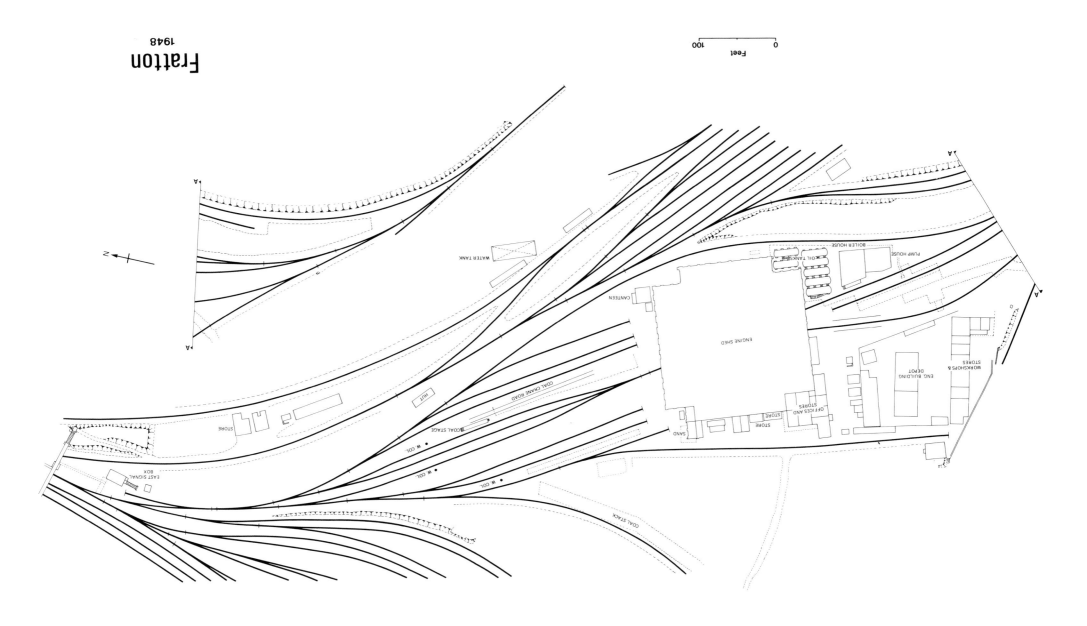

Fratton 1948

Feet
0   100

N

ENGINE SHED

BOILER HOUSE
PUMP HOUSE
OIL TANK STORE

WATER TANK

CANTEEN

COAL CRANE ROAD

COAL STAGE

HUT

STORE

SAND
STORE
STORE
OFFICES AND
STORES

ENG. BUILDING
DEPOT
WORKSHOPS &
STORES

W. COL.
W. COL.
W. COL.

EAST SIGNAL
BOX

COAL STACK

38

Variety of engine types at Fratton.   *A.B. McCleod*

Fratton shed on 10th May 1959.   *P.J. Kelley*

The preserved locos in 1963.

J. Scrace

Fratton shed replaced a variety of locomotive facilities sited near the station. The line into Portsmouth was worked jointly by the LSWR and LBSCR and in 1868 a four road shed stood on the north side of the line and a turntable with siding to the south, by the goods depot. Plans were submitted in 1889 for a jointly owned LBSC/LSW depot on spare ground at Fratton. The shed was of the roundhouse type and despite having to use the common 50 ft. turntable, the Brighton and South Western companies maintained separate offices and coal stages and their engines used separate stalls within the shed. After 1923 of course the depot was unified under a single management. It was built in brick with a slated and glazed pitched roof.

Each company normally maintained thirty to forty locos at the shed, LBSC engines working along the coast to Brighton and to London via Horsham, and the LSW working to Eastleigh and via the 'Direct Line' to Waterloo. Several 'Schools' class locomotives were delivered new in the 'thirties and in 1937 the total allocation numbered over seventy locos, including those required for a sub shed at Gosport. The 'Schools' and other passenger engines, however, were transferred away with electrification in that year and by 1950 the allocation had been very nearly halved.

Fuel tanks were installed during the 1946-47 oil-firing débâcle when Fratton, along with Exmouth Junction, was to be converted to an entirely oil-fuel depot. The scheme soon collapsed but the pump buildings survived for many years until final demolition of the shed. Despite suffering considerable bomb damage during the war, Fratton continued in use until the late 1950s and did not officially close until November 1959. The buildings survived for a number of years afterwards and as well as stabling the occasional steam visitor, housed for many years a handful of ex-SR locos scheduled for preservation. A light pacific stabled in the yard as late as October 1966 by which time the shed was decrepit and completely roofless, and demolition finally took place in 1969. Only the offices now remain.

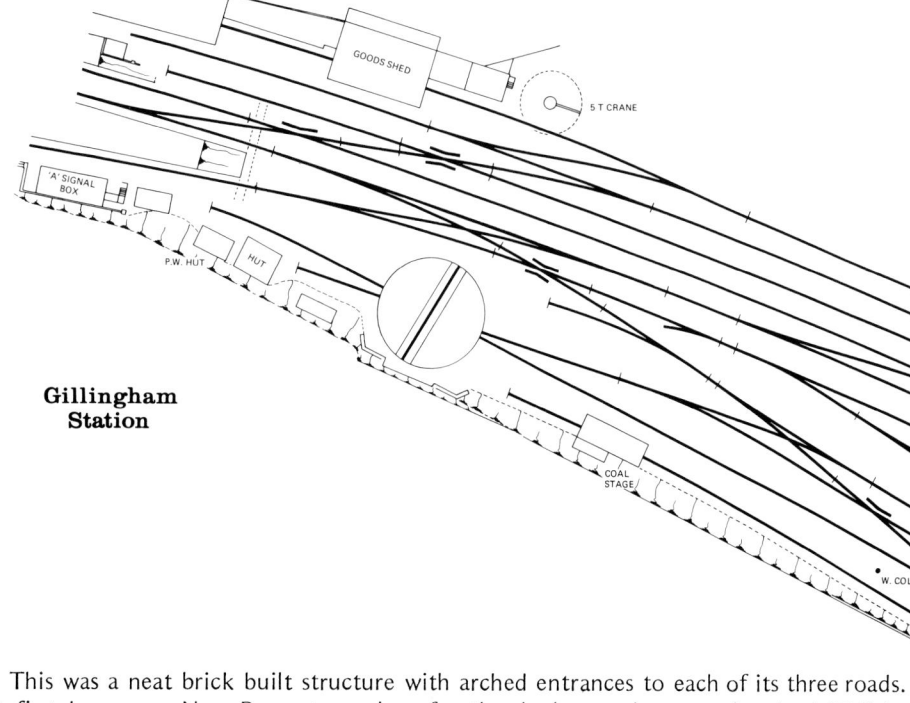

Gillingham Station

GOODS SHED

5 T CRANE

'A' SIGNAL BOX

P.W. HUT

HUT

COAL STAGE

W. COL.

W. COL.

LOBBY

BIN

Old and new steam designs at Gillingham in the 'fifties.

Lens of Sutton

Dock Branch

W. COL.

OFFICES AND STORES

WATER TANK OVER

ENGINE SHED

MESS OFFICES & STORES

SAND

to Faversham

Gillingham

1953

N

COAL STACK

0   Feet   75

This was a neat brick built structure with arched entrances to each of its three roads. At first known as New Brompton, plans for the shed were drawn up by the LCDR in 1884. Construction of the shed began shortly afterwards on a site just east of the station. A pitched slated roof was installed with offices, stores and a water tank, with well underneath, on the north side. At first a single ended building, two roads were later extended through the rear of the shed, probably during SECR ownership. A 50 ft. turntable and a coaling stage were provided in the yard. In 1899 the depot was amalgamated for operating purposes with the nearby ex-SER Strood shed, both of them subsequently using the same number 10 code. The Southern ended this arrangement, running down Strood during the 'twenties and eventually closing it altogether. Under the Southern Faversham and Gillingham were under the same local management, residing at Gillingham, and the fifty or so locos were freely exchanged, engines from one depot often working from the other for quite prolonged periods.

The allocation had halved by 1950 and consisted almost entirely of 'C' 0-6-0s. The 'D' 4-4-0s and 'H' passenger tanks of the early 'thirties had all but disappeared, but the shed retained still a solitary 'Z' 0-8-0T. They worked a variety of secondary turns along the coast line and around the Medway towns. The Southern had provided a new roof in 1931 and approved a new coal shelter in 1947. This was improved by BR in 1955 with the addition of a coaling gantry enabling coal to be hoisted and loaded over several tracks. The shed lost its remaining engines on electrification in 1959 and the handful afterwards required for local duties were supplied from Tonbridge. The depot closed completely following the dieselisation of the Sheerness branch in June 1960 and has since been demolished to make way for industrial development.

Gosport

1919

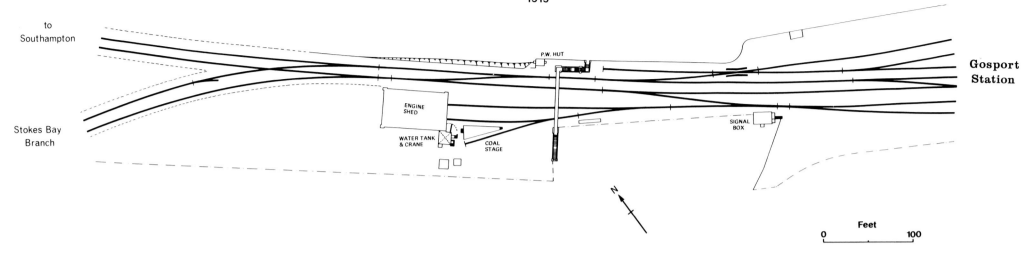

to
Southampton

Stokes Bay
Branch

P.W. HUT

ENGINE
SHED

WATER TANK
& CRANE

COAL
STAGE

SIGNAL
BOX

**Gosport
Station**

N

Feet

0   100

The shed from the footbridge with the track of the Stokes Bay Pier branch in the background.

Lens of Sutton

The LSWR opened the line to Gosport, the first railway to Portsmouth, in 1842 and the shed was probably built at this time to serve this 'Portsmouth terminus'. It was a two road brick built shed with a pitched slated roof and had a water tank provided on the southern side. The water was originally pumped from a nearby well. Until the 1860s, at least, a wagon table was installed outside the shed and this, together with a stub siding, was probably used in connection with coaling. In later years, a coal stage was provided in its place, but ash disposal was carried out using wagons left on the road adjacent to the main line.

The LSWR outstationed 'M7s' at Gosport from Fratton depot for shunting the station and Clarence yard and working the Meon Valley line to Alton. As no turntable was provided at the shed, visiting engines turned on the triangle of the Stokes Bay Pier Branch. This facility was in fact retained after the closure of the Pier branch and indeed after closure of the shed itself.

The depot continued as a sub shed of Fratton under the Southern but it seems to have declined even further in status. It was partly demolished by 1953 when the passenger service was withdrawn but it served as an engine siding for some time afterwards. By 1962 it was completely out of use, although engines still occasionally turned on the triangle, and it has now been completely demolished.

This shed was opened by the LSWR in 1887 on the site of a former chalk pit and replaced a two road straight shed which previously stood at the side of the station. The new depot was built in brick with a slated roof of several pitches and was unusual in taking the form of a semi-roundhouse, thirteen stalls radiating from the 50 ft. turntable. The original shed was demolished and a coal stage for the new depot, as well as additional station platforms, built on the site.

The shed grew in importance over the years, being on a major junction on the Portsmouth main line between the LSWR, SECR and LBSCR. Under LSW ownership the allocation rapidly reached over sixty engines. A severe gale had put paid to the small Brighton shed at Bramley in 1882, and subsequently a few LBSCR locos were stabled at the SW depot for which privilege the Brighton company made regular payment. Some major alterations were carried out at Guildford around the turn of the century, the most notable being the conversion of part of the building into a straight shed. This increased accommodation was authorised in 1896 at a cost of £8,000 and obviated the need to rebuild the near-defunct shed at Woking. Several roads were extended to form the straight shed, but access continued to be via the turntable. Around 1904 new hydraulic cranes were erected on the coaling stage and about the same time a larger 55 ft. table was installed at the shed.

Guildford continued to grow in importance after 1923, providing for London commuter routes via the Alton and Cobham lines and via Woking until electrification. Ten years after the grouping its allocation numbered some ninety engines, including twenty-five 'U' 2-6-0s, mainly for Redhill-Reading workings, and twenty-six 'M7' 0-4-4Ts. The depot underwent a second series of major improvements in Southern days, and these involved the complete renewal of the coal stage, with electric cranes replacing the old hydraulic apparatus and alterations to the pits and approach roads. This was complete by 1934 at a cost of over £7,000 and in the same year the small ex-SER shed at Ash joined Bordon as Guildford's second sub shed.

Shortly after nationalization the by-now decrepit roof was rebuilt using the customary corrugated sheeting and within a few years BR standard types began replacing the old designs. Guildford took over a number of duties when Reading partially closed in 1954 and ten years later received further engines following the closure of Horsham. The shed continued to be a stronghold of the Maunsell 2-6-0s but towards the end the loco stud consisted largely of BR standard stock. The peculiar layout of the depot necessitated a shed pilot, for many years the 0-4-0ST No. 458 *Ironside*, but 'B4' and later 'USA' tanks took over the regular pilot duties. The shed finally closed in July 1967 with the end of steam and the site is now occupied by the station car park.

Guildford with new BR roof.

Ken Fairey

Guildford

1955

Feet

0   100

to London

Guildford Station

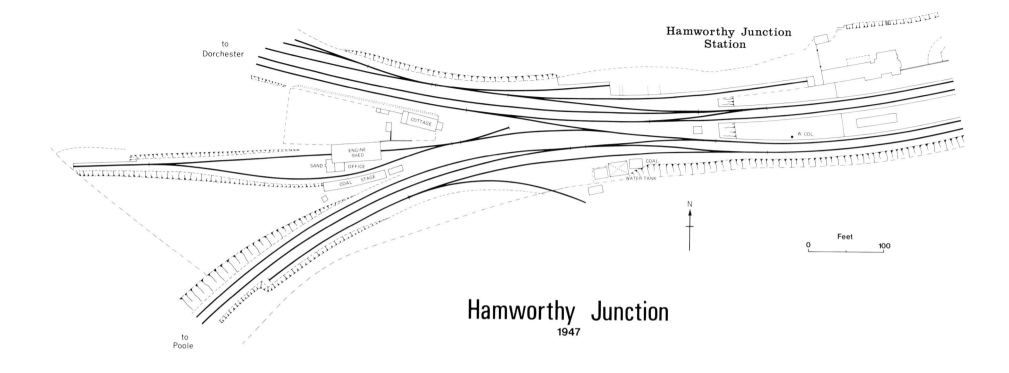

to
Dorchester

Hamworthy Junction
Station

COTTAGE

ENGINE
SHED

SAND   OFFICE

COAL   STAGE

COAL

WATER TANK

W. COL.

N

Feet
0   100

Hamworthy Junction
1947

to
Poole

This single road building has been described as similar in design to the shed at Swanage, but was actually quite different. Built in brick with a pitched slated roof, it was sited at the down end of Hamworthy Junction station and was presumably built when the LSWR opened the line to Hamworthy in 1847. No turntable was ever installed but a coal stage was provided on a siding adjacent to the shed. Towards the end of the century the shed was altered to a through building and the coaling road was extended to form a run-round loop. The coal stage was enlarged at the same time.

Four engines for branch work and shunting were outstationed at Hamworthy from the parent depot at Bournemouth in LSWR days and this number had risen to six in 1937. Three 0-4-4Ts worked the various local turns and three 'B4' 0-4-0Ts performed the shunting duties, all travelling to Bournemouth for repairs and washouts. A general decline in local traffic after the war, however, led to rundown of the shed and in the last few years only two engines, a 'B4' and an 'M7' were kept at Hamworthy. The depot closed completely in May 1954 and the remaining duties were transferred to Bournemouth. The building was used as a store for a time but has now been completely demolished.

Hamworthy Junction in 1937. On shed on this April day were Adams' tanks Nos. 364, 362 and 92.

W.A. Camwell

Hither Green

1945

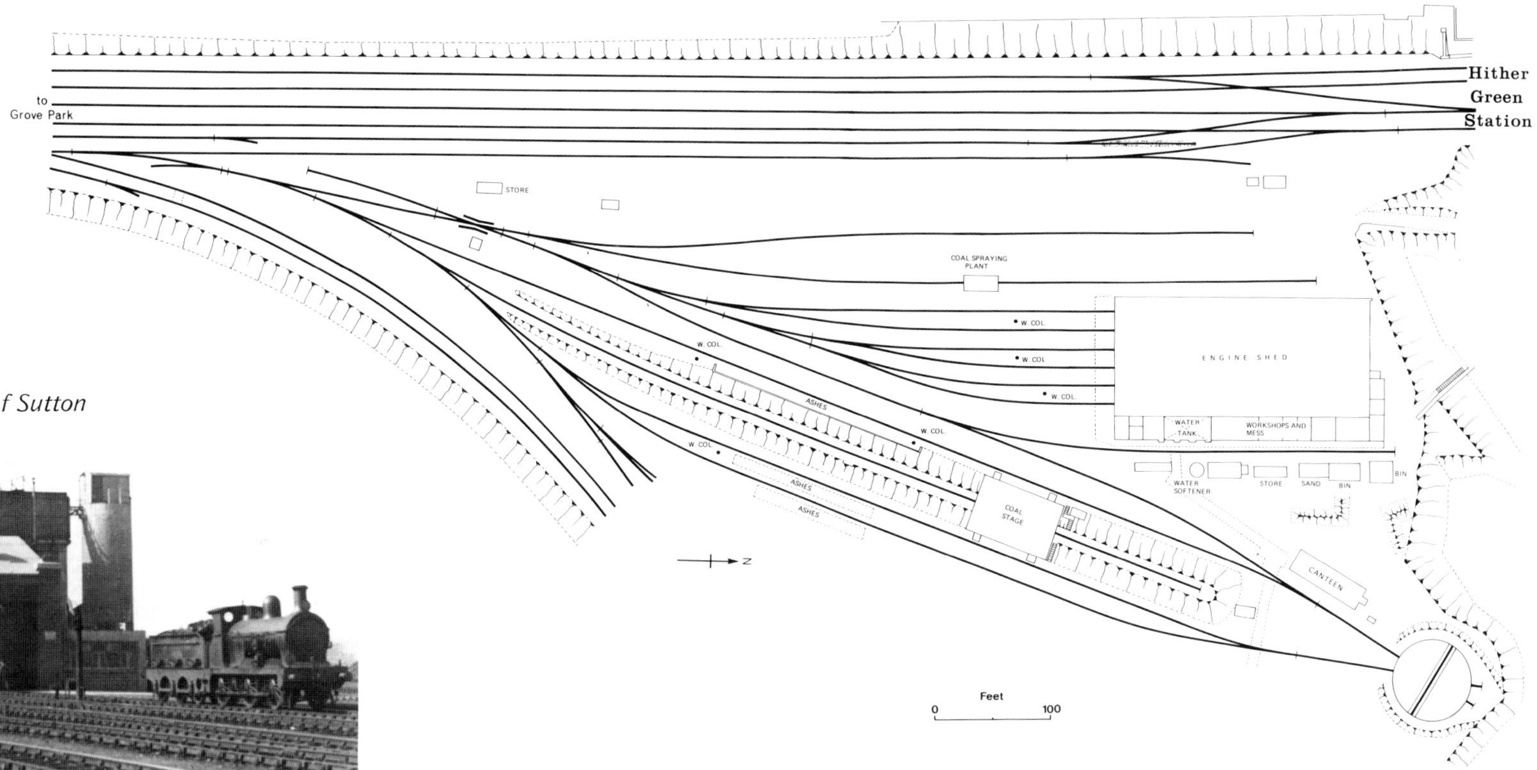

to Grove Park

STORE

COAL SPRAYING PLANT

ENGINE SHED

W COL

ASHES

WATER TANK

WORKSHOPS AND MESS

WATER SOFTENER

STORE

SAND

BIN

COAL STAGE

CANTEEN

ASHES

Feet
0 — 100

The shed shortly after completion.

Lens of Sutton

The Type 3 diesel takeover in 1961.

Ken Fairey

This was a modern well laid out shed opened by the Southern in 1933, and built at a cost of over £100,000. The site, just to the south of Hither Green station, had to be raised about fifteen feet on concrete piles, and the shed itself was constructed in concrete on steel framing. It was a single ended building with six roads, including a wheel drop covered by a northlight pattern roof. A coaling ramp enabling four engines to be coaled simultaneously was built, with the roads leading onto a 65 ft. turntable. A 5,000 gallon water softener was also provided.

The depot was intended primarily for locomotives working to and from the nearby yards and the allocation consequently consisted mainly of freight engines, including a number previously operated from Bricklayers Arms. The construction of Hither Green immediately preceded that of Norwood Junction and it is interesting to note the similarities between the two sheds. They were closely similar in construction and layout details, indeed being virtually the 'same model', and both were built to serve nearby yards. As at Norwood, shunting tanks, Moguls and 0-6-0s formed by far the majority of the locomotive stud of about forty to fifty engines.

Apart from improvements to the water supply in 1938 after problems with the well sunk into the chalk, the shed passed unchanged into British Railways ownership and diesels soon began to arrive in force. By 1951, ten diesel shunters were at Hither Green and by 1961 a considerable fleet of type 3 diesels had been built up. No steam duties remained by that year but a handful of class 'C' 0-6-0s were retained for special work for a while. The shed continued to serve as a diesel depot and the building itself can be seen in use today. The coal ramp has been demolished but the turntable remains in operational condition.

Horsham

1941

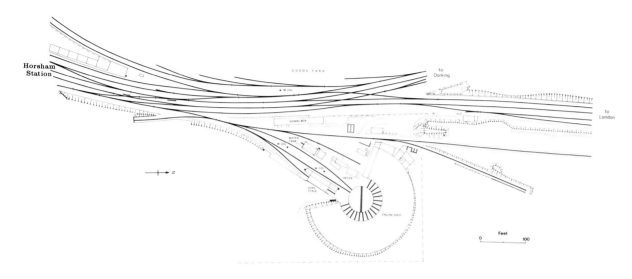

The original shed at Horsham was a small wooden building with three roads, leading directly onto a turntable installed immediately outside. The LBSCR replaced this with a ten road semi-roundhouse sited on the opposite side of the line, very similar in design to the second depot at Eastbourne. A plan of 1896 shows the new shed virtually complete and it would seem the roundhouse came into use about this time. The shed was brick built and contained a 46 ft. turntable, with coal stage and water tank supplied alongside the two approach roads. The building was extended shortly after the turn of the century, eight further roads being added in a contract of 1900.

Horsham was an important depot in LBSC days and was the headquarters of a locomotive district which included Three Bridges, Midhurst, Littlehampton and Bognor. It stood on a major junction and its allocation of 'Terriers', 0-4-2Ts and various 0-6-0s worked over most of the Brighton system. A slow decline began after 1923, however, with Littlehampton and Bognor gaining their independence and Midhurst closing completely, the Portsmouth No. 2 electrification via Horsham considerably reducing the depot's work. By 1947 the allocation at Three Bridges actually exceeded that of its former parent depot.

In 1927 it was decided to replace the somewhat undersized turntable and with the closure of Orpington it was intended that the redundant 55 ft. table should be transferred to Horsham. Various improvements to the yard were also carried out as part of this scheme.

Under BR the shed housed about twenty-five small, mainly tank engines for local duties in the area, the most modern in 1950 being a pair of 'Q' 0-6-0s. A travelling crane supplemented the coal stage after a few years and Ivatt 2-6-2Ts began to replace the old Brighton types. Only a handful of engines remained at closure in June 1964 and the shed was demolished shortly afterwards, the site now being occupied by industrial development.

Hard work but immaculate engine in 1926.

H.C. Casserley

A general view in 1959.

J. Scrace

Ilfracombe

1904

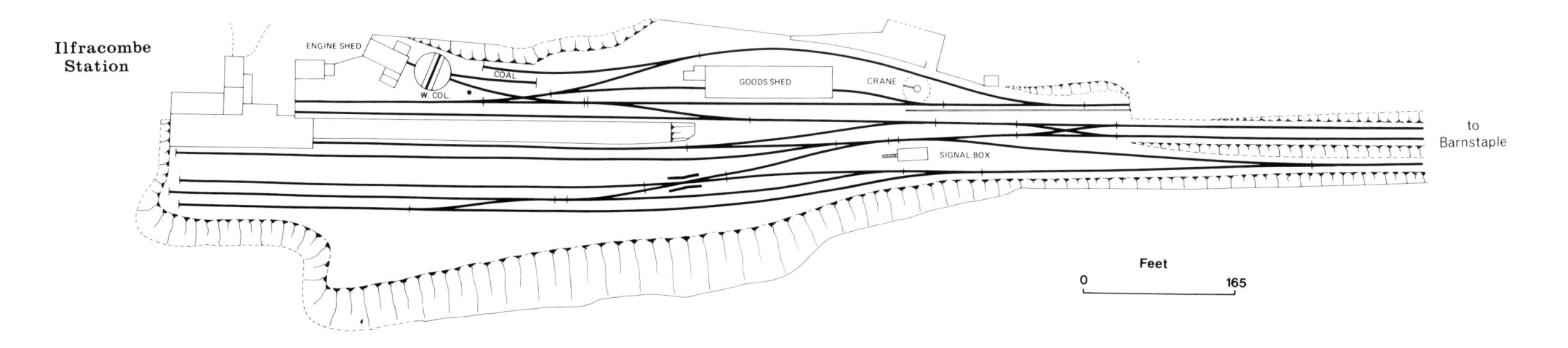

Ilfracombe Station

ENGINE SHED

COAL

W. COL.

GOODS SHED

CRANE

SIGNAL BOX

to Barnstaple

Feet
0   165

The original shed at Ilfracombe stood at the east side of the station. It was a single road building with a small turntable immediately in front to accommodate the 'Barnstaple Goods' and 4-4-0s that served the line in LSWR days. A subsidiary company of the LSW, the Barnstaple and Ilfracombe, opened the line and the shed in 1874. A replacement turntable was approved in 1895 and in 1910 a new 60 ft. engine pit was provided. In the same year, repairs costing £40 had to be made after an engine ran through the rear wall of the shed. It was closed after the grouping, however, when the Southern carried out extensive improvements and alterations to the station in 1929. A replacement building, again a single road shed but this time of the through type, opened on a site excavated in the rock some distance to the south. The new shed was built in concrete blocks with a pitched roof of corrugated asbestos, and a 65 ft. turntable with run-round loop was installed at the rear. A coaling platform and water tank were provided on the east side.

From the turn of the century, the line was operated by various LSWR classes, notably T9s and M7s, SR Moguls appearing in the 1930s and, after the war, light Pacifics. Improvements in coaling and watering equipment around this time were probably meant to coincide with the introduction of the larger engines, one of which usually was stabled overnight. Enlargement of the turntable to 70 ft. would also date from this time. Towards the end, the parent depot, Barnstaple Junction, supplied Ivatt 2-6-2Ts for most of the workings. Closure came in 1964 and shortly afterwards the shed was completely demolished.

'N' class Mogul outside the shed in 1935.

W.A. Camwell

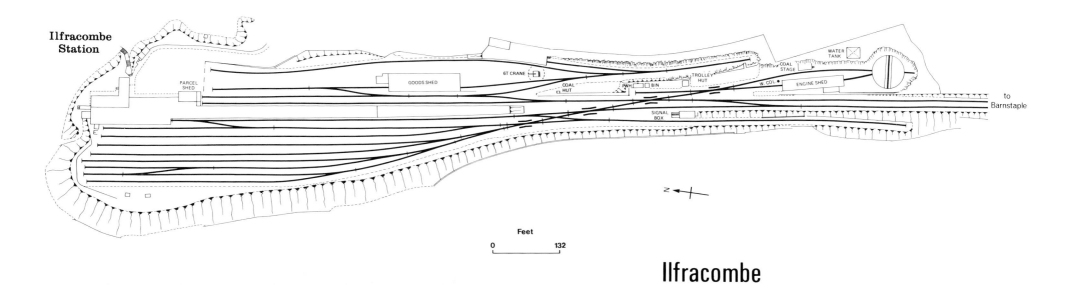

Ilfracombe
Station

PARCEL SHED

GOODS SHED

6T CRANE

COAL HUT

PWH   BIN

TROLLEY HUT

COAL STAGE

WATER TANK

W. COL.

ENGINE SHED

SIGNAL BOX

to Barnstaple

Feet

0   132

Ilfracombe

1952

The shed surviving intact into 1965, with standard 2-6-4T No. 80039 backing onto its train.

John H. Meredith

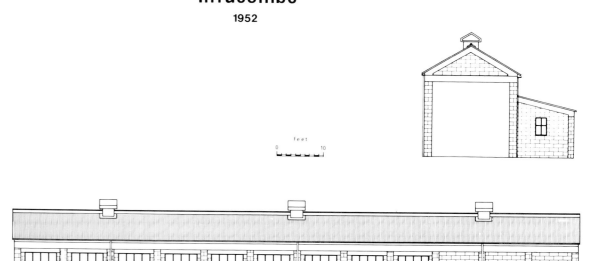

Feet

0   10

The original shed. The offices soon after opening were slightly altered.

47

Launceston

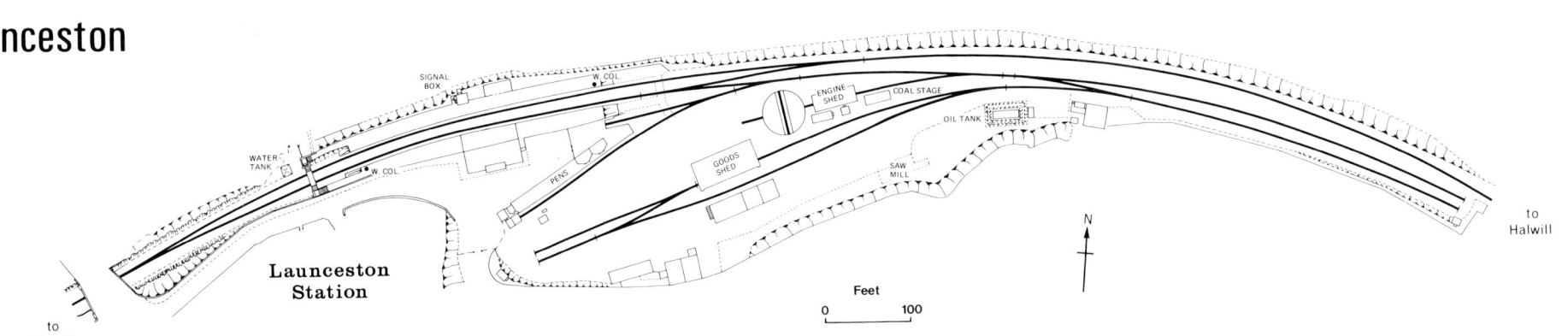

The LSWR opened its North Cornwall line through to Launceston in 1886 and the shed would seem to date from the same year. It was a tiny through building, even smaller than the nearby GWR sub shed and was of much less substantial construction than its neighbour, being a simple steel frame structure clad in corrugated sheeting. The pitched roof with raised vent was covered in similar material. A coal stage was provided outside the eastern end of the shed.

It was sub to Wadebridge under the LSWR and this arrangement continued under the Southern, 'M7' and 'O2' 0-4-4Ts being regular visitors. By 1932 a 50 ft. turntable had been installed, mainly for the use of visiting 'T9s' and Moguls. Sited at the rear of the shed, access was through the actual building, resulting in a somewhat inconvenient layout.

The last years of the shed are a little difficult to describe in any detail, but it was certainly of very little status. The building, though not the turntable, was already out of use and in very poor condition when the WR took over in 1962, closing the entire line four years later. The whole station area has since been redeveloped and no trace of the shed now remains.

The shed and turntable at Launceston.

W.A. Camwell

The derelict shed out of use in 1961. Engines still used the turntable at this time, including ex-GW types, as this picture shows. The turntable at the GWR stone built shed, in the background, had ceased operating by 1961.

R.C. Riley

Lyme Regis

1914

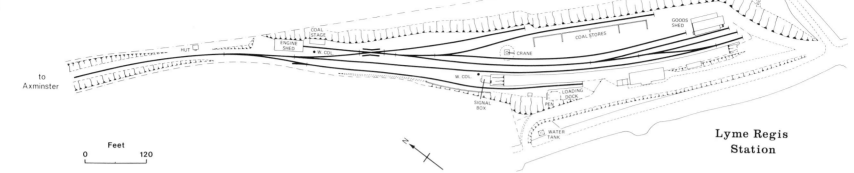

to Axminster

Feet
0 ———— 120

Lyme Regis Station

The original shed at Lyme Regis was a small single ended building, constructed in wood and opened when the Axminster and Lyme Regis Light Railway was completed in 1903. It was acquired by the LSWR in 1907 who afterwards normally stabled one or two tanks in the single road building. A new structure, this time in asbestos on steel framing, appeared in 1913 at a cost of £400, following the destruction of the old shed by fire. It was built on the same site but was slightly shorter and had a pitched roof, again in asbestos sheeting. A coal stage and water column stood immediately outside the shed.

The line became famous for the prolonged use of the Adams radial tanks, and one of these usually stabled at the shed, even well into BR ownership. The other two engines of the class when not at Lyme Regis, stabled at the parent depot, Exmouth Junction. The building was in rather a sad state in its final years, settling of the foundations causing it to lean considerably. The shed passed to the WR in 1962 and soon closed with the ensuing dieselisation, together with Exmouth and Seaton in November 1963, and has now been demolished.

Lyme Regis shed on 22nd April 1962. *P.J. Kelley*

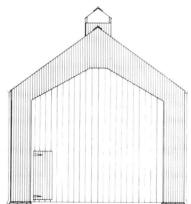

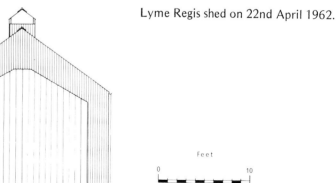

Feet
0 ———— 10

49

Lymington
1946

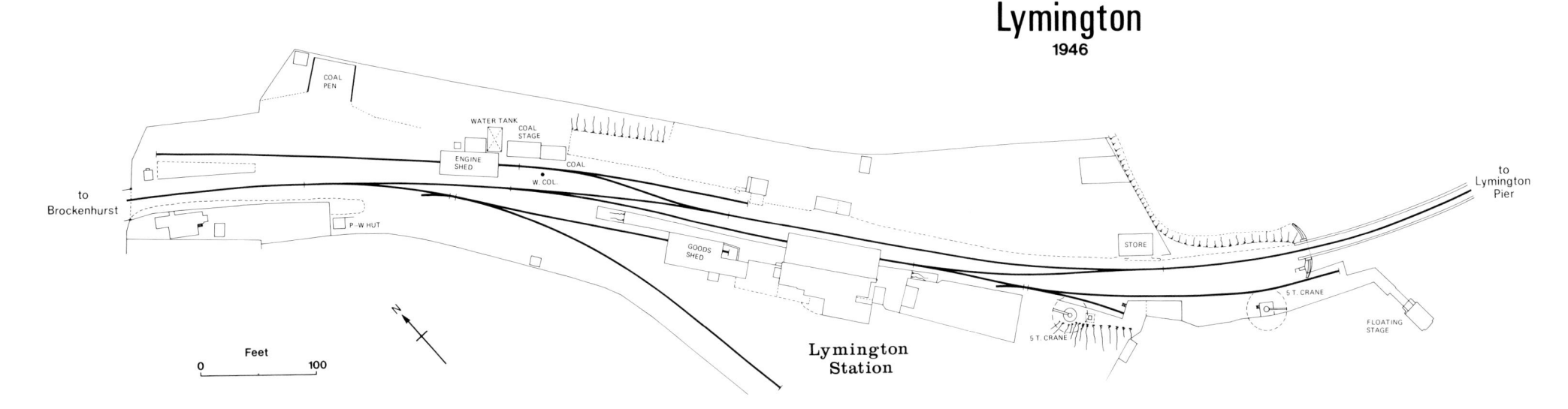

to
Brockenhurst

COAL PEN

WATER TANK

COAL STAGE

ENGINE SHED

COAL

W. COL.

P-W HUT

GOODS SHED

STORE

5 T. CRANE

5 T. CRANE

FLOATING STAGE

to
Lymington
Pier

Lymington
Station

N

Feet
0   100

This was a small single road shed opened, with the station, by the Lymington Railway Co. in 1858. It was brick built with a slated pitched roof and offices and a water tank were provided on the east side. Approach to the shed was originally from the north, but this was later reversed, probably coinciding with the extension of the line to Lymington Pier by the LSWR in 1884. The original approach road became a siding and a new coal stage was erected at the same time.

No turntable was installed at the shed, tank engines normally being employed on the branch workings, but the running of through trains to Lymington Pier necessitated servicing facilities for main line engines and in 1888 the provision of a turntable and water tank was approved at Brockenhurst, the junction of the branch with the main line.

Lymington was a sub shed of Eastleigh and normally a single tank locomotive was outstationed from the parent depot. 'M7' 0-4-4Ts were the regular engines for many years until they were replaced by the larger Ivatt tanks in the 1950s. The line gained a fleeting fame in 1966 when it became the last steam worked branch in southern England and the shed continued to house the branch engine, a 2-6-2 or 2-6-4 tank. Within a few months, however, the steam service was withdrawn prior to electrification and the shed closed at the same time. It has since been completely demolished.

Lymington shed.
J. Scrace

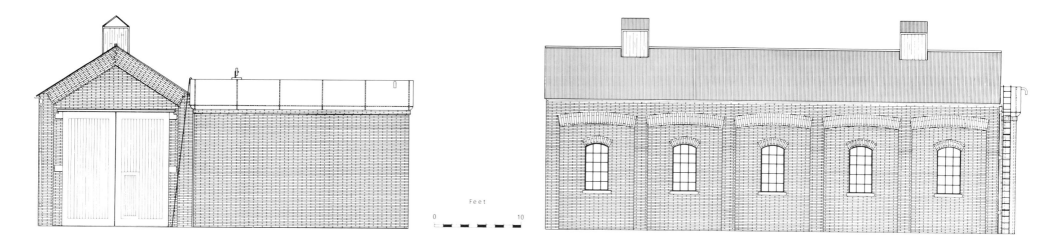

M7 0-4-4T No. 60 is just visible, stabled in the shed in 1936.
W.A. Camwell

New Cross Gate
1910

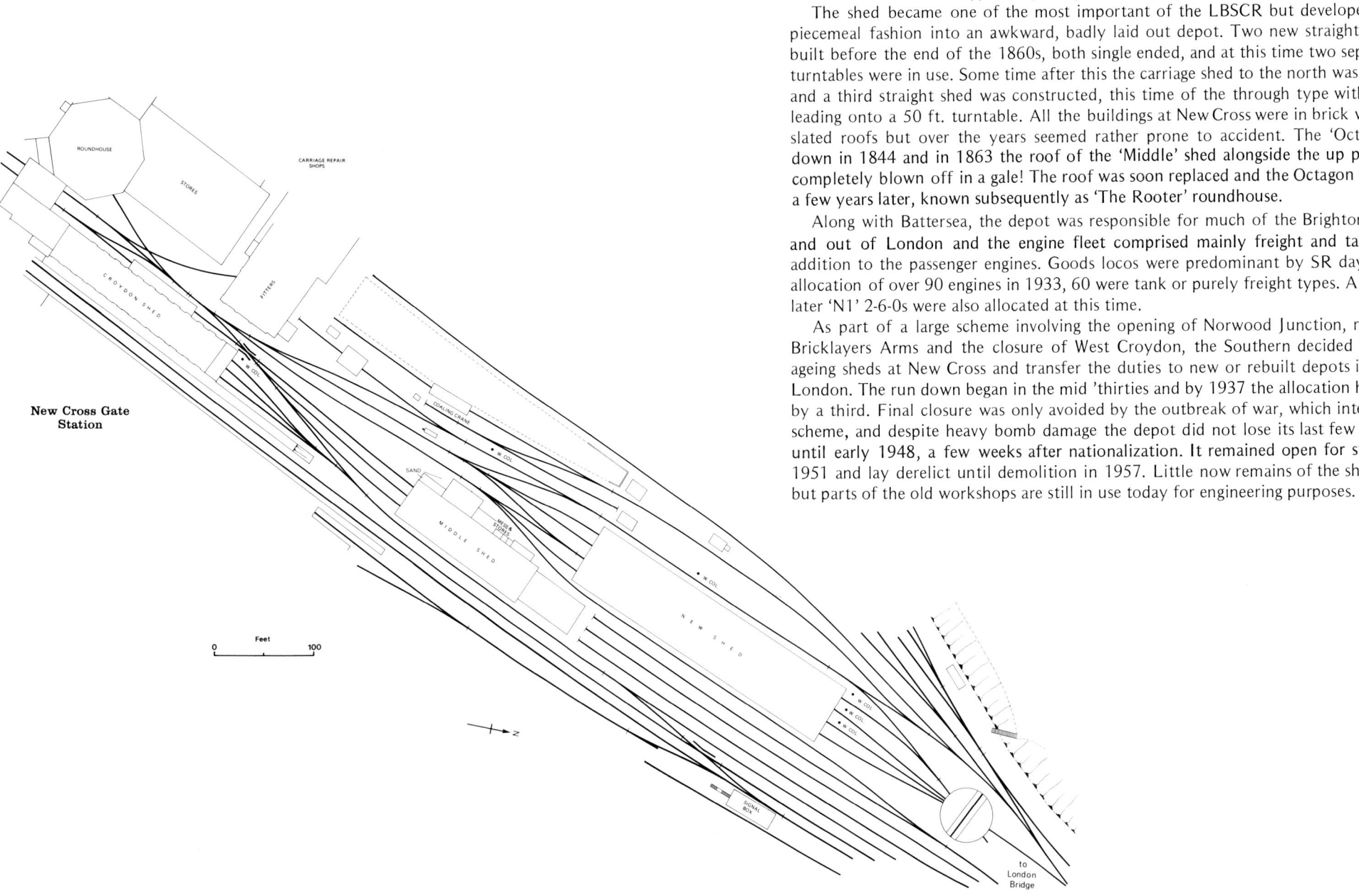

**New Cross Gate
Station**

Feet
0   100

The first buildings at New Cross Gate were the locomotive shed and workshops of the London and Croydon Railway and were opened in 1839. For many years it was known simply as New Cross, the name changing on grouping to avoid confusion with the ex-SER station. The depot was notable in that the first shed building was a roundhouse, one of the earliest in the country, subsequently known through its shape as the 'Octagon'.

The shed became one of the most important of the LBSCR but developed in a very piecemeal fashion into an awkward, badly laid out depot. Two new straight sheds were built before the end of the 1860s, both single ended, and at this time two separate 40 ft. turntables were in use. Some time after this the carriage shed to the north was demolished and a third straight shed was constructed, this time of the through type with four roads leading onto a 50 ft. turntable. All the buildings at New Cross were in brick with pitched slated roofs but over the years seemed rather prone to accident. The 'Octagon' burnt down in 1844 and in 1863 the roof of the 'Middle' shed alongside the up platform was completely blown off in a gale! The roof was soon replaced and the Octagon itself rebuilt a few years later, known subsequently as 'The Rooter' roundhouse.

Along with Battersea, the depot was responsible for much of the Brighton's traffic in and out of London and the engine fleet comprised mainly freight and tank types in addition to the passenger engines. Goods locos were predominant by SR days and of an allocation of over 90 engines in 1933, 60 were tank or purely freight types. All five of the later 'N1' 2-6-0s were also allocated at this time.

As part of a large scheme involving the opening of Norwood Junction, rebuilding at Bricklayers Arms and the closure of West Croydon, the Southern decided to close the ageing sheds at New Cross and transfer the duties to new or rebuilt depots in south east London. The run down began in the mid 'thirties and by 1937 the allocation had dropped by a third. Final closure was only avoided by the outbreak of war, which interrupted the scheme, and despite heavy bomb damage the depot did not lose its last few locomotives until early 1948, a few weeks after nationalization. It remained open for stabling until 1951 and lay derelict until demolition in 1957. Little now remains of the shed buildings but parts of the old workshops are still in use today for engineering purposes.

The 'New' shed.

Collection of R.C. Riley

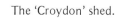

The 'Croydon' shed.

Lens of Sutton

The 'Middle' shed.

Lens of Sutton

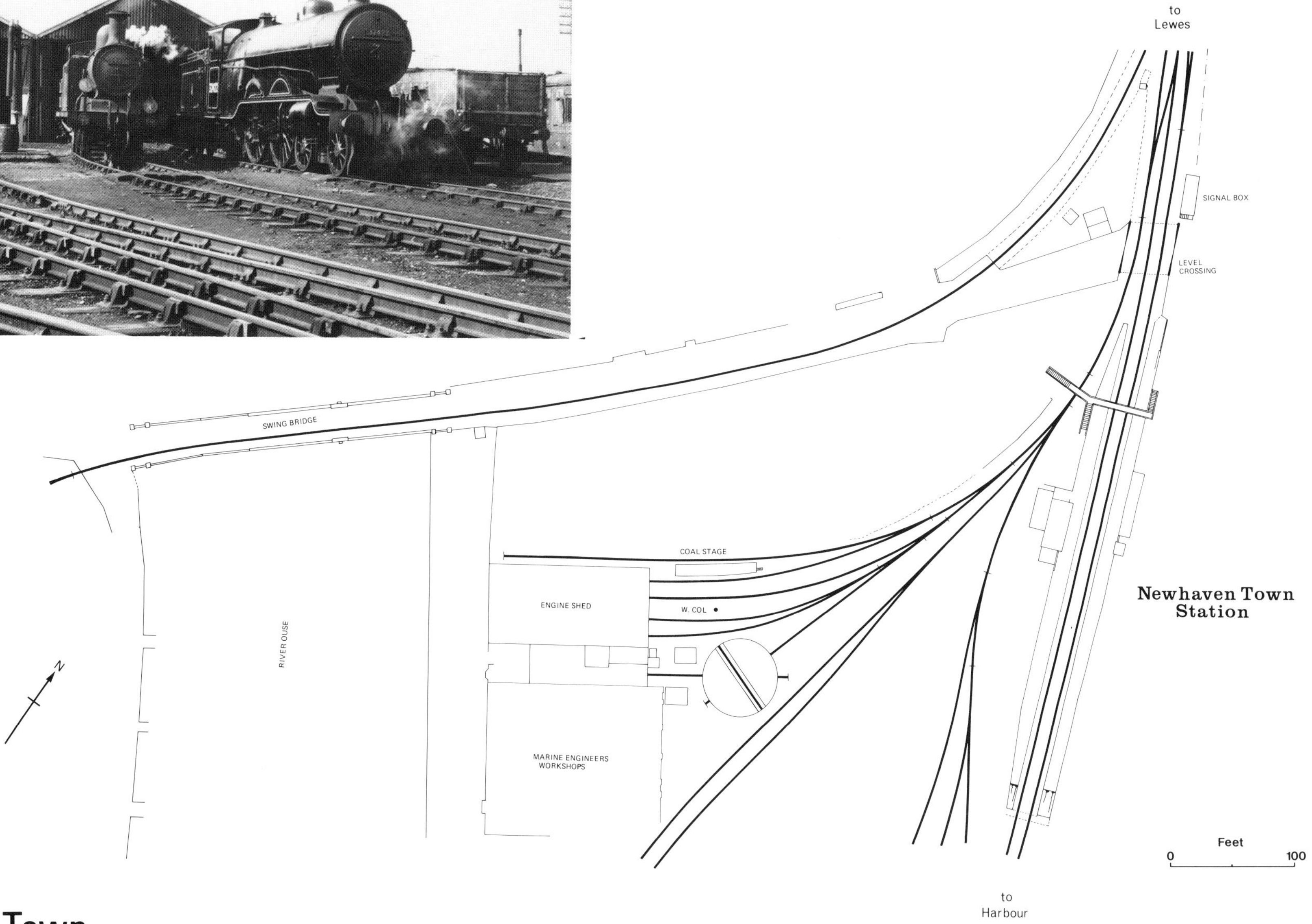

to
Lewes

SIGNAL BOX

LEVEL
CROSSING

SWING BRIDGE

COAL STAGE

ENGINE SHED

W. COL

RIVER OUSE

N

MARINE ENGINEERS
WORKSHOPS

**Newhaven Town
Station**

Feet
0   100

to
Harbour

Newhaven Town
1950

The contract for the building of a new depot at Newhaven was drawn up by the LBSCR in 1887 and the fairly cheaply constructed shed was built shortly afterwards. Corrugated sheeting was used for the main parts of the building, which had four roads covered by a roof of two pitches. It replaced an older two road shed near the Harbour station and was built alongside a marine engineers depot. In 1917 a larger 60 ft. turntable was installed, presumably for the new 'K' 2-6-0s then beginning to work freight trains to Newhaven.

The main duties of the small depot were the various dock shunting turns, most of its regular allocation of around 16 engines being small tanks, and the servicing of visiting freight and boat train engines. Two or three 'Terriers' were always to be found at the shed and one, No. 32636, served continuously for 57 years. The shed was administered from Brighton but maintained its separate allocation throughout Southern ownership. Under BR it was officially regarded as sub to Brighton and shared the same code. Light Pacifics were authorised to enter the shed yard in 1950 but traffic was already declining and in 1955 the depot was reduced to a stabling point, and the remaining duties transferred to Brighton. The last 'A1X' became redundant in 1963 and the shed closed in September of that year. Although the turntable has been removed and the yard cleared, the shed itself was taken over by a private concern and is still in use today.

An early Victorian view of the shed showing the original smoke ventilators. *Lens of Sutton*

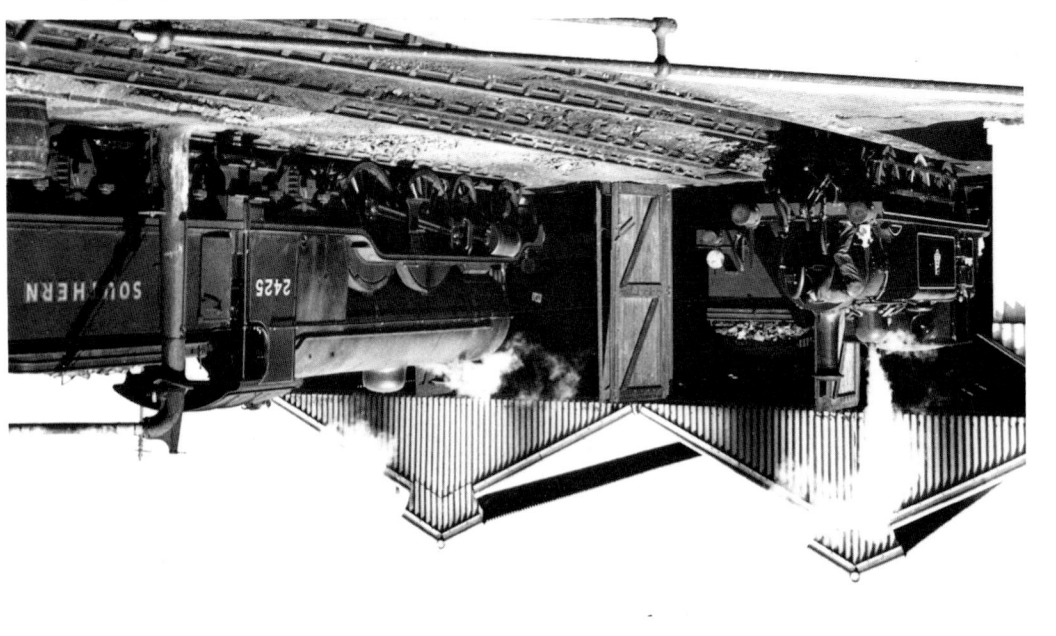

The shed in early BR days. *Pamlin Prints*

The converted shed today. *Author's collection*

Newport
1935

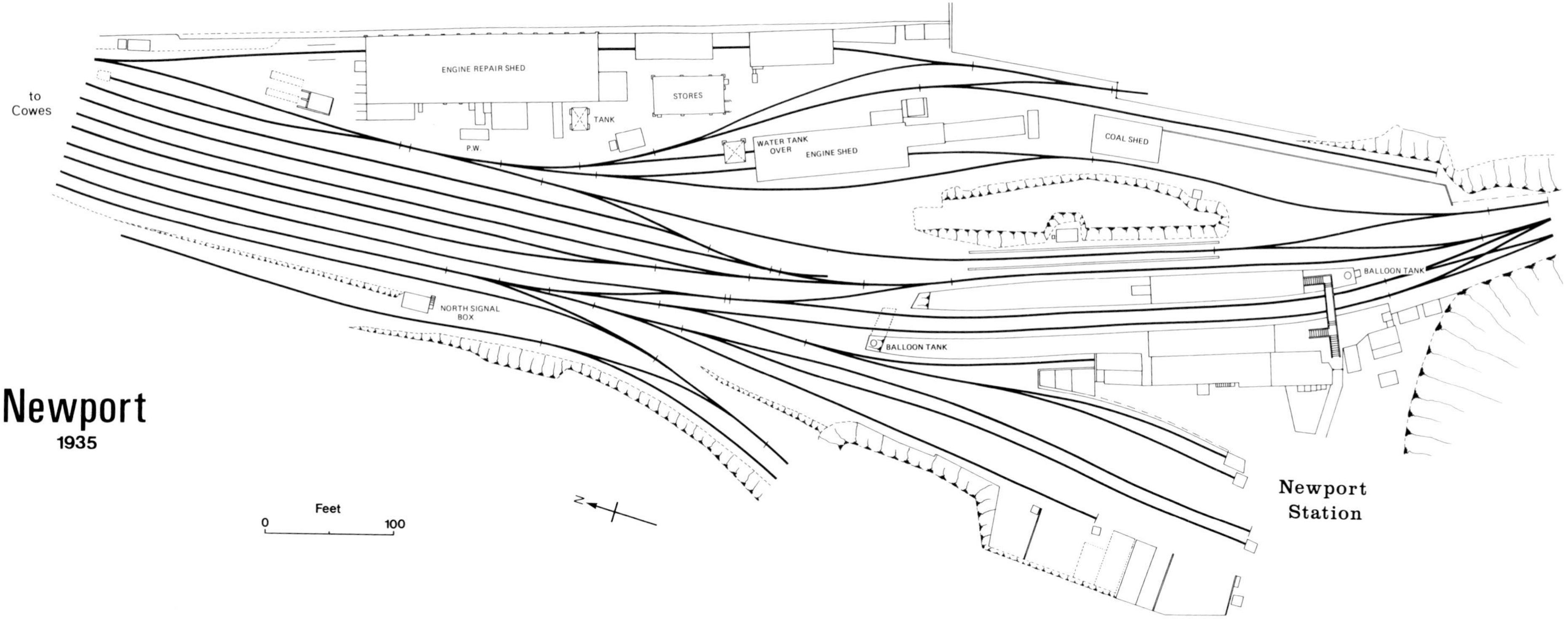

to Cowes

ENGINE REPAIR SHED

STORES

TANK

P.W.

WATER TANK OVER ENGINE SHED

COAL SHED

BALLOON TANK

NORTH SIGNAL BOX

BALLOON TANK

Newport Station

Feet
0   100

N

The Isle of Wight Central Railway built the shed at Newport, probably in the late 1870s after the lines from Ryde and Merstone were completed. The building stood slightly to the north of the station, and was built in wood and corrugated sheeting, its two roads covered by a pitched roof with central raised vent. It was a through building with a water tank built over one of the roads immediately outside the shed. There was no turntable, the company's locos being all tank engines.

The premises at Newport, like Ryde, had a rather general operating function, repairs being carried out to wagons and carriages as well as to locomotives. The nearby loco repair shop, however, began to fall out of use under the Southern and in 1929 it was decided to convert the by-now disused shop to carriage painting, at a cost of some £423. The engine hoist inside the works was removed just prior to the war and installed at the south end of the shed yard, near the new coal stage approved in 1930.

The depot continued in use through the 'fifties, its duties steadily decreasing, 'E1' 0-6-0Ts and 'O2s' being the usual engines. The lines to Merstone and Yarmouth had closed by 1956 and the shed itself closed in November the following year, Ryde taking over the remaining duties. The remaining two routes closed in 1966 and the depot has now been completely demolished.

Yarmouth and *Bembridge* alongside the shed in 1956, a year before closure.

S.C. Nash

This was the principal locomotive depot of the LSWR and an engine shed on the site dates from the earliest years of the railway, probably when the extension was completed to Waterloo in 1848. This early building, sited alongside the main line near to the works, was a seven road through shed with a pair of coal stages and 40 ft. turntables provided at each end. This was later replaced by a semi-roundhouse building set at right angles to the main line, the site of the earlier depot disappearing under additional running lines. The new roundhouse was provided with twenty-six roads radiating from a pair of 42 ft. turntables, and two large covered coal stages were built alongside the shed approach roads.

The shed and yard, seen from the nearby flats.
Lens of Sutton

Nine Elms
1939

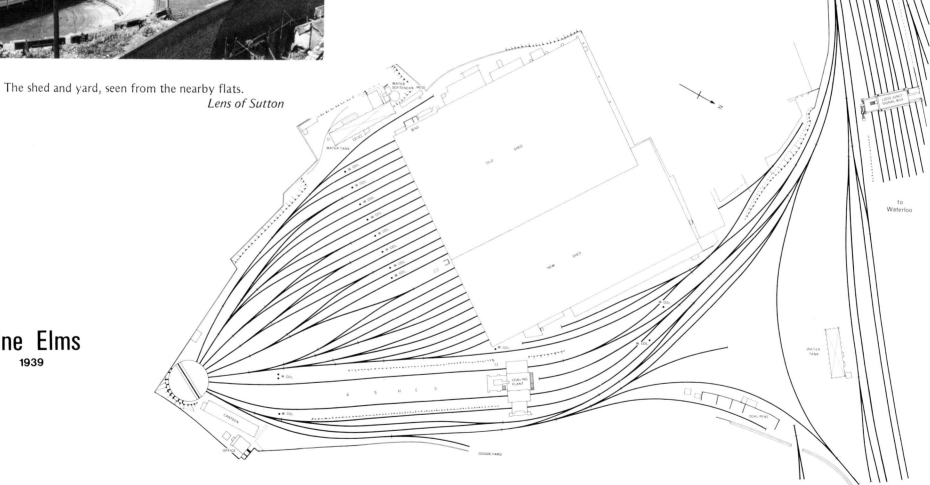

2168

The old shed at Nine Elms c1910; the construction of the new shed is taking place at the right.

The next development at Nine Elms was the construction of the first part of the modern depot. This took the form of a huge fifteen road single ended shed measuring 365 ft. by 235 ft. sited just to the west of the semi-roundhouse. It was brick built and had a pitched slated roof similar in design to the later constructions at Salisbury and Eastleigh. A large new coal stage supported on brick arches was provided and all fifteen roads led onto a new 50 ft. turntable. The shed was brought into use around 1889 and by the turn of the century some two hundred locomotives were stationed at the depot. Despite a decline of about a fifth by 1922 this total made it by far the most important LSWR shed, its locos working all kinds of freight and passenger services over the main lines of the system, as well as the numerous pre-electrification suburban services.

Nine Elms was to see still further rebuilding, however; the semi-roundhouse, used solely for suburban tank engines since the opening of the straight shed, was demolished on the transfer of the works to Eastleigh in 1909. Its demolition now enabled an eleven road extension to be made alongside the 'old' straight shed. This latest building was authorised in 1910 at a cost of over £26,000 and two years later the installation was also approved of a new 65 ft. turntable, costing £845. This final building, now in its turn known as the 'new shed' was constructed somewhat differently from its neighbour. Although the walls were again of brick, the roof pitches and central vents were transverse to those of the original building. The coal stage now serving a vast twenty-five road depot was retained for several years but in the last months of its existence the LSWR decided to replace it with modern ferro-concrete apparatus. The 400 ton coaling plant, costing over £9,000 did not actually come into use until after the formation of the Southern Railway.

The Southern initiated little in the way of structural alteration at Nine Elms but it continued to be the principal depot of the Western Section, and in terms of total allocation ranked second only to Stewarts Lane on the system as a whole. The number of engines stationed at Nine Elms steadily declined throughout the 'twenties and 'thirties, however, and had fallen to around a hundred and twenty by the outbreak of war in 1939. The depot must have presented severe difficulties to the maintenance department with seventeen separate classes being present even as late as 1933, from a solitary 'T9' 4-4-0 to a stud of twenty-eight 'M7' 0-4-4Ts. Large numbers of mixed traffic 4-6-0s, 'H15' and 'S15' were also allocated, as well as of course, the 'King Arthurs' and 'Lord Nelsons'.

The construction of a water softener, at a cost of over £1,400 around 1930 and the provision of an engine washing plant in 1936 were about the only improvements carried out by the Southern until the bombing of 1940-43 reversed many of the advances of the previous decades. The depot was bombed on many occasions and suffered severe damage, particularly to the roof. Repairs were effected in asbestos sheeting after the war but much of the original 'old shed' roof was never replaced.

Apart from the introduction of more modern locomotives by British Railways, the period after 1948 again saw little in the way of rebuilding. The allocation declined still further and the variety of locomotive types also decreased. Oddities were a stud of ten ex-GW pannier tanks allocated in 1959, but by the mid-'sixties the various standard types and Bulleid Pacifics greatly outnumbered the handful of Moguls and 'S15's. The depot's duties had undergone a gradual contraction over the years, local turns disappearing and shunting duties going over to diesel traction. Towards the end the locomotives were used principally on the main lines to Bournemouth, Southampton and Salisbury, with several 2-6-2Ts for the Waterloo empty stock workings. The shed closed completely in July 1967 when steam services were withdrawn and after standing empty for a couple of years was demolished to make way for the new Nine Elms Market, no trace now remaining of the last London steam shed.

The old shed at Nine Elms from the nearby flats.

Lens of Sutton

The 'old' shed. The girder on the right formed part of the original entrance to the shed.

Lens of Sutton

The 'new' shed.

Lens of Sutton

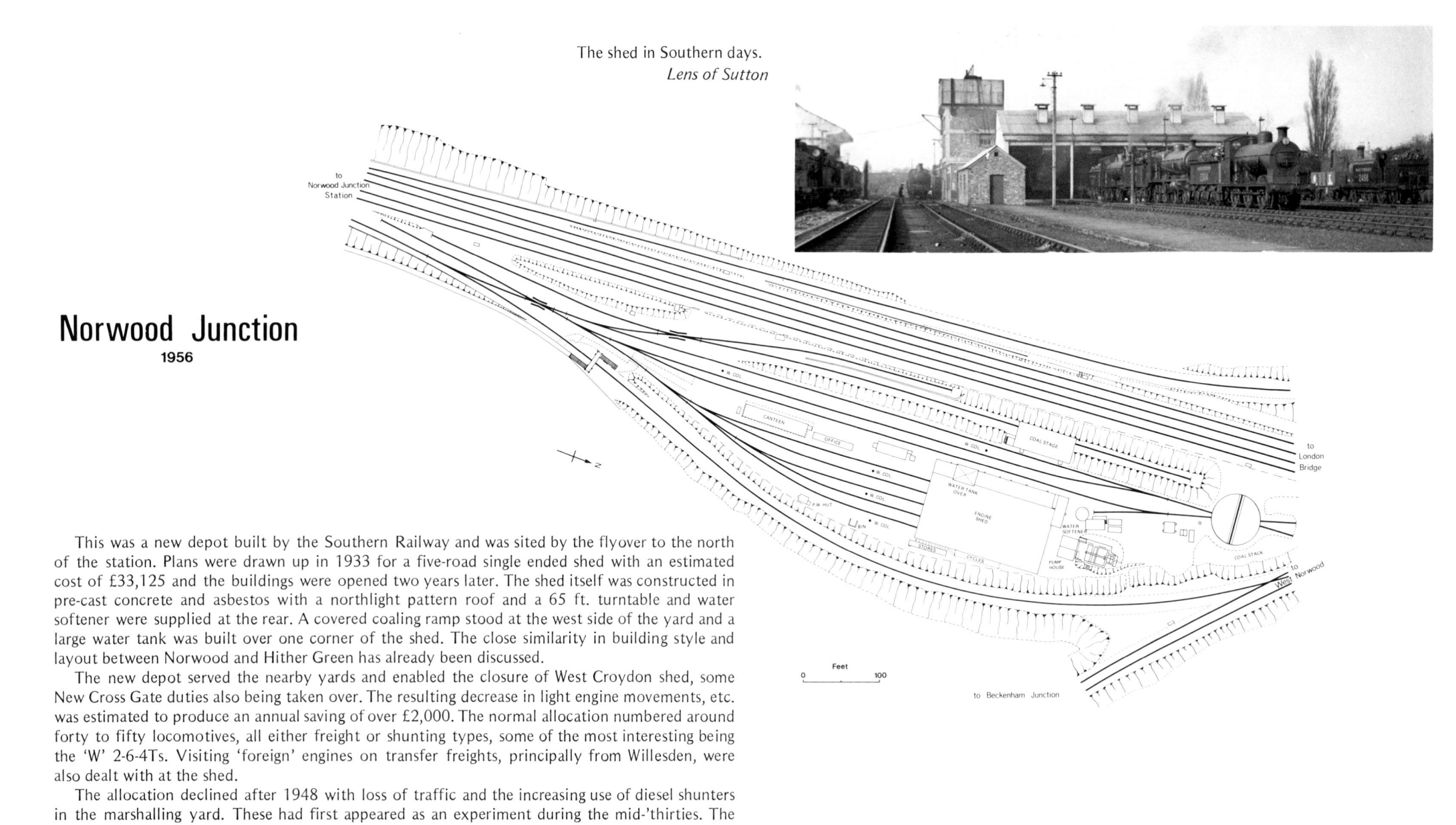

The shed in Southern days.
Lens of Sutton

Norwood Junction
1956

Feet
0   100

to Norwood Junction Station

to London Bridge

to West Norwood

to Beckenham Junction

This was a new depot built by the Southern Railway and was sited by the flyover to the north of the station. Plans were drawn up in 1933 for a five-road single ended shed with an estimated cost of £33,125 and the buildings were opened two years later. The shed itself was constructed in pre-cast concrete and asbestos with a northlight pattern roof and a 65 ft. turntable and water softener were supplied at the rear. A covered coaling ramp stood at the west side of the yard and a large water tank was built over one corner of the shed. The close similarity in building style and layout between Norwood and Hither Green has already been discussed.

The new depot served the nearby yards and enabled the closure of West Croydon shed, some New Cross Gate duties also being taken over. The resulting decrease in light engine movements, etc. was estimated to produce an annual saving of over £2,000. The normal allocation numbered around forty to fifty locomotives, all either freight or shunting types, some of the most interesting being the 'W' 2-6-4Ts. Visiting 'foreign' engines on transfer freights, principally from Willesden, were also dealt with at the shed.

The allocation declined after 1948 with loss of traffic and the increasing use of diesel shunters in the marshalling yard. These had first appeared as an experiment during the mid-'thirties. The shed received an influx of locos as Bricklayers Arms and Stewarts Lane were run down in 1962-3 but was itself closed when its last remaining steam engine was withdrawn in January 1964. The buildings were demolished in 1966 and the site is now occupied by a BR engineering department.

A general view from the footbridge in 1958.
Photomatic

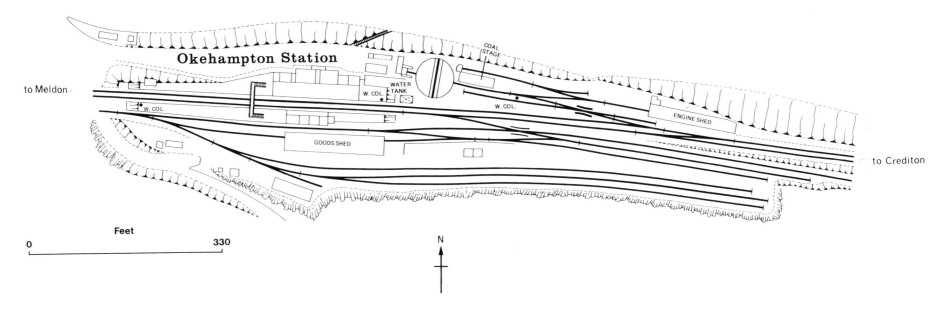

Okehampton Station

to Meldon

COAL STAGE

WATER TANK

W. COL.

W. COL.

W. COL.

ENGINE SHED

GOODS SHED

to Crediton

Feet

0   330

N

Okehampton

1953

No shed was built at Okehampton at first but a turntable for visiting engines was provided on the site for many years. A shed was proposed in 1894 however, and shortly afterwards a small single road wooden shed with a slated roof appeared, only to be entirely destroyed by fire in 1920. Seven years previously, enlargements costing over £600 had been authorised. The replacement shed, again with only one road, was built within a few months but was constructed this time in concrete blocks with an asbestos roof, at the cost of £1,500. The LSWR obviously did not want to see the disastrous fire repeated! The shed was single ended with a coal stage and 50 ft. turntable immediately outside.

Okehampton regularly serviced and turned visiting engines, notably those used on the ballast trains to and from the nearby Meldon Quarry. The service department shunter was housed in a separate shed in the quarry itself.

Okehampton was sub to Exmouth Junction and this remained the situation right through into BR ownership, when the engines outstationed were a 'T9' and two 'N' 2-6-0s. In 1947 a new 70 ft. turntable was installed a few yards to the west, enabling larger types like 'S15' 4-6-0s to work the ballast trains and a new covered coaling canopy was provided around the same time. The shed was transferred to the WR along with the parent depot in 1962 and was still in use two years later, but was demolished following the closure of the lines to Wadebridge and Bude in 1966.

'T9' class 4-4-0 No. 30717 at the shed in 1953.
J.H. Meredith

An elevated view of the shed in Southern days.
W.A. Camwell

'T9' class No. 30709 outside Okehampton shed.
E. Crawforth

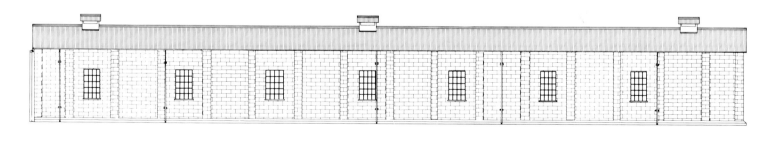

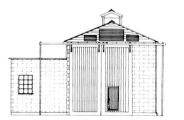

The shed as built with only three smoke vents and sliding doors.

Plymouth Friary
1940

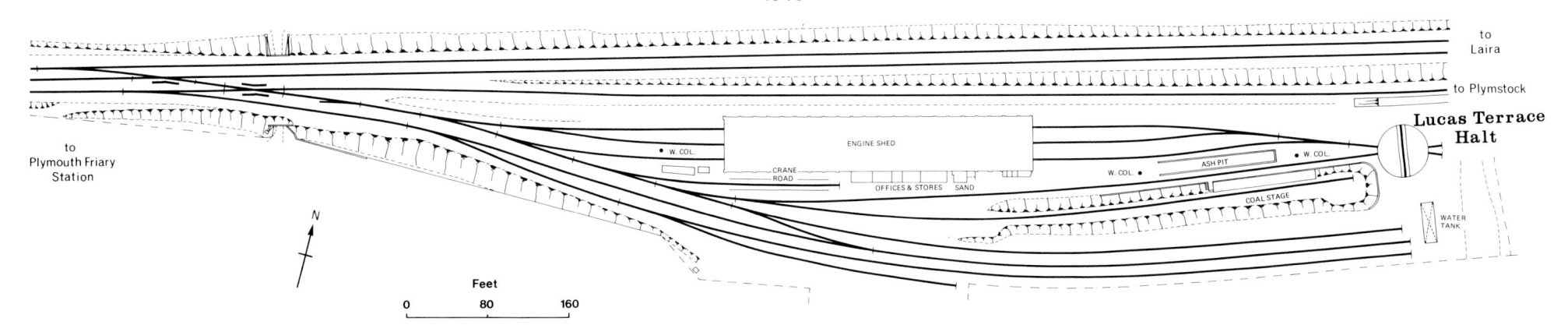

A typical LSWR depot, the gable glazing, as at many similar ex-SW sheds, has been re-placed by corrugated sheeting in BR days.

Ken Fairey

The original shed at Friary was a small two road building sited near the goods shed by the station. It housed only four engines and this being considered inadequate the LSWR authorised a replacement shed in 1905, this time to house fifteen locos. The new depot, costing over £19,000 was built on spare ground near the station and was virtually complete by 1908. It was a long through shed built in brick with a slated pitched roof covering three roads. These led onto a 50 ft. turntable at the eastern end of the yard where a covered coaling ramp and water tank were also provided.

Friary was principally a servicing depot for locomotives working in on the main line from Exeter but the allocation of about twenty-five engines included 'B4' tanks for dock work and 'O2' passenger tanks for minor lines like the Turnchapel branch. 'T9' 4-4-0s handled the bulk of the passenger duties. The depot was also responsible for a small sub shed at Callington and, particularly in later years, the ex-PD&SWJR 0-6-2Ts from that shed frequently appeared at the main depot for washout and repairs.

Few changes occurred under the Southern but a lifting crane had appeared by 1933 and in 1938 it was decided to alter the coal ramp to deal with the 'high modern tenders'. Friary was damaged several times by bombs in 1940 and 1941 and after nationalization the various standard types and light Pacifics became increasingly common at the shed. It was transferred to the WR, along with Callington, in 1958 and after being run down for several years, finally closed in May 1963, the remaining locos transferring to Laira. Shortly afterwards the buildings were demolished and the site is now occupied by commercial development.

A post-war view, the glazing showing evidence of bomb blast damage.

S.C. Townroe

Ramsgate Town

1910

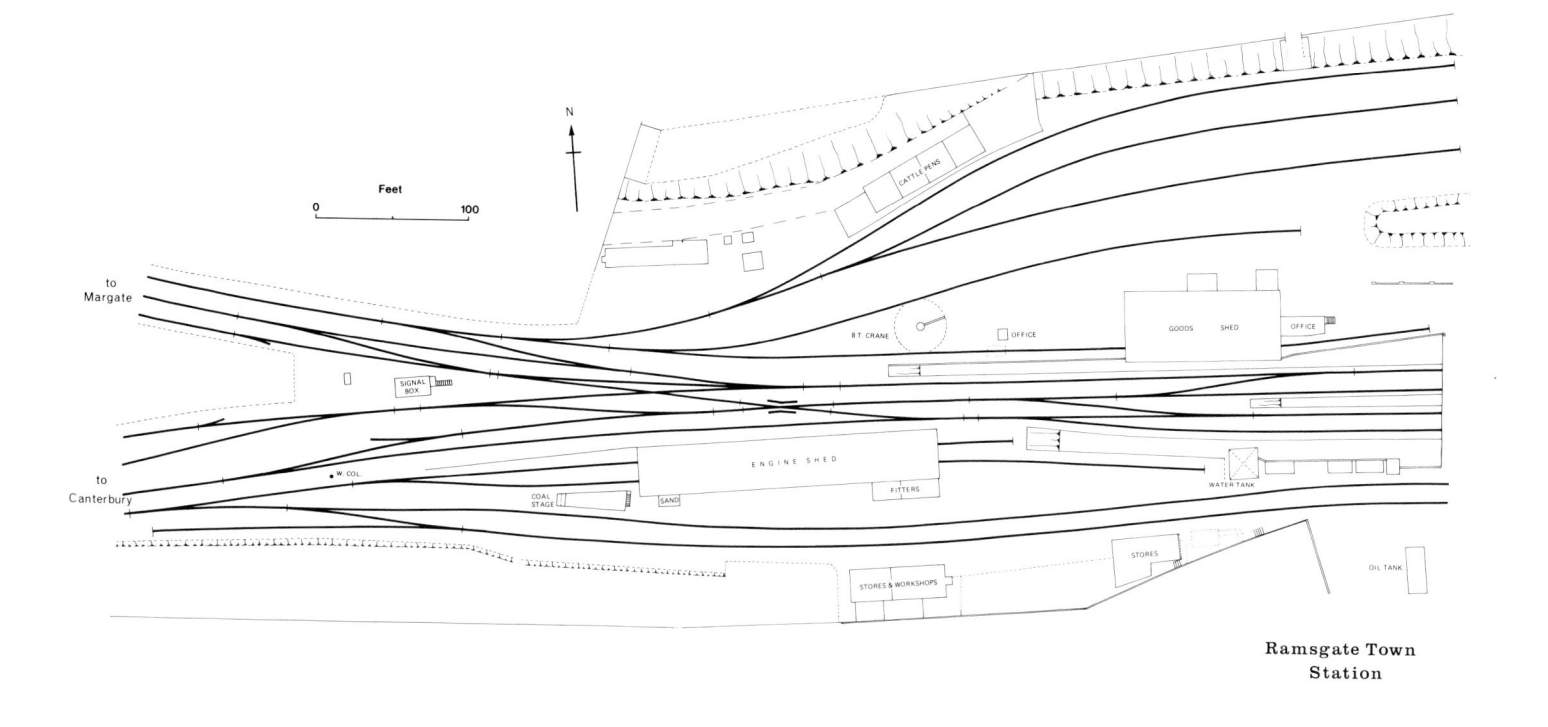

N

Feet
0   100

to
Margate

to
Canterbury

SIGNAL
BOX

W. COL.

COAL
STAGE

SAND

ENGINE SHED

FITTERS

B.T. CRANE

OFFICE

GOODS   SHED

OFFICE

WATER TANK

CATTLE PENS

STORES & WORKSHOPS

STORES

OIL TANK

**Ramsgate Town
Station**

Ramsgate was one of several large modern depots built by the Southern between grouping and the Second World War. Authorised in 1926 at a cost of £55,000, it was a six road single ended structure built mainly in concrete with a northlight pattern roof. A brick built water tower was provided on the northern side and a 65 ft. turntable and mechanical coaling plant were installed in the yard. Originally, it was intended to construct a coaling ramp, costing £7,000, but this was later altered to a coaling plant, involving a further £3,000.

The opening of the new depot brought about the closure of several smaller sheds, Margate West and Ramsgate Town disappearing in 1926, and Deal in 1930. Ramsgate Town, the ex-SER shed was a long through building, in brick, with offices and workshops housed in a second building separated by a pair of tracks. Fifteen engines were allocated in 1898. It presumably dated from the opening of the station in 1846 and although situated at the end of a branch, no turntable seems to have been provided. It went out of use in 1926 and, along with the old station, was completely demolished.

The LCDR also maintained an establishment at Ramsgate alongside Harbour station, consisting simply of offices and a water tank labelled 'loco department' on a very early plan. It was used by the station pilot from the opening of the line in 1863. A turntable was also provided at the far end of the station. However, these facilities were never regarded as a separate depot and Ramsgate Harbour does not appear on any LCD or subsequent lists.

The new SR depot did not eventually come into use until 1930 and normally around forty locomotives were allocated. 'King Arthurs' and 'Schools' were sent there on opening along with eleven 'D1' 4-4-0s. With a dozen 'H' 0-4-4Ts this meant that only six of the engines were specifically freight types. The available water supply at the shed was particularly unsuitable for steam locomotives and in order to remedy this a 10,000 gallon water softener was authorised in 1933 at a cost of £2,500.

The depot became part of the Ashford district under BR and in the 'fifties Bulleid Pacifics and standard types became common. The Kent Coast electrification project of 1959 meant the loss of Ramsgate's regular allocation and its designation as a mere stabling point, servicing visiting locos from Ashford, Bricklayers Arms and Dover. By the following year the shed building itself had been taken over for conversion to e.m.u. maintenance and locos were serviced and stabled in the open. It closed completely in December 1960, steam servicing in the Thanet area being concentrated at Margate for the final few months. Although partially demolished during conversion work, much of the shed building can still be seen.

The shed in 1958.

A 1939 view of the shed yard with twenty-seven engines on view.
W.A. Camwell

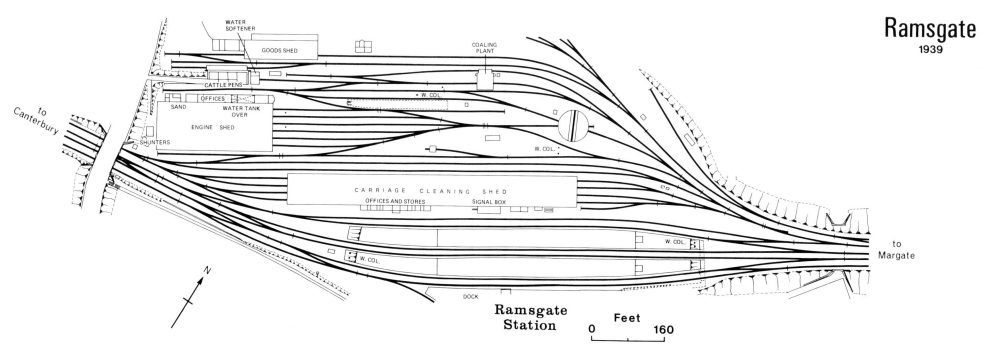

Ramsgate
1939

WATER SOFTENER

GOODS SHED

COALING PLANT

CATTLE PENS

OFFICES

to Canterbury

SAND

WATER TANK OVER

ENGINE SHED

SHUNTERS

W. COL.

W. COL.

CARRIAGE CLEANING SHED

OFFICES AND STORES

SIGNAL BOX

to Margate

W. COL.

W. COL.

DOCK

N

Ramsgate Station

Feet

0   160

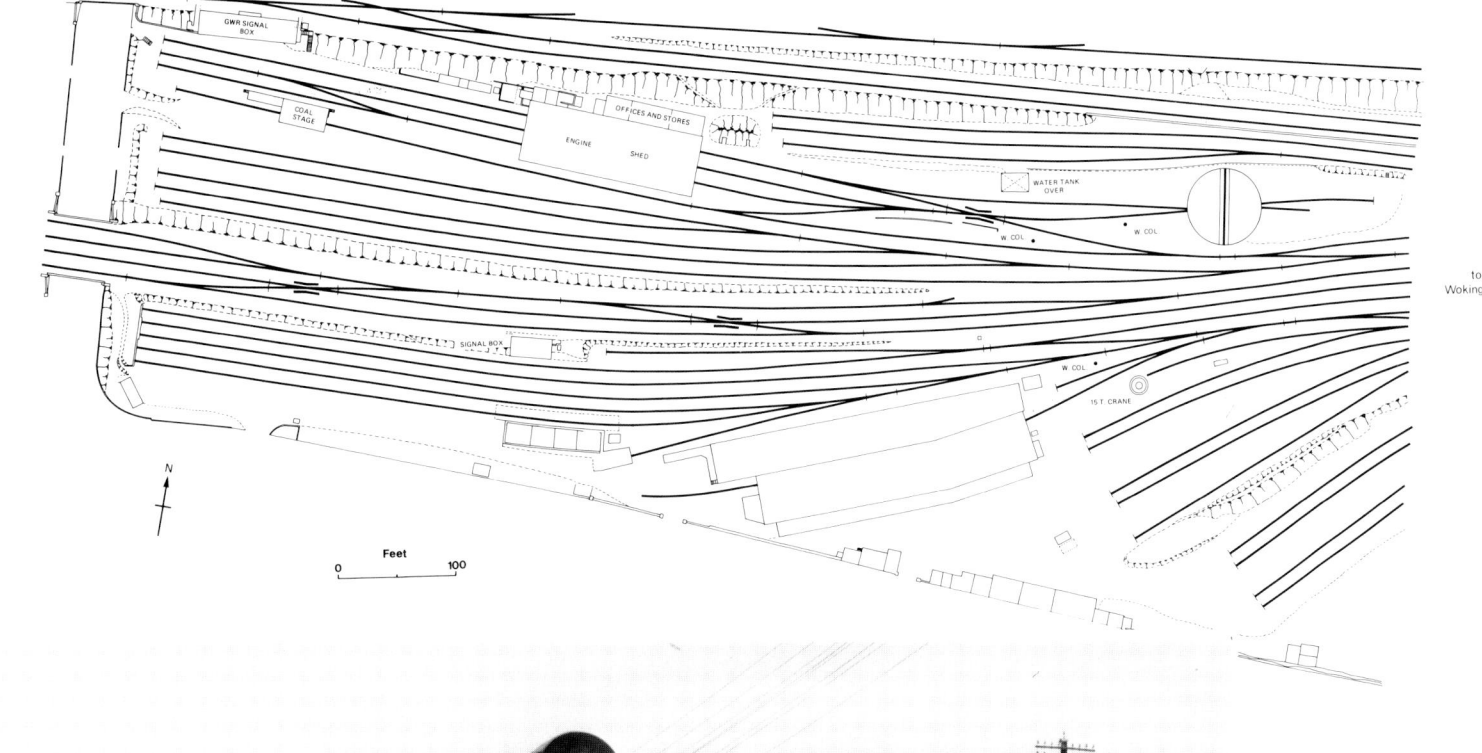

G.W.R. Running Lines

GWR SIGNAL BOX

COAL STAGE

OFFICES AND STORES

ENGINE SHED

WATER TANK OVER

W. COL.

W. COL.

SIGNAL BOX

W. COL.

15 T. CRANE

N

Feet
0   100

to Wokingham

Reading
1943

This was a brick built shed with a pitched slated roof, presumably constructed in the 1850s, when the SER took over the line from the Reading Guildford and Reigate Company. Three roads ran right through the building and until 1923 one was always reserved for visiting LSWR locomotives. The SER stationed about twenty locos at the shed with a further four housed in the small sub shed at Ash, near Aldershot. The SECR continued these arrangements but in 1933 the Southern transferred responsibility for the sub shed to Guildford. Twenty-two engines, nearly half of them 'F1' 4-4-0s, were allocated in 1933 for the Waterloo workings but after electrification in 1937 this total fell to seventeen.

Improvements to the shed, estimated at £35,000, were approved in 1925 but these were delayed for some years and by 1933 only £6,701 of the total allocated had been spent. A new 65 ft. turntable had replaced the old table and a new coal stage had been built. During the War, the Southern installed a water softening plant near the turntable and improved the coal stage. There was to have been a completely new shed building but by now this was not felt to be justified and the only further improvements were alterations to the layout of the sidings. Redhill, a depot with close operating links with Reading, suffered in a similar way, proposals for a complete rebuilding subsequently being restricted to just the yard and facilities.

For much of its life the shed maintained a small stud of Maunsell 2-6-0s but many of the locos were comparatively ancient. It was notable in the 'fifties for housing some of the last remaining Stirling locos, 'F1s' and 'R1s'. Reading was never considered of much importance by British Railways, and in 1954 all but two engines, both shunters, were transferred away, principally to Redhill and Guildford. The shed continued in use as a stabling point and became officially sub to Guildford in 1962, until complete closure in January 1965. Engines continued to visit the shed for a while but the whole site has by now been redeveloped.

Reading shed on 23rd April 1961 showing modifications to the entrance and roof ventilation.   *P.J. Kelley*

The shed and yard in 1937.

W.A. Camwell

Redhill

1955

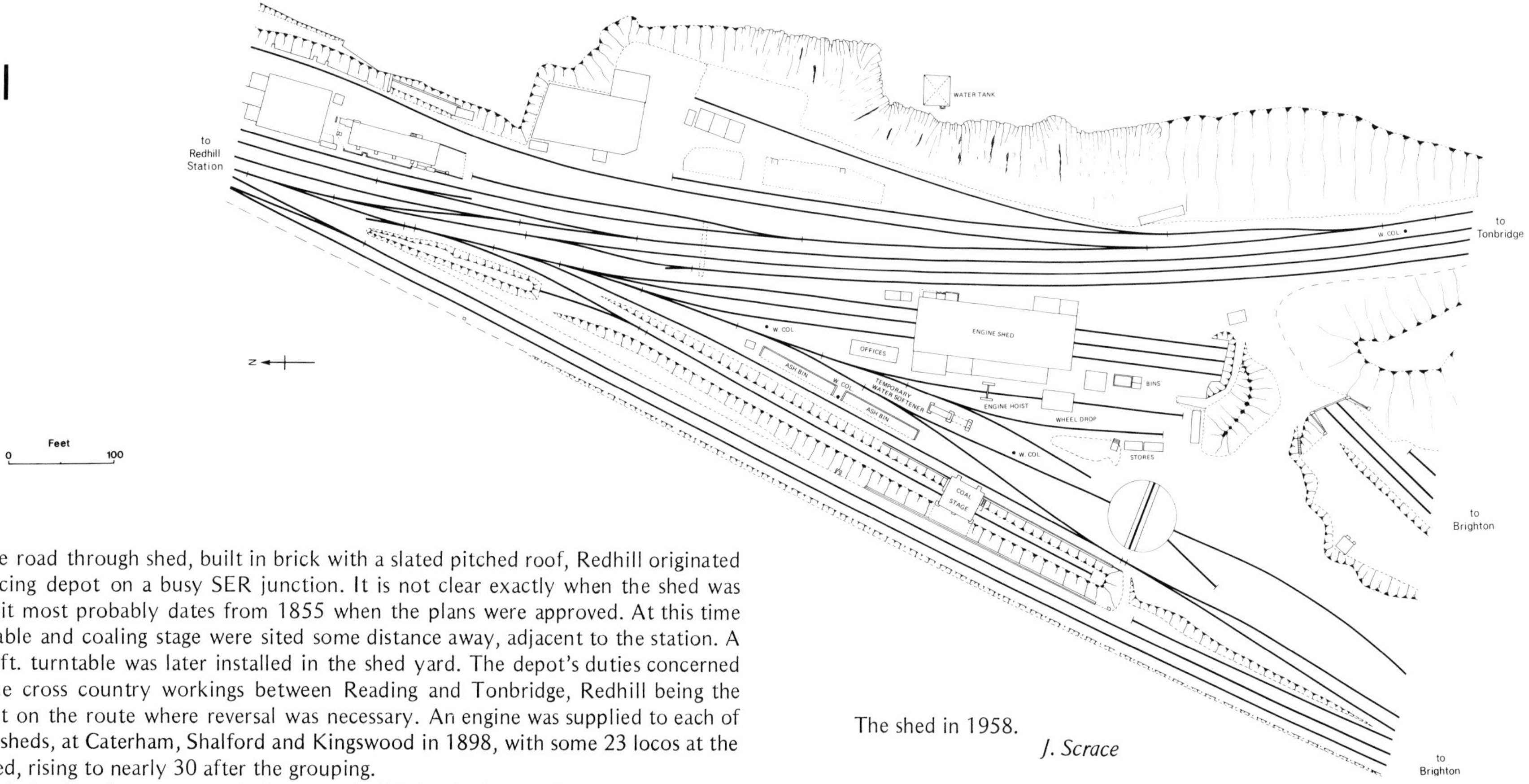

to
Redhill
Station

WATER TANK

to
Tonbridge

W. COL.

ENGINE SHED

W. COL.

OFFICES

ASH BIN

TEMPORARY
WATER SOFTENER

ENGINE HOIST

BINS

ASH BIN

WHEEL DROP

W. COL.

STORES

COAL
STAGE

to
Brighton

to
Brighton

Feet

0   100

A three road through shed, built in brick with a slated pitched roof, Redhill originated as a servicing depot on a busy SER junction. It is not clear exactly when the shed was built but it most probably dates from 1855 when the plans were approved. At this time the turntable and coaling stage were sited some distance away, adjacent to the station. A larger 45 ft. turntable was later installed in the shed yard. The depot's duties concerned mainly the cross country workings between Reading and Tonbridge, Redhill being the only point on the route where reversal was necessary. An engine was supplied to each of three sub sheds, at Caterham, Shalford and Kingswood in 1898, with some 23 locos at the parent shed, rising to nearly 30 after the grouping.

In 1924 the Southern approved plans to rebuild the shed, providing a new turntable and coaling ramp at a cost of £9,700 and putting aside a further £26,800 for a new shed building. A 65 ft. turntable and modern coal stage were provided alongside the ex-LBSC main line, these being completed in 1928. The coal stage was eventually built to a higher standard than originally intended and this involved the expenditure of a further £3,000. The planned replacement shed building, like the one at Reading, was abandoned in 1930 and the old structure remained unaltered, apart from the eventual provision of a new standard asbestos roof by BR in 1950.

A number of Maunsell 2-6-0s were normally kept at Redhill for the Reading—Tonbridge workings but in later years were increasingly replaced by BR standard types, particularly the 76XXX series Moguls.

The shed was interesting for its frequent 'foreign' visitors, and 'Black 5s', 'B1s' and 'Manors' were by no means infrequent arrivals. The shed was reported closed in January 1965, along with Reading, but remained open for visiting locos, the sole remaining Central Division steam depot. It finally closed with the dieselisation of the Tonbridge line in June of that year. The buildings were still intact over four years later but have now been partially demolished. The offices on the eastern side have been retained and diesels are still stabled in the old yard.

The shed in 1958.

J. Scrace

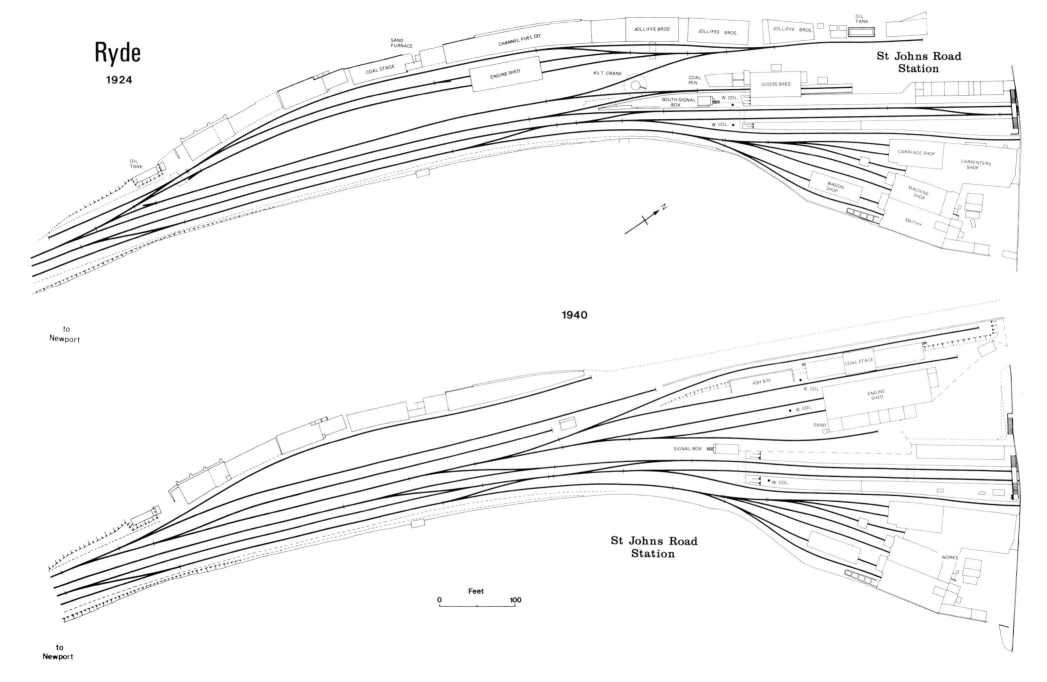

Ryde

1924

SAND FURNACE

COAL STAGE

CHANNEL FUEL CO.

ENGINE SHED

JOLLIFFE BROS.

JOLLIFFE BROS.

JOLLIFFE BROS.

OIL TANK

St Johns Road Station

4½ T. CRANE

COAL PEN

GOODS SHED

SOUTH SIGNAL BOX

W. COL.

W. COL.

OIL TANK

CARRIAGE SHOP

CARPENTERS SHOP

WAGON SHOP

MACHINE SHOP

SMITHY

N

1940

to Newport

COAL STAGE

ASH BIN

W. COL.

ENGINE SHED

W. COL.

SAND

SIGNAL BOX

W. COL.

St Johns Road Station

WORKS

to Newport

Feet

0   100

The first shed at Ryde was a simple two road building constructed in brick and subsequently incorporated into the works. A replacement shed was opened by the Isle of Wight Railway in 1874 and although larger, it was not of the same quality as its predecessor. It was a two road through building and was constructed mainly in corrugated iron, a covered coaling stage being provided alongside the run-round loop.

This crude building sufficed for many years until 1930 when a third shed was opened by the Southern Railway. This was a considerable advance on its predecessor. The new depot was sited about a hundred yards to the east and was single ended with two roads. The 1874 building had become very cramped and the new shed was capable of housing eight of the 'O2' tanks. It was constructed in asbestos on steel framework, some of the girders originating as LBSCR electrification gantries. A large new coal stage was also built in the yard. All repair work was performed by Ryde Works.

IOWR 2-4-0Ts were the dominant engine type until the grouping when ex-LSW 0-4-4Ts began to appear. There was always a shortage of engines at Ryde, which had to provide a locomotive for a sub shed at St. Helens in addition to the regular daily duties. This situation was eased with the closure of St. Helens in 1921 and the influx of SR locos after 1923. The new engines at first worked only the ex-IOWR lines but of course were soon used all over the island. Ten 'O2's and two 'Terriers' formed the allocation in 1933. Traffic declined after the war and line closures in the western half of the island led to the demise of Newport shed in 1957, the remaining locos transferring to Ryde. Nineteen 'O2s' were now allocated but on closure in 1967 only ten and a diesel shunter remained. The shed was used as a wagon shop for a year or two but has now been demolished.

Ventnor undergoing repairs outside the original engine shed at Ryde, now incorporated into the works.

E. Crawforth

The second shed at Ryde in 1928.   *A.B. Macleod*

Ryde shed in 1964.   *Ken Fairey*

St. Leonards was the LBSCR's Hastings depot and was sited just to the west of the Bo-Peep Tunnel. The first shed was a small two road structure, single ended and built in brick, with a small turntable provided on the northern side. This building was rather small and although the yard was later enlarged and a 50 ft. turntable installed, in 1898 a contract was let to build a much larger depot on the same site.

The 50 ft. turntable was retained and three roads led off it to a large through shed, built in brick with a northlight pattern roof. It remained much in its original condition throughout LBSC and subsequent Southern days, apart from the appearance by the 1930s of a second approach road, leading directly on to the turntable from the east.

The depot increased in importance following the demolition of the ex-SER shed at Hastings, the entire allocation transferring to St. Leonards in 1929. The shed thereafter provided locos for both the ex-SER and ex-LBSCR routes to London. A new wheel drop, costing £1,680 was approved in the same year to help cope with the increased number of locomotives. The first of twelve 'Schools' arrived in 1931, and some twenty other 4-4-0 locos, 'F1s' and 'Ls' made up the rest of the allocation, apart from a handful of tank and 0-6-0 types.

After electrification of the coast line in 1935 the shed's considerable stud of 4-4-0s were used primarily on the London service via Ashford. The predominance of this type of locomotive probably made St. Leonards unique in the mid 'fifties, no comparable main line passenger depot relying exclusively on 4-4-0s for express work.

A new asbestos roof with brick gables was added shortly after nationalization, but by 1957 the depot's duties had become severely reduced. The first stages of dieselisation had been completed in that year, leading to the closure of the servicing point at Hastings station and the withdrawal of most of St. Leonard's engines. In June 1958, after further dieselisation, the depot effectively closed although engines were still serviced and occasionally stabled in the yard. Diesel locomotives were stabled in the empty shed for a number of years, into the mid 'sixties, but the buildings have now been completely demolished.

St. Leonards with new BR style roof.   *Ken Fairey*

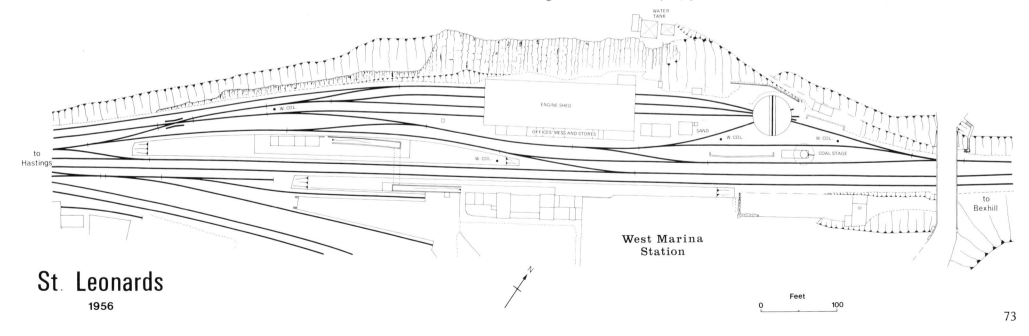

St. Leonards

1956

West Marina Station

Feet
0   100

The shed with original roof in 1938.
S.C. Townroe

to Exeter

G.W.R. RUNNING LINES

to Salisbury Station

W. COL.

W. COL.

COAL STAGE

W. COL.

W. COL.

COAL STACK

COAL STACK

TANK HOUSE

SEWER

ENGINE SHED

OFFICES AND STORES

P-W HUT

Salisbury
1942

Feet
0   100

N

The shed with original roof in 1926.   *H.C. Casserley*

Salisbury was a large, and for the time, modern shed opened by the LSWR in 1901. It was brick built with a slated roof of five pitches covering ten roads. A huge water tank, forming the roof of what was originally the enginemen's dormitory, and a 55 ft. turntable with coaling stage were provided on the northern side. This large new depot replaced some much older buildings sited near the station and followed an agreement with the GWR to exchange land enabling the enlargement of the LSWR station.

The original depot dated from 1847 and by 1900 consisted of a pair of three road sheds, built alongside each other with a 42 ft. turntable and coal stage at the western end of the yard. These buildings were swept away in the rebuilding of the station and all locomotives were concentrated at the new depot.

Initially, some forty locomotives were stationed at the shed, this large number being mainly due to the LSWR practice of changing engines of all main line trains at Salisbury. The shed was also responsible for local turns to Portsmouth, Bournemouth, Southampton, etc. The number of engines had grown to over sixty by 1922 and under the Southern this even increased slightly. Eleven 'King Arthurs' were allocated in 1933 and the rest of the fifty or so locos were made up of eighteen classes, six represented by only a single engine. This situation was obviously not designed for maximum servicing efficiency and although perhaps an extreme case, was by no means unusual on the railway.

To cope with the increasing size of locomotives, around 1912, a new 65 ft. turntable was installed, enabling the old 55 ft. table to be transferred to Waterloo, but the next major alteration did not take place for many years until a standard corrugated asbestos roof was fitted. The ex-GWR shed on the opposite side of the line closed in 1950 and after this visiting WR engines were often stabled and serviced at the SR depot. Salisbury survived until the very end of steam on the Southern Region, Pacifics and standards predominating in the final years. Condemned locos were stored in the yard for nearly a year after closure in July 1967 but the whole site has now been completely cleared.

The shed in early BR days. *Author's Collection*

The BR roof in 1957. *H.C. Casserley*

The 1912, 65 ft. turntable. This later gave way to an undergirder type. *Lens of Sutton*

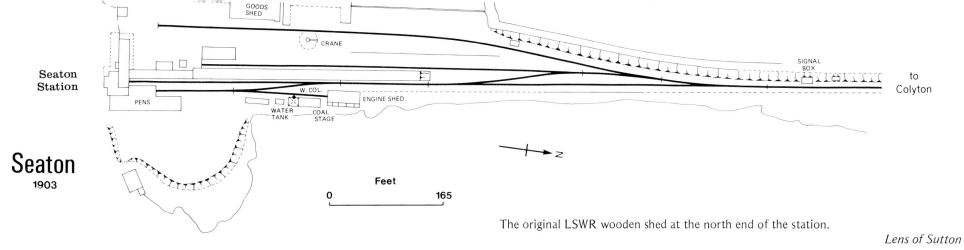

Seaton
1903

Seaton Station

GOODS SHED

CRANE

PENS

W. COL.

WATER TANK

COAL STAGE

ENGINE SHED

SIGNAL BOX

to Colyton

Feet
0   165

The original LSWR wooden shed at the north end of the station.

Lens of Sutton

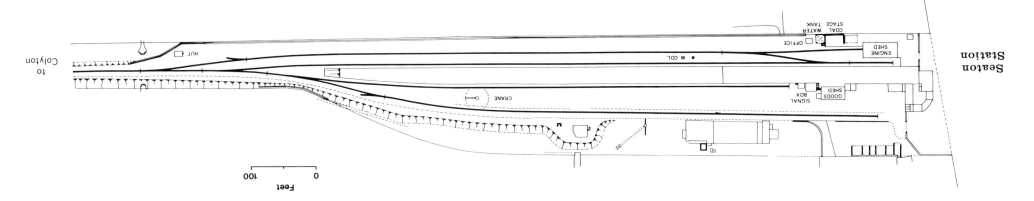

The shed would have been built when the Seaton and Beer Railway opened in 1868, but services were worked from the first by the LSWR, who officially absorbed the line in 1885. The original shed was a tiny building only just able to accommodate a 'D1' 0-4-2T, and was sited at the east side of the station close by the River Axe.

This structure was later demolished by the Southern and rebuilt further to the south, by the cattle pens at the side of the station. The old shed was swept away in the extensive rebuilding of the station in 1937 and its successor, built in concrete blocks with a corrugated asbestos pitched roof, opened around the same time. The second shed was again single ended, with a coal stage and water tank provided directly outside, ex-LSW 0-4-4Ts and Adams 4-4-2Ts powering most of the services. Along with the parent depot, Exmouth Junction, Seaton was transferred to the WR in 1962 and was closed in November of the following year. The line itself was closed three years later and the entire station area, including the shed, was afterwards demolished.

The 1937 replacement. Early contract drawings incorporated a water tank into the roof, but this was later abandoned in favour of the customary tower.

H.C. Casserley

Seaton Station

1959

to Colyton

Feet 100 0

HUT · W. COL. · CRANE · SIGNAL BOX · GOODS SHED · ENGINE SHED · OFFICE · WATER TANK · COAL STAGE TANK

Southampton

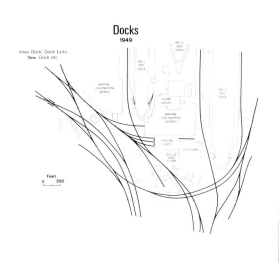

Docks
1949

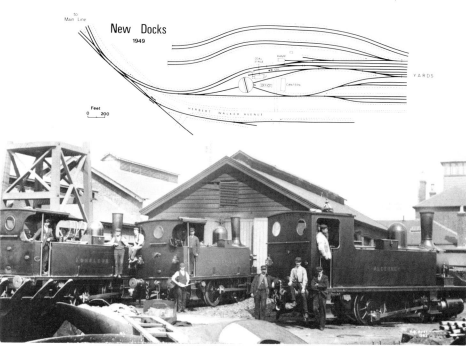

New Docks
1949

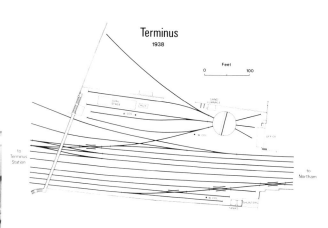

Terminus
1938

Southampton Docks loco shed, August 1903.
Left to right: *Honfleur, Granville* and *Alderney*.

R. Randell Collection

The Southern maintained three separate locomotive establishments at Southampton; an independent shed in the old docks, a sub-depot of Eastleigh at Terminus station, and a servicing point located to the west in the New Docks. The LSWR took over dock workings from the Southampton Dock Company in 1892 and with it a small one road engine shed, shortly afterwards enlarged to include a second road. It was single ended and built in brick. By 1907 one of the roads had been extended through the rear of the shed and later yet another, third, road was added to the building. By the 'thirties it was fitted with a northlight pattern roof and an overhead water supply in the shed entrance. Coal and sand bunkers were incorporated inside the building.

From the LSWR takeover 'B4' 0-4-4Ts, around fourteen of them, were responsible for all the duties and despite occasional incursions by other types, maintained a virtual monopoly until the arrival of the 'USAs' in 1947.

The principal engine depot in Southampton was originally at Northam but this closed on the opening of Eastleigh in 1903. Servicing facilities were retained at Terminus station, however, a 50 ft. turntable with coal stage, sidings and offices being provided at the end of Western Terrace, north of the station. The tiny sub depot incorporated in the goods shed, dating from the 1840s, and its associated turntable had gone out of use some years prior to this. The depot was sub to Eastleigh and a small tank loco was normally supplied for pilot duties in the engine yard. A new 70 ft. table was provided at Terminus shortly after the war.

After the opening of the vast New Docks in 1933, a 65 ft. turntable with sidings, water column, coal stage and offices was built to service visiting locos, the system having independent access to the Dorchester line at Millbrook. It was not officially regarded as a depot by the Southern but it was certainly a busy site, passenger engines from Terminus even making use of it on occasions. After nationalization its status was raised to that of a sub shed of Southampton Docks depot. A 70 ft. turntable was eventually installed, probably around 1949.

The old docks shed was re-roofed in modern style in 1955 and its fourteen 'USA' tanks remained until diesel shunters began arriving in 1962. Rail traffic in the docks was declining drastically at this time and the shed officially closed in January 1966, the twelve 0-6-0 diesels transferring to Eastleigh. Locos continued to stable in the old shed, however, and nearly ten years after closure it was still standing virtually intact.

The engine yard at Terminus was reported closed in 1955, when a 'C14' 0-4-0T was yard pilot, but this seems highly unlikely and the table probably did not turn its last loco till 1966, when the station closed. It has since been removed and the facilities demolished. New Docks depot continued to service visiting freight engines including ex-GWR types till the end of steam on these trains around 1966-7. In 1974 the facilities were all still intact and the turntable in perfect working order. It has since been sold to the Great Western Society for use at Didcot.

The original northlight pattern roof under repair in 1947.

H.C. Casserley

The shed in 1957.

Ken Fairey

Derelict offices and stores at Southampton Terminus in 1974. The depot now permanently quiet.
Author's collection

The 70 ft. turntable at New Docks still in occasional use in 1974.

Author's collection

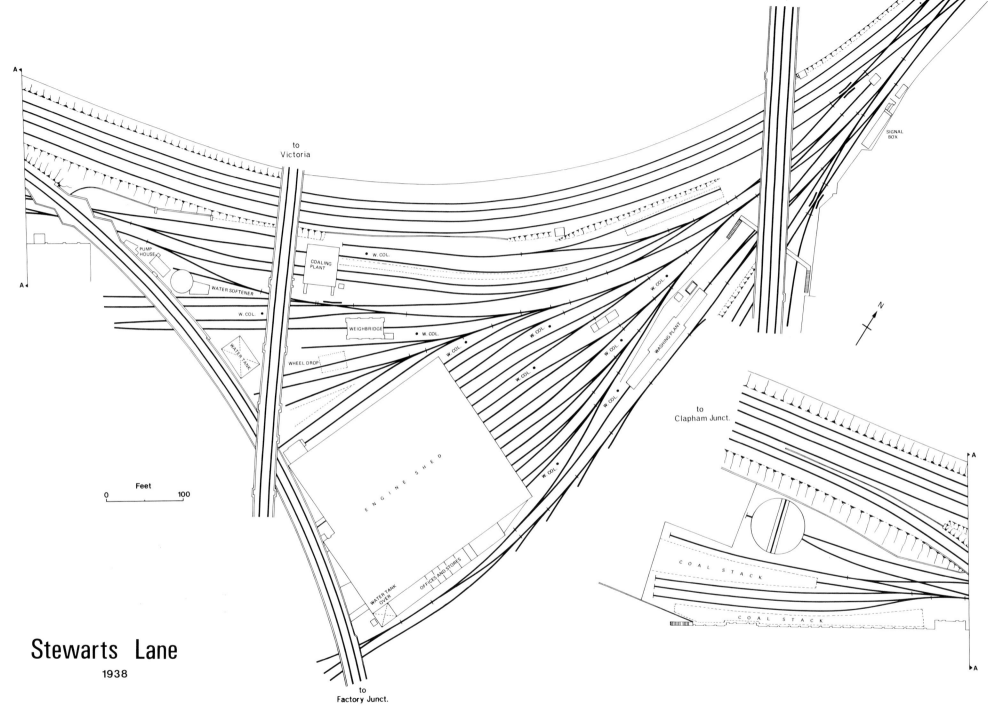

to Victoria

to Victoria

to Clapham Junct.

to Factory Junct.

SIGNAL BOX

PUMP HOUSE

COALING PLANT

W. COL.

WATER SOFTENER

W. COL.

WEIGHBRIDGE

W. COL.

WATER TANK

WHEEL DROP

W. COL.

W. COL.

W. COL.

W. COL.

WASHING PLANT

W. COL.

W. COL.

W. COL.

E N G I N E   S H E D

WATER TANK OVER

OFFICES AND STORES

COAL STACK

COAL STACK

N

Feet
0   100

Stewarts Lane

1938

An interesting posed photograph taken from the viaduct in 1901, with early coal stage in right foreground.

W. Palmer

This large shed was set in the maze of lines just north of Factory Junction alongside the Longhedge Works and became the principal depot of the LCDR. The original shed, dating from the first days of the LCD's line to Victoria in 1862, was of the semi-roundhouse type with forty roads, half of them covered, radiating from a 45 ft. turntable. The workshops were situated in a building adjoining the south side.

This old semi-roundhouse was removed and a new straight shed built on the site in 1881, the nearby Longhedge works being enlarged at the same time. This second building was completely different in style, being a sixteen road single ended shed constructed in brick with a slated pitched roof, and resembling the nearby works in architectural style. A large coaling ramp was sited centrally in the yard and a wheel drop and lifting crane were provided nearby.

Stewarts Lane, with around a hundred engines, became the main depot of the LCD's successor, the SECR, and at the time had always been known as 'Battersea' or 'Longhedge' the modern title not coming into general use until rebuilding by the Southern in 1933. Electrification by the SR during the 'twenties led to a decline in the importance of the depot and of the ex-LBSCR sheds at Battersea Park. In 1932 a plan was approved to transfer the remaining engines to Stewarts Lane providing power for both eastern and central sections from one depot. The scheme was eventually to cost over £56,000 and to deal with the increased allocation a number of improvements were carried out at 'The Lane'. The approach roads were modified, the turntable resited and a 300-ton capacity mechanical coaling plant was constructed. Ten water columns replaced the original two, their supply being pumped from a new 20,000 gallon water softener. Unfortunately, the site restrictions prevented an ideal layout and engine disposal times were longer at Stewarts Lane than most other sheds.

These improvements, together with a new roof of a northlight pattern, meant the emergence in 1934 of a virtually new depot, equipped to house and service an allocation of some one hundred and seventy locomotives. Although this number fell in the succeeding years it was the highest of any shed on the Southern, the locos working all over the south east of England. A considerable number of 'Lord Nelsons' and 'King Arthur' 4-6-0s powered the prestigious *Golden Arrow* and *Night Ferry* boat trains as well as other principal passenger services, to Margate, Ramsgate and Dover. Several dozen Moguls and 0-6-0s, including twenty-four 'C' class worked the large number of freight turns, while ex-Brighton engines worked the services to Littlehampton, Bognor and Portsmouth. The succession of top express power culminated in the 'fifties in the 'Merchant Navy', and 'Britannia' Pacifics, the condition in which some were kept being legendary.

Surviving several direct hits during the war, Stewarts Lane lasted into the early 'sixties as a steam depot. Third rail had been installed in the yard in 1959 when the first electric locomotive arrived and some alterations were made at the shed for dealing with the new motive power. Diesels and electrics continued to arrive and by 1961 the depot was left with only two regular Pacific duties. It was closed to steam in 1963 and despite partial demolition and the destruction of the roof by fire in 1967 it appears to still be partly in use for locomotive stabling purposes.

The shed and its diminishing steam locomotive stud in 1961.

J. Scrace

A variety of locos in Southern days.

Photomatic

Swanage

1912

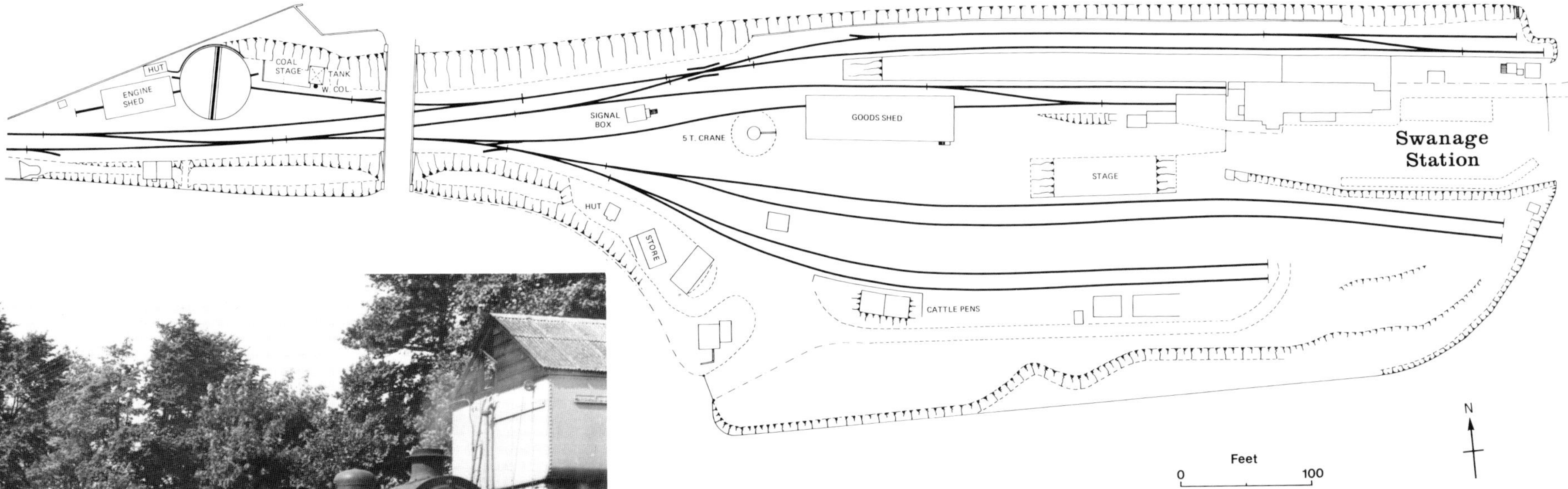

to
Wareham

HUT

ENGINE
SHED

COAL
STAGE

TANK
W. COL.

SIGNAL
BOX

5 T. CRANE

GOODS SHED

STAGE

HUT

STORE

CATTLE PENS

**Swanage
Station**

N

Feet

0   100

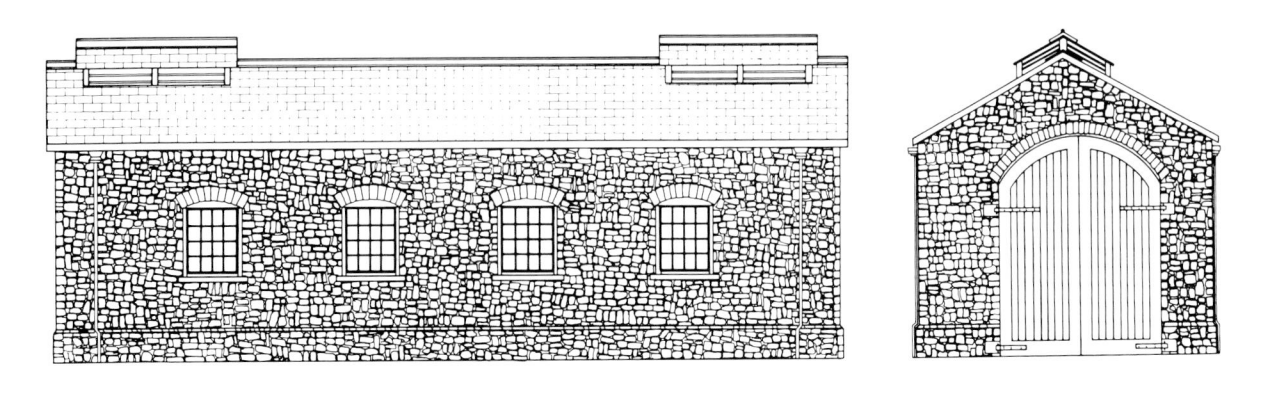

The shed in the 1950's.

Collection of R. Randell

The shed as originally built.

Feet

0   10

This was an attractive single road shed, built in the local stone with a pitched slated roof. The small building was of the through type, with access via a 50 ft. turntable sited immediately outside. The slightly cramped site meant that engines could not enter the shed without operation of the turntable. Water was pumped to a tank by the coal stage using steam pressure from the locomotive.

The LSWR built the shed when they opened the line in 1885 and one engine was normally supplied to work the branch, Bournemouth being the parent depot. 'M7s' were the regular engines for many years and were not really supplanted until the 'sixties, when BR 2-6-2 and 2-6-4Ts came to monopolise the services. Swanage was a popular venue for excursions in earlier years, often from the Bath and Bristol areas, and S&D locos frequently made use of the shed. It stood next to the cemetery and engine cleaners disliked being left alone at night! Until 1958 the building possessed arched doorways but the entrance was altered to incorporate a simple lintel, when an 'M7' tank, overshooting the turntable, collided with the building. Swanage fell out of use with dieselisation in September 1966 but although the turntable has been removed the shed itself is still standing in good condition. The Swanage Railway Society eventually hope to repair the building and turntable and restore the shed to its original use.

'M7' 0-4-4T No. 30328 comes off the turntable in March 1962.

C.L. Caddy

Templecombe Upper

1930

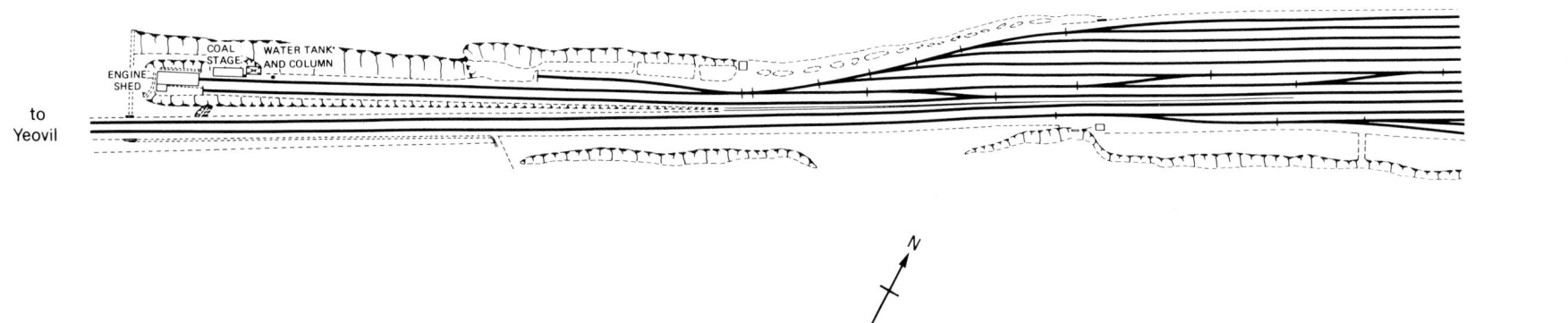

to
Yeovil

**Templecombe
Station**

N

The small shed at Templecombe Upper was provided by the LSWR principally for the shunting engines working the nearby exchange yards. It was sited on the north side of the main line, connected to the western end of the yard by a long siding and probably dates from the opening of the western connecting spur to the S&D in 1870.

The shed was constructed in timber with a pitched roof and stood on a dwarf brick wall. A small office was provided at the side and a coal stage with water tank directly outside. No turntable was ever installed but the shed did stable tender locos from places like Yeovil and Salisbury.

Water supply was a problem for both railways in the Templecombe area and the LSW tank and reservoir often came near to running dry in the summer months. The Southern improved the coal stage at Templecombe and continued to station an engine, often a Yeovil 'G6' 0-6-0 tank, to shunt the exchange freights. Yeovil Town was responsible for the small sub shed but with nationalization Templecombe ex-S&D shed became the natural host of the SR engines. The shed appeared to go out of use around 1951 and the site has since been completely cleared.

Even a 'K10' 4-4-0 is too large for the diminutive shed at Templecombe Upper.

W.A. Camwell

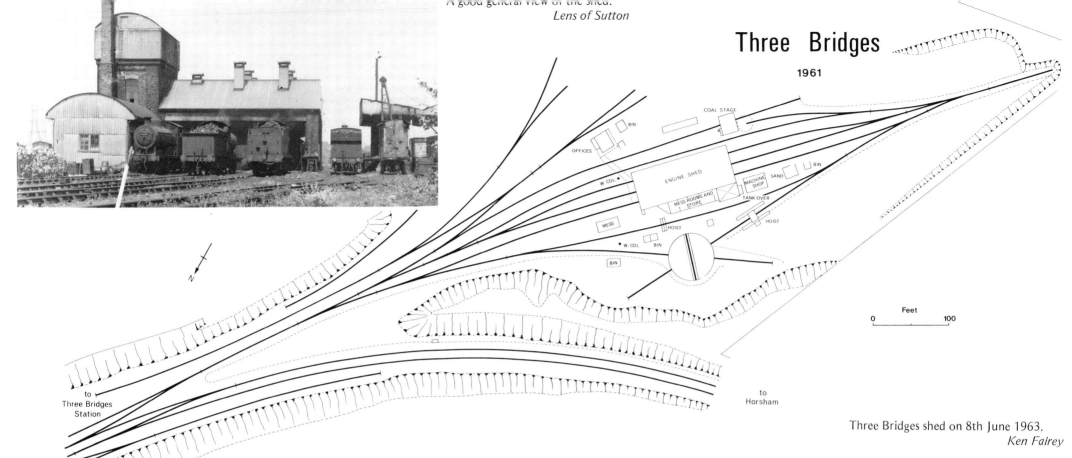

A good general view of the shed.
Lens of Sutton

Three Bridges

1961

COAL STAGE

BIN

OFFICES

W. COL.

ENGINE SHED

BIN

MACHINE SHOP

SAND

BIN

MESS ROOMS AND STORE

TANK OVER

MESS

HOIST

HOIST

W. COL

BIN

BIN

Feet

0   100

to
Three Bridges
Station

to
Horsham

Three Bridges shed on 8th June 1963.
Ken Fairey

The LBSC built its first shed at Three Bridges at the west side of the station. The small two road shed had a slated pitched roof and a 45 ft. turntable and water tank were located in the fork of the Horsham and Brighton lines. These arrangements were later superseded by a much larger three road structure sited further to the south.

The new shed, built in brick with a northlight pattern roof and an adjacent water tank, was virtually complete by 1909. A 60 ft. turntable and coal stage were provided on the north and south sides of the yard respectively. The coal stage was later improved with the addition of a canopy and crane. The depot was part of the Horsham locomotive district in the early years and the twenty-five or so locomotives stationed at the shed were mainly 0-6-2 and 0-6-0Ts, used principally on local passenger and goods work. The allocation increased under the Southern, eventually exceeding that of Horsham and shortly before the War the depot gained complete independence. Standard tanks began to join the varied Brighton types in the early 'fifties but little over ten years later the in-evitable run-down was in progress.

The shed effectively closed in June 1964, Brighton taking over the remaining duties, but diesels continued to be stabled in the yard. The building was apparently used for rolling stock repairs for a number of years and survived for some ten years before being finally demolished.

Tonbridge

1938

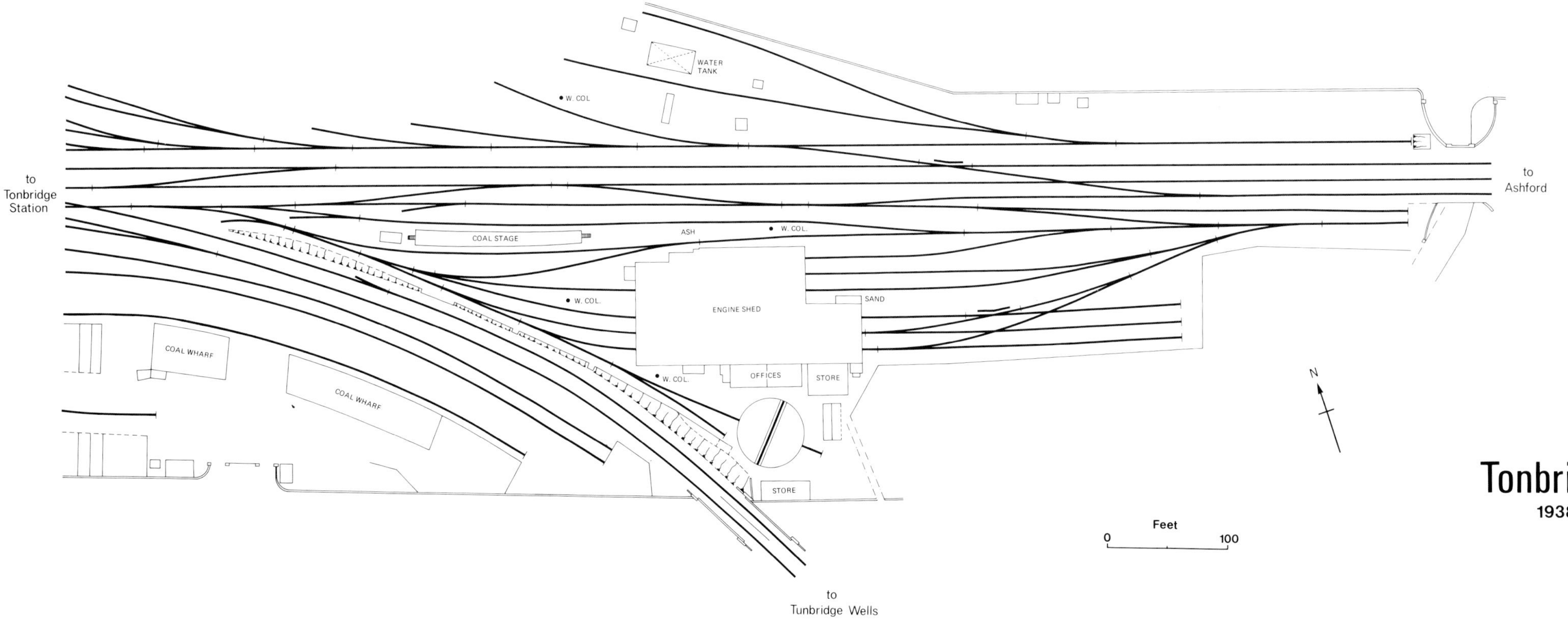

WATER TANK

W. COL.

COAL STAGE

ASH

W. COL.

W. COL.

ENGINE SHED

SAND

to
Tonbridge
Station

to
Ashford

COAL WHARF

COAL WHARF

W. COL.

OFFICES

STORE

STORE

N

Feet
0   100

to
Tunbridge Wells

Coal stage and new BR roof in the 1950s.

Lens of Sutton

The original depot at Tonbridge was a three road single ended building with adjacent carriage shed and probably dated from the opening of the station in 1842. The SER later carried out extensive alterations incorporating much of the original buildings. The new depot consisted of a six road through building, in brick, with a pitched slated roof and a 55 ft. turntable with coal stage. A large oil store was also built at the same time.

Various improvements after 1945 included structural alterations at the west end of the shed and in 1952 a new asbestos roof with brick gables was installed. The location of the turntable was altered, presumably by the Southern, its final position being at the south side of the shed near the location of the old SER oil store.

The SER stationed over thirty locos at Tonbridge, including a single tank for a sub shed at Westerham, and this made it one of the most important on the system. Some fifty engines, including a dozen 'D' 4-4-0s for the main line passenger work and some twenty 'C' and 'O1' 0-6-0s were at Tonbridge in the 'thirties.

Westerham had been closed in the 'twenties but the depot briefly regained a sub shed when Gillingham was being run down in 1960. Many of the old Stirling and Wainwright 0-6-0s were replaced by 'Q1s' in the 1950s and by 1962 several 'N1' Moguls had arrived at the shed, which by this time was the last in Kent with regular steam passenger and freight workings. The number of engines had dwindled to about ten by 1962 and steam finally disappeared from June 1964. The shed building has now been demolished but the offices remain and diesels are still serviced in the yard.

Torrington
1950

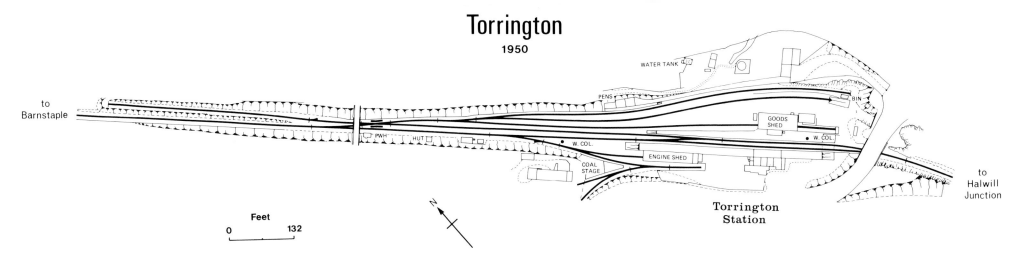

WATER TANK

PENS

BIN

GOODS SHED

W. COL.

W. COL.

to Barnstaple

PWH HUT

COAL STAGE

ENGINE SHED

to Halwill Junction

Torrington Station

N

Feet
0   132

The shed was almost certainly built in 1872, to serve the branch terminus which opened in that year. The LSWR constructed the single ended shed adjacent to the up platform, and at first a small turntable was provided immediately outside the entrance. The shed was built in timber, on a dwarf brick wall, with a pitched slated roof. Torrington was a sub shed of Barnstaple and 4-4-0s and 0-6-0s worked much of the traffic in LSWR days. The Southern extended the branch southwards to Halwill in 1925, converting several Stroudly 'E1s' to 0-6-2Ts for the new line. The 'E1/Rs' subsequently based at Torrington worked between Halwill Junction and Barnstaple Junction. 'M7' 0-4-4Ts were among the three or four engines outstationed at the shed, and these survived the 'E1/Rs', the allocation in 1958 comprising two Ivatt tanks and a single 'M7'.

Closure came in November of the following year, however, the engines and crews going to Barnstaple Junction, but it is probable that the building was used for stabling purposes for a further few years. It has now been demolished.

A Halwill train passes the shed in 1949.

J. Meredith

A view in 1925 with original over-girder turntable.

H.C. Casserley

The first shed at Tunbridge Wells West was a small two road through building sited at the south side of the station. One road ran onto a turntable sited immediately to the west of the shed. The first proposal for a new depot emerged in 1889, for a single ended shed with four roads leading directly onto a 48 ft. turntable. The design eventually accepted and largely completed the following year was a four road single ended shed built in brick with a slated pitched roof. A 46 ft. turntable was installed at the far end of the yard, and a water tank was later provided at the rear of the shed. The building stood on the opposite side of the line from the original depot and needed to be partly raised on brick arches.

The shed, a sub depot of Tonbridge in the SR organization, was responsible primarily for passenger turns to Three Bridges and Victoria via Oxted, the allocation consisting mainly of tank engines. The older Brighton 4-4-2 and 0-4-4 tank types were the mainstay of the services for many years, giving way to 'I1X' rebuilds under the Southern and in the 'fifties, ex-LSW 'M7' tanks. The allocation declined by a third to around twenty engines at the outbreak of war and fell still further after 1947. The shed yard had suffered bomb damage during the war and a new roof in the normal asbestos sheeting was later installed.

Some of the first BR 2-6-4Ts were delivered to Tunbridge Wells in 1951 and these powerful engines must have seemed revolutionary compared to the various pre-grouping tanks then in use at the shed. They came to virtually monopolise the depot's workings, the turntable eventually being removed around 1961. The shed closed in September 1963 but engines continued to use the shed for some time afterwards. The buildings are intact today and remain in use for rolling stock storage.

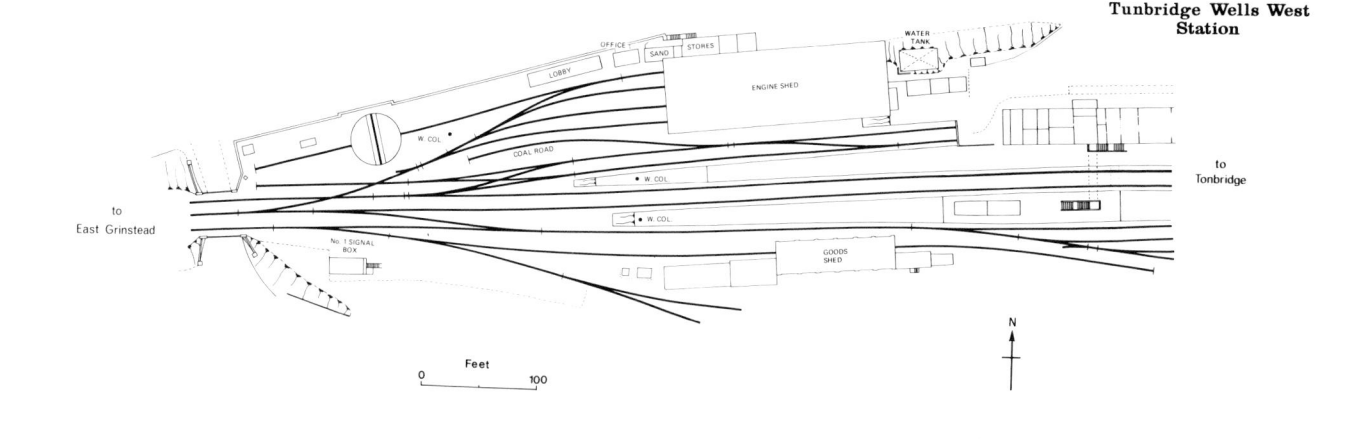

Tunbridge Wells West Station

Tunbridge Wells West
1956

Five years later with the new BR roof.

Ken Fairey

The shed in 1953, with original roof.   *Photomatic*

Wadebridge

1906

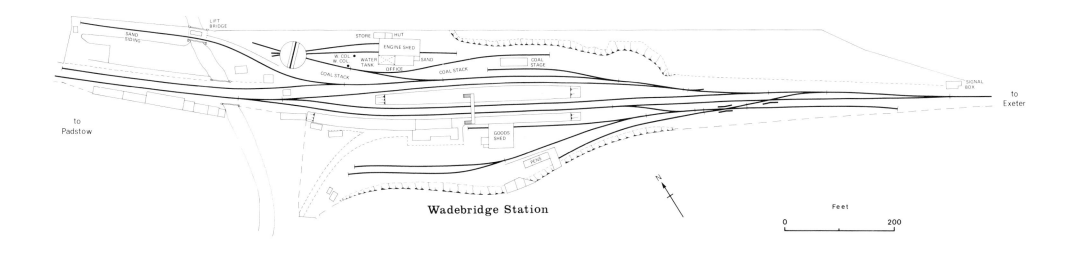

Wadebridge Station

Feet
0   200

North western end of the shed in the 1930's

W.A. Camwell

The LSWR finally connected with its Bodmin and Wadebridge line in 1895 and in the same year enlarged the station to handle the North Cornwall traffic. The shed dates from this year and was built in timber and brick with a slated pitched roof. Offices and water tank were built on the south side of the building. A coal stage was provided to the east of the shed and at first access to the building was via a 50 ft. turntable. In 1907 plans were approved for the enlargement of the building and the extension of the two roads through to provide a second exit via the coal stage. Two other sheds perhaps should also be mentioned in connection with Wadebridge, both closed on the opening of the new depot. The first was the original 1834 building of the B&WR, sited to the north, and the second an LSW building at Delabole, former terminus of the line to Wadebridge.

The LSWR stationed eight locomotives at Wadebridge, which was also responsible for a sub shed at Launceston. The engines by the 'thirties were normally two 4-4-0s for passenger work and two 0-4-4Ts for lesser services, with of course, the trio of Beattie well tanks for the Wenford Bridge workings. This situation remained little changed for many years, even well into British Railways ownership.

Light Pacifics after their introduction were turned on a new 70 ft. table at Padstow, but along with ex-SR Moguls regularly appeared at the shed in BR days. In 1962 the well tanks gave way to '1366' pannier tanks, the depot becoming part of the Western Region in that year. The line was dieselised in 1965, the building afterwards simply stabling a diesel shunter provided by St. Blazey for the china clay workings. The shed was eventually demolished in 1969.

91

A general view of the shed in 1936 complete with adverts!

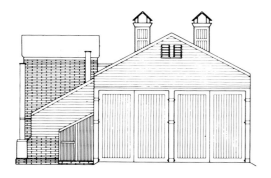

Feet
0   10

The rebuilt shed of 1907.

A superb posed shot showing the coal stage and the trio of Beattie tanks in 1962.

R.C. Riley

No. 30586 alongside the shed in the 1950's.

OPC Collection

93

Winchester City Station

Winchester City
1941

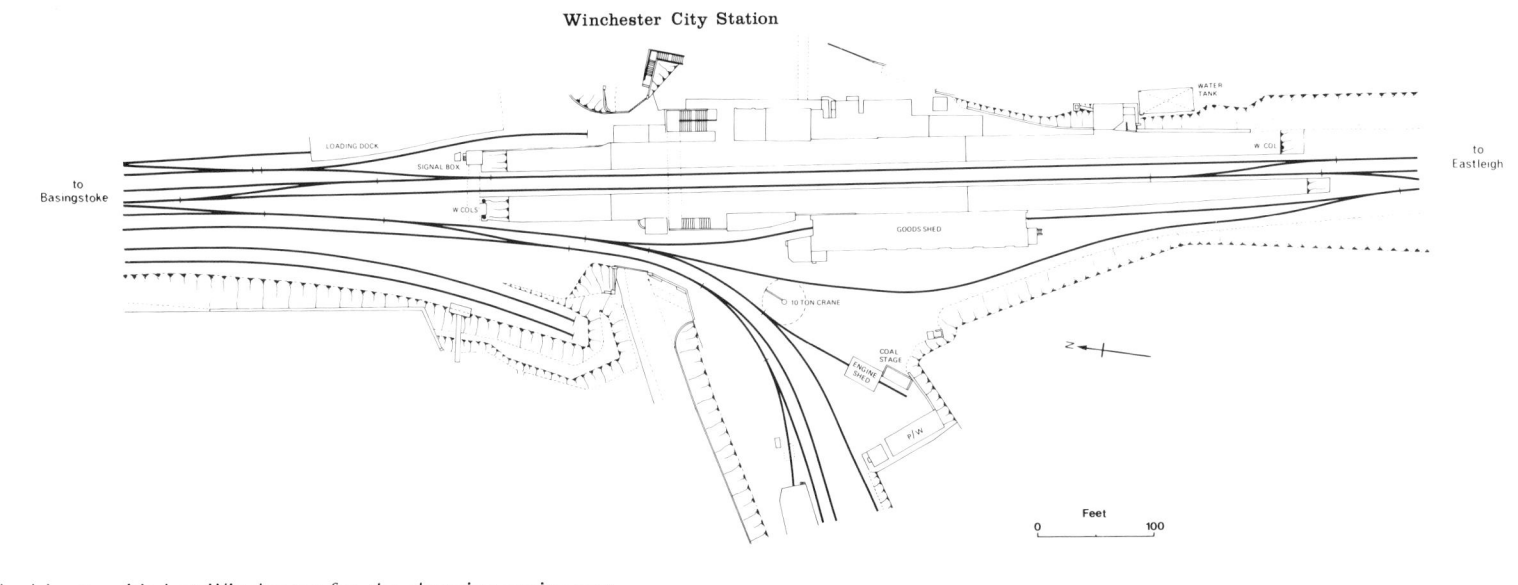

to
Basingstoke

to
Eastleigh

The recommendation that a small shed be provided at Winchester for the shunting engine was approved in 1927 at a cost of £598. There was an extensive and important goods yard at Winchester reached by a sharp curve which could only be negotiated by a short-wheelbase loco. A shunter had been outstationed there from Eastleigh for many years, a coal stage being constructed for its use in 1920. The new shed, built in corrugated iron on a timber frame, had a pitched roof with central vent and appears to have opened in 1928. Throughout its existence, the building simply stabled the 'B4' 0-4-0T supplied from Eastleigh. The loco returned to the parent depot at weekends for servicing or changing and apart from occasional incursions by ex-SECR 'P' tanks, the 'B4's remained until 204 hp diesels arrived in 1963.

It seems probable that the building was retained to house the diesel shunter for two or three years, but it would have been demolished when the goods yard closed in 1969.

The tiny garage-like shed at Winchester only just accommodates its 'B4' 0-4-0T.
Photomatic

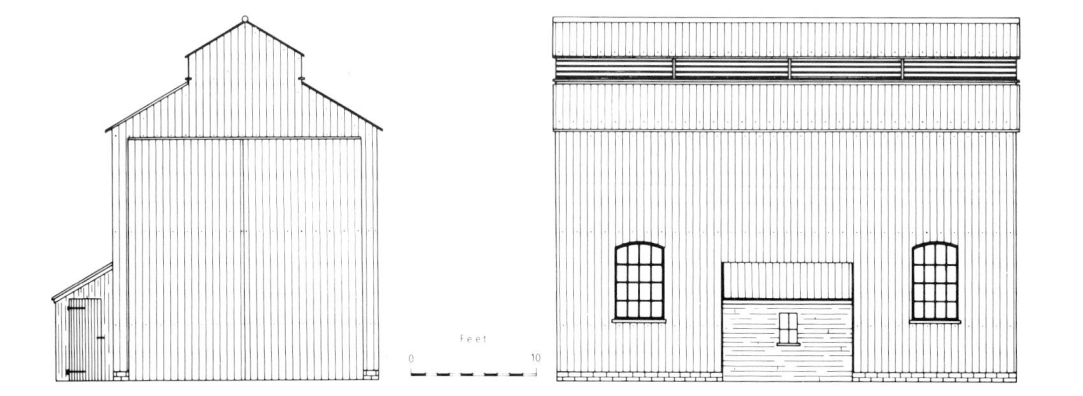

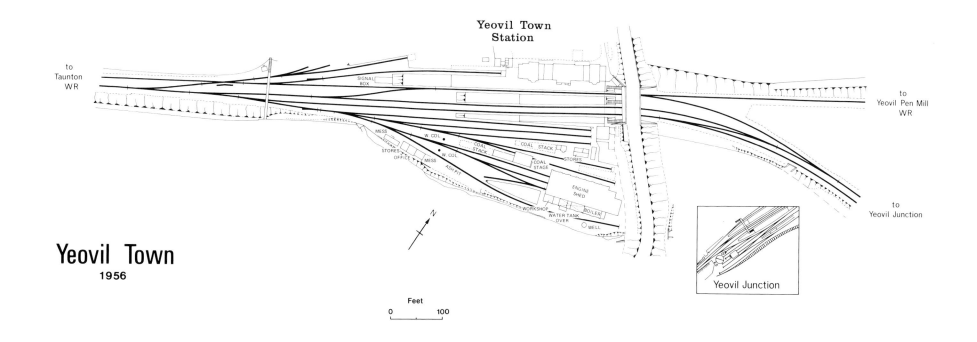

Yeovil Town Station

to
Taunton
WR

to
Yeovil Pen Mill
WR

to
Yeovil Junction

SIGNAL BOX

MESS
STORES
OFFICE
MESS
W. COL
W. COL
COAL STACK
COAL STACK
COAL STAGE
STORES
ASH PIT
ENGINE SHED
WORKSHOP
WATER TANK OVER
BOILER
WELL

N

Yeovil Town

1956

Feet
0   100

Yeovil Junction

The shed was sited by Yeovil Town station, on a short branch off the Salisbury—Exeter main line, and was built in brick with a slated pitched roof. From the look of the building, it probably dates from the arrival of the Salisbury and Yeovil Railway, worked from the first by the LSWR, in 1861. It was a three road building with arched entrances, and a coal stage was built on the station side of the yard.

Main line engines came to use the 50 ft. turntable installed at Yeovil Junction, and the 43 ft. table originally provided at the shed fell out of use, eventually being removed in 1917. The LSW added a canopy to the coal stage in 1920 and later the Southern appears to have installed a new roof, lower than the original. BR installed a new girder water tank in 1957. The shed's twenty or so locos worked an assortment of duties between Salisbury and Exeter. A 'G6' tank was sent to Templecombe Upper, while a stud of some ten assorted Drummond 4-4-0s handled the passenger and freight traffic. 'O2' tanks worked the push-pull service to Yeovil Junction. After the grouping a handful of 'U' 2-6-0s arrived to handle the freight traffic. Ex-GWR engines regularly used the shed after the closure of Pen Mill in 1959, and Yeovil Town itself passed to the Western Region in 1962. Dieselisation soon made the depot redundant and it closed in June 1965. The turntable at Yeovil Junction, enlarged after the war to 70 ft., continued in occasional use and still survives in a usable condition; the shed has now been completely demolished, the site being used as a car park.

The shed in 1964.
Ken Fairey

Southern Railway Engine Sheds closed prior to 1947

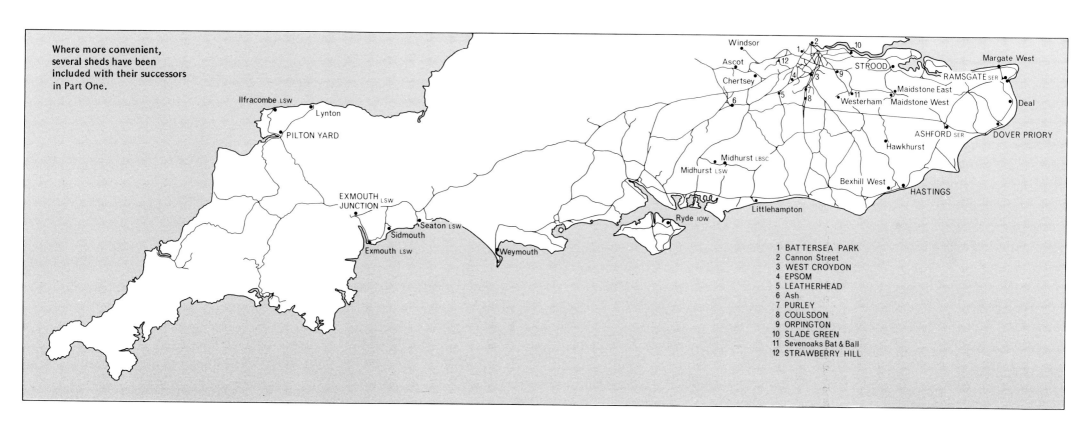

Where more convenient,
several sheds have been
included with their successors
in Part One.

Windsor

Ascot

Chertsey

Ilfracombe LSW

Lynton

PILTON YARD

Midhurst LBSC

Midhurst LSW

EXMOUTH
JUNCTION LSW

Seaton LSW

Sidmouth

Ryde IOW

Littlehampton

Exmouth LSW

Weymouth

STROOD

Margate West

RAMSGATE SER

Maidstone East

Westerham   Maidstone West

Deal

ASHFORD SER

DOVER PRIORY

Hawkhurst

Bexhill West

HASTINGS

1 BATTERSEA PARK
2 Cannon Street
3 WEST CROYDON
4 EPSOM
5 LEATHERHEAD
6 Ash
7 PURLEY
8 COULSDON
9 ORPINGTON
10 SLADE GREEN
11 Sevenoaks Bat & Ball
12 STRAWBERRY HILL

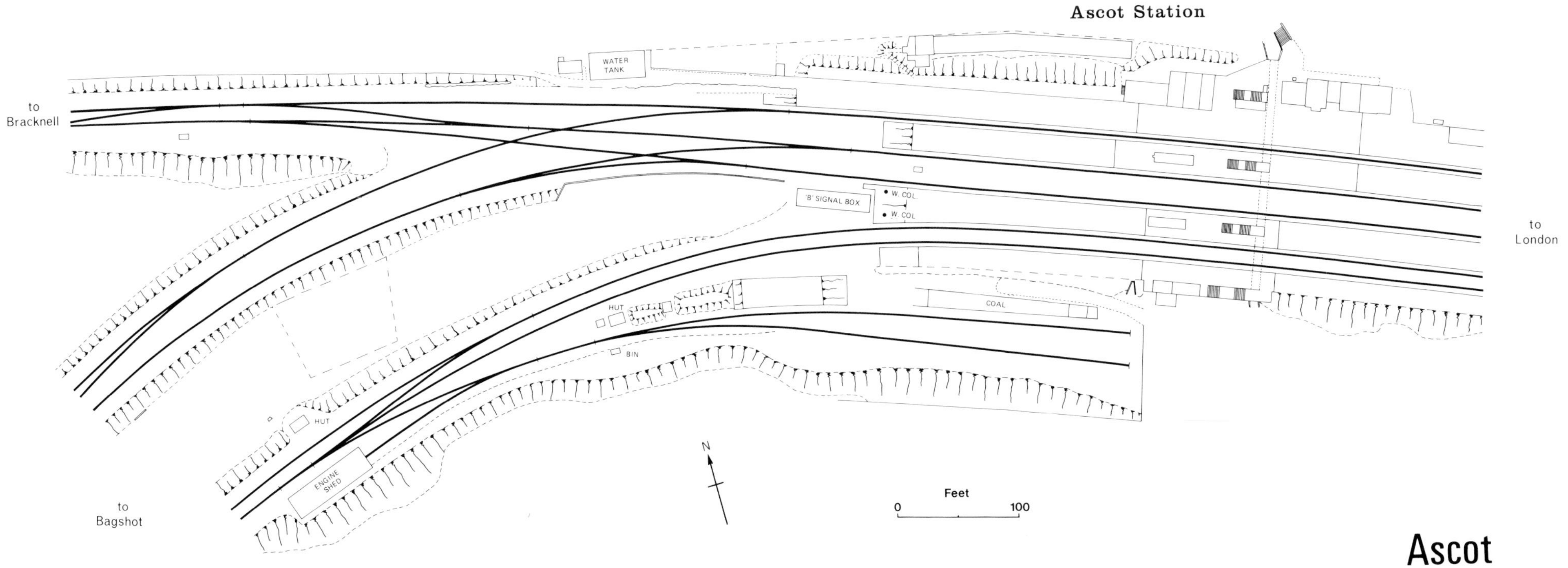

WATER
TANK

to
Bracknell

'B' SIGNAL BOX

• W. COL
• W. COL

to
London

HUT

COAL

BIN

N

HUT

ENGINE
SHED

to
Bagshot

Feet
0   100

Ascot
1936

The first engine facilities provided at Ascot were sited in the station yard and comprised simply a 40 ft. turntable. A small one-road shed was later constructed in the yard with access via a larger 50 ft. turntable.

Drawings for a new shed were approved in 1889 and later a single road structure was built some distance away alongside the Camberley line. Constructed in wood with a pitched slated roof, the LSWR kept a handful of engines there for various duties in the area, on the lines to Reading, Guildford and Waterloo. The small turntable, in the station yard, was retained for visiting locomotives and the site of the former shed was occupied by a new goods shed.

Only two engines were allocated when the Southern Railway was formed but the building continued in use for quite a few years under its new ownership. It was made sub to the new depot at Feltham but with increasing electrification saw less and less use. By 1936 it was noted that the shed was virtually disused, being visited by only one engine daily, and it was decided not to incur any expense in renovation. Electrification of the line had been approved the previous year and the shed did not survive the completion of the scheme. It closed in 1937 and was subsequently demolished; industrial development now occupies the site.

Feet
0   10

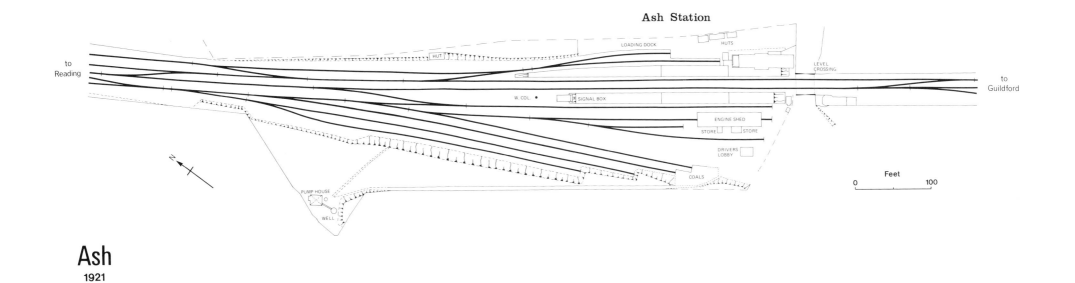

Ash Station

to Reading

LOADING DOCK

HUTS

HUT

LEVEL
CROSSING

to
Guildford

W. COL.

SIGNAL BOX

ENGINE SHED

STORE

STORE

DRIVERS
LOBBY

COALS

PUMP HOUSE

WELL

N

Feet

0   100

Ash

1921

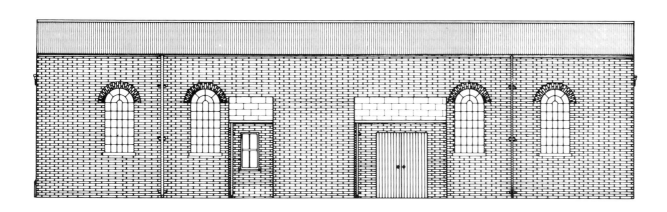

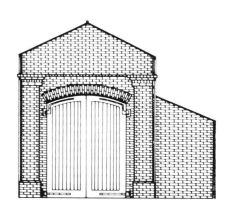

feet

0   20

The shed today in use as a private store.   *Author's collection*

The SER built the line through Ash to Guildford in 1849 and the original building, sited in the station yard, was built seven years later. It was a two road structure, incorporating both the engine and goods sheds. Constructed in brick with a slated pitched roof, it was radically altered in 1905. At a cost of some £220 the goods side was removed and the rest of the building converted to a single road shed. It was also used by the LSWR who normally stabled one engine there, a small tank from Guildford to work the Tongham line.

The SECR listed the shed as sub to Reading, and this arrangement was continued by the Southern Railway, the Aldershot–Guildford workings becoming the responsibility of ex-SECR 0-4-4Ts. These duties passed to Guildford in 1933 and ex-LSWR 'M7s' became the usual passenger tanks on the line. Closure of the shed was considered in 1937 because of the troublesome water supply, but the stabling facilities it provided were considered too important and it continued in use for some time afterwards. It is not included in any British Railways lists and it appears to have closed around 1946, although engines continued to use the yard for two or three more years. The shed is virtually intact today and is still in use as a store.

One of Ash's tank engines on shed in Southern Railway days.   *A.B. Macleod*

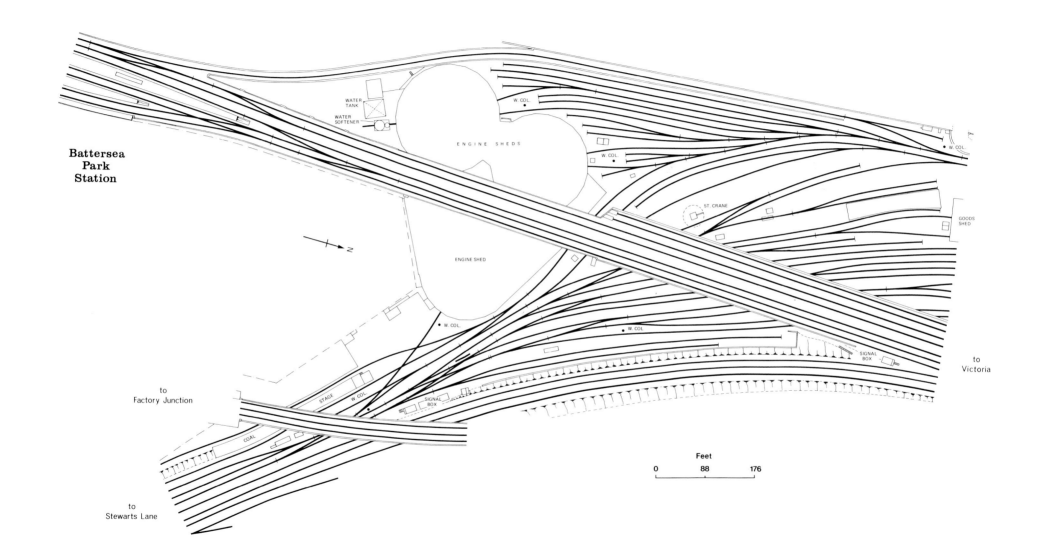

Battersea
Park
Station

WATER
TANK

WATER
SOFTENER

W. COL.

W. COL.

ENGINE SHEDS

W. COL.

ENGINE SHED

5T. CRANE

GOODS
SHED

W. COL.

W. COL.

W. COL.

to
Factory Junction

STAGE

W. COL.

SIGNAL
BOX

SIGNAL
BOX

to
Victoria

COAL

to
Stewarts Lane

Feet

0   88   176

The more northerly of the two roundhouses on the up side at Battersea Park in 1924, with No. 192 still in LBSCR livery.

H.C. Casserley

This interesting depot was constructed by the LBSCR in the 1870s, the company probably choosing roundhouses in preference to a straight shed because of the restricted site. Three roundhouses were built, two on the up side of the high level viaduct and one on the down side. The buildings were of the circular type, constructed in brick with slated roofs completely covering the turntables, and their construction enabled the closure of a small three road shed sited to the south. 55 ft. turntables were installed in the two up buildings and a smaller 45 ft. table in the third roundhouse.

The sheds originally housed large numbers of tank engines for suburban work in south

London, seventeen 'Terriers' being allocated in 1880 as well as 0-4-2 and later 0-4-4 tank types. Main line engines were also housed at the depot for working out of Victoria but increasing electrification in the twentieth century led to a gradual reduction in the numbers of locos required, and from 1933 the remaining engines began to be transferred to the newly-modernized ex-LCD shed at Stewarts Lane. The roundhouses were completely closed in the following year and partially converted into a lorry maintenance depot, and remain in this use to the present day.

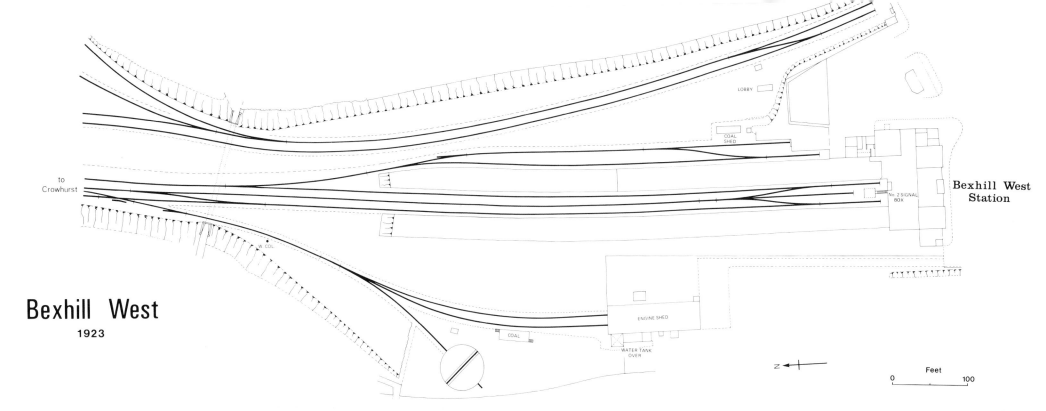

Bexhill West

1923

to Crowhurst

LOBBY

COAL SHED

W. COL

COAL

ENGINE SHED

WATER TANK OVER

No. 2 SIGNAL BOX

Bexhill West Station

Feet
0   100

This two road building, constructed in brick with a northlight pattern roof, opened in 1902 with the nominally independent Crowhurst Sidley and Bexhill Railway, but was worked from the start by the SECR. It was a single ended building but doors were provided at the rear, possibly to enable future extension. A water tank stood over the north-west corner of the building and a 55 ft. turntable and coal platform were provided in the yard, with water pumped from some distance down the line. The shed was designed to house four locomotives, and for many years office accommodation was provided in the form of an ex-LBSCR coach.

The shed was sub to Hastings throughout most of its existence and apart from a period of temporary closure during the First World War, 'H' class 0-4-4Ts were the usual engines. It was at first the policy of the Southern to concentrate Bexhill traffic at the West station but after electrification of the coastal route this was revised and traffic on the branch steadily declined, the shed becoming virtually disused after 1929, when the ex-SECR Hastings depot was demolished.

Engines continued to be coaled and watered for a number of years afterwards, the shed itself serving as a store for withdrawn locomotives, but the building was taken over by a private company in 1938. It was in use for over twenty years but since final closure of the line in the 'sixties all traces of the depot have been eliminated by industrial development.

The shed in 1936.

W.A. Camwell

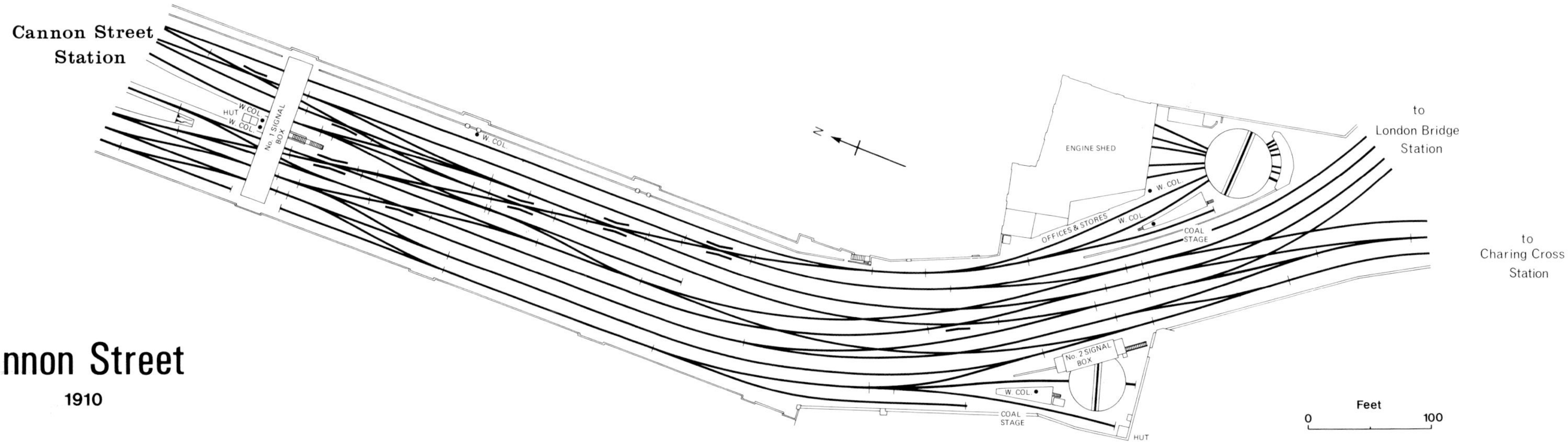

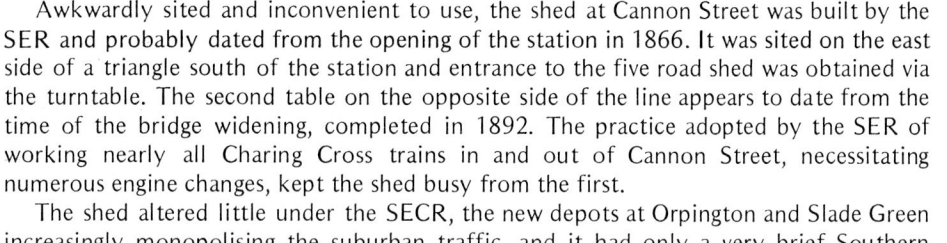

Cannon Street Station

to London Bridge Station

to Charing Cross Station

N

ENGINE SHED

W. COL

HUT

W. COL

W. COL

No.1 SIGNAL BOX

W COL

W COL

OFFICES & STORES

W. COL

COAL STAGE

No. 2 SIGNAL BOX

W. COL

COAL STAGE

HUT

Feet

0   100

Cannon Street

1910

Awkwardly sited and inconvenient to use, the shed at Cannon Street was built by the SER and probably dated from the opening of the station in 1866. It was sited on the east side of a triangle south of the station and entrance to the five road shed was obtained via the turntable. The second table on the opposite side of the line appears to date from the time of the bridge widening, completed in 1892. The practice adopted by the SER of working nearly all Charing Cross trains in and out of Cannon Street, necessitating numerous engine changes, kept the shed busy from the first.

The shed altered little under the SECR, the new depots at Orpington and Slade Green increasingly monopolising the suburban traffic, and it had only a very brief Southern Railway history. It was one of a number of sheds made redundant by Eastern Section electrification and was demolished, along with turntable and coaling stage in 1926, visiting engines afterwards having to use the surviving table on the west side of the line or run to the sub-depot at Ewer Street. An electricity sub station was subsequently built on the site.

This photo of the site in 1926 shows the rear of the shed surviving along with the derelict turntable. *Author's Collection*

Chertsey
1931

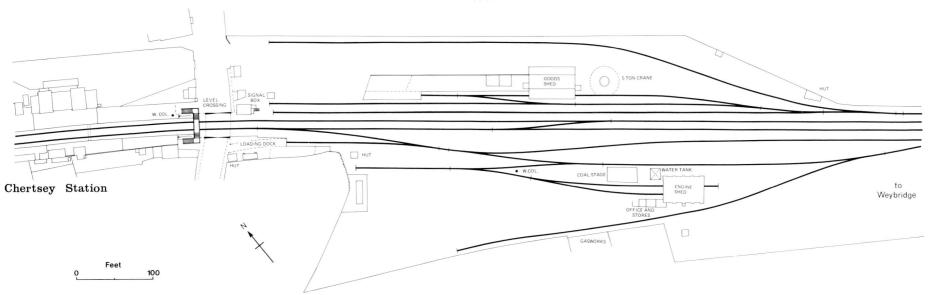

Chertsey Station

to Weybridge

1931 view with 'M7' 0-4-4T No. 106.   *H.C. Casserley*

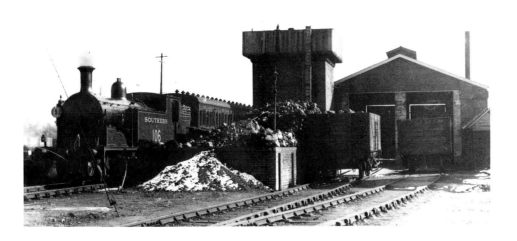

Little is known of the early history of this LSWR shed but it probably opened with the line from Weybridge in 1848 and was certainly in existence in the 1860s when the line was extended to Virginia Water.

It was a two road shed but additional doors were provided at the rear and later one of the roads was extended through. It was built in brick and had a pitched slated roof. Water was supplied from a well in the yard and a pump house was built adjacent to the shed to get the water from below ground. No platform was provided at first and coaling was probably carried out directly from wagons using a small wagon table at the side of the shed. This was removed before the turn of the century and a platform provided outside the shed.

Chertsey is not even mentioned in a 1922 list of LSWR sheds and may not have had any locos allocated at that time, but it would have normally housed a handful of tank engines for local services in the area. As no turntable was provided it is unlikely that tender engines were ever allocated. Under the Southern a pair of locos were supplied from Feltham, and before this Strawberry Hill would have been the parent shed. Chertsey became completely redundant with electrification and was finally closed in January 1937.

Coulsdon

1927

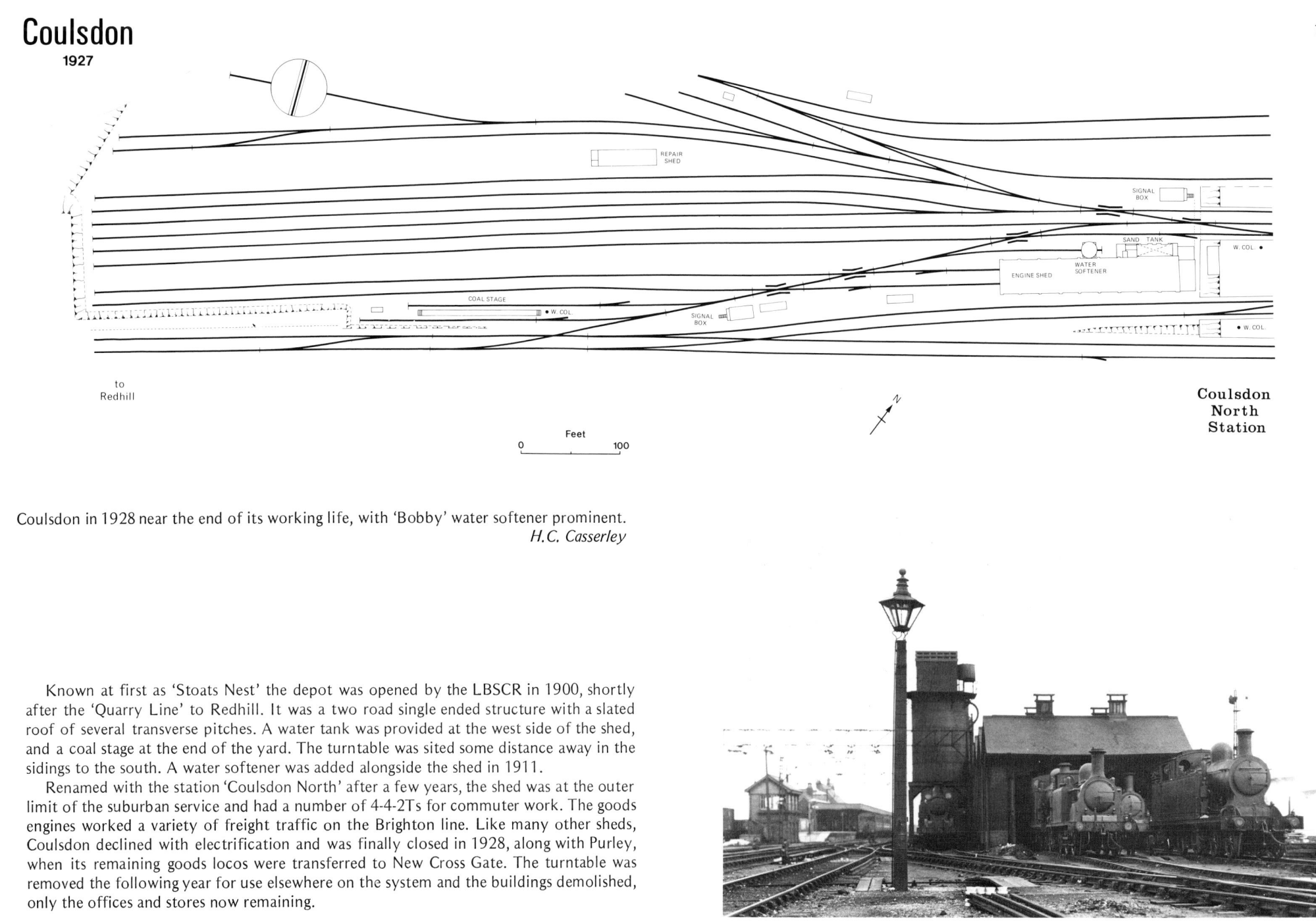

to
Redhill

Feet
0   100

N

**Coulsdon
North
Station**

Coulsdon in 1928 near the end of its working life, with 'Bobby' water softener prominent.

H.C. Casserley

Known at first as 'Stoats Nest' the depot was opened by the LBSCR in 1900, shortly after the 'Quarry Line' to Redhill. It was a two road single ended structure with a slated roof of several transverse pitches. A water tank was provided at the west side of the shed, and a coal stage at the end of the yard. The turntable was sited some distance away in the sidings to the south. A water softener was added alongside the shed in 1911.

Renamed with the station 'Coulsdon North' after a few years, the shed was at the outer limit of the suburban service and had a number of 4-4-2Ts for commuter work. The goods engines worked a variety of freight traffic on the Brighton line. Like many other sheds, Coulsdon declined with electrification and was finally closed in 1928, along with Purley, when its remaining goods locos were transferred to New Cross Gate. The turntable was removed the following year for use elsewhere on the system and the buildings demolished, only the offices and stores now remaining.

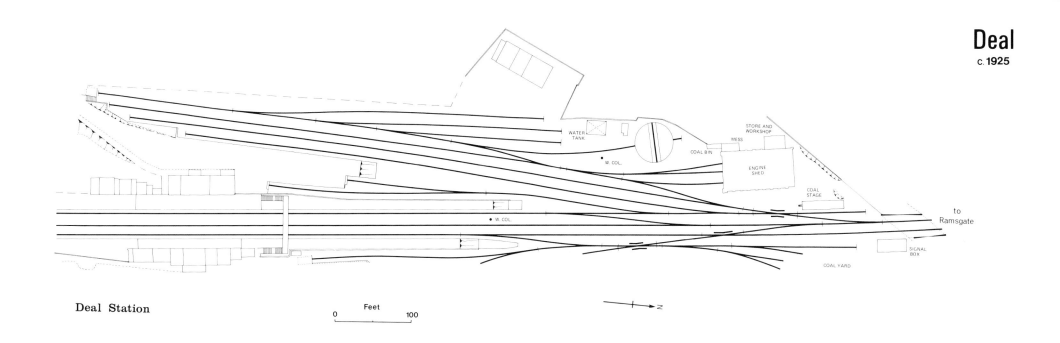

Deal Station

Feet
0   100

An early view of the shed, the roof and brick gable latterly being replaced in corrugated sheeting.

Collection of R.C. Riley

The first shed at Deal was opened by the SER when it constructed its branch from Minster to a terminus at Deal in 1847, and was a two road single ended building constructed in brick, sited north of the station. It was a small shed, measuring only 33 ft. by 50 ft., but the offices, stores and smithy were housed in a separate building sited at the far end of the yard. The shed was later rebuilt, however, to include a third road and a turntable, probably to coincide with the arrival of the line from Dover in 1881.

The shed was sub to Ramsgate in SER days but after 1899 it became a sub shed of Dover. The depot seems to have been regarded as more important under the SECR and SR, having only three locos in 1898 but including several of the famous 'Schools' class in its allocation in 1930. This must have been a welcome change for the staff as before the First World War the shed was noted as a last resting place of elderly, obsolete engines. It was not to keep its modern 4-4-0s for long however, as in September 1930 the new depot at Ramsgate came into operation and as a result Deal shed was closed. The building though continued to be used by the CME's department and after surviving several bomb attacks in 1941 was still being used for goods purposes in the mid 'fifties. It has since been demolished

Dover Priory

1917

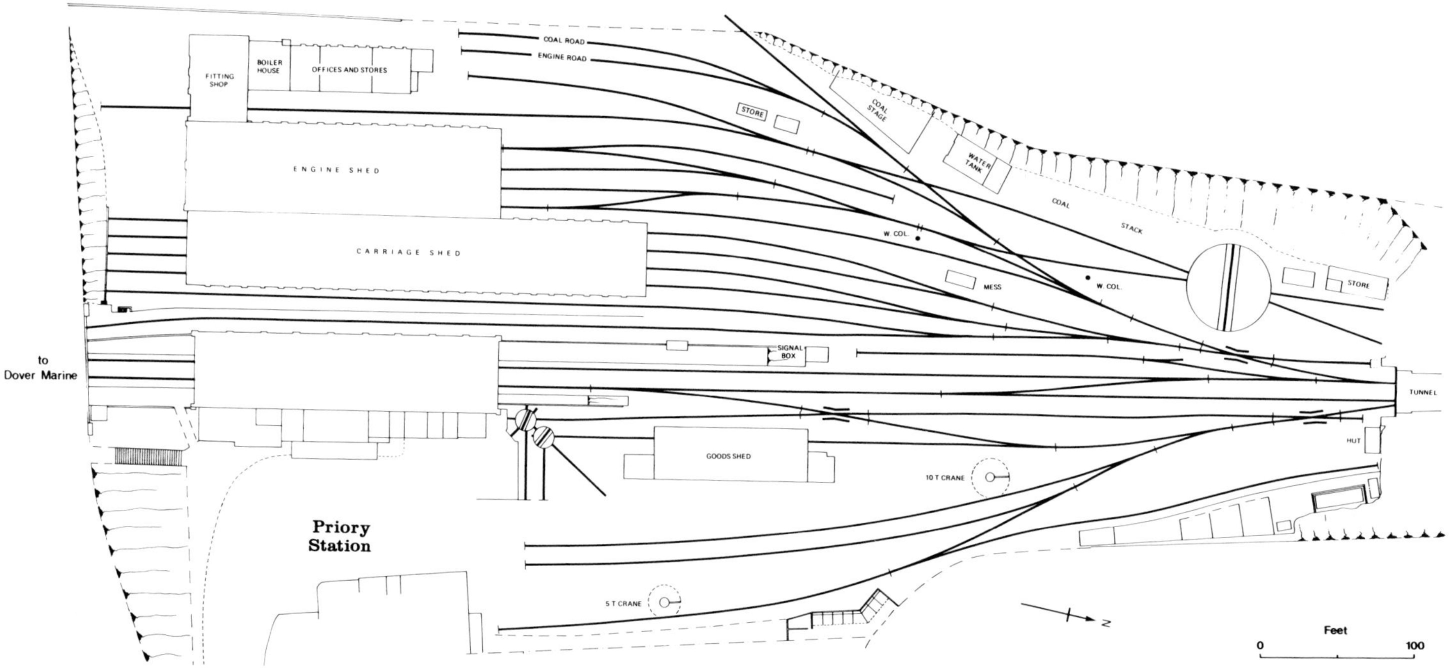
COAL ROAD
ENGINE ROAD
FITTING SHOP
BOILER HOUSE
OFFICES AND STORES
STORE
COAL STAGE
WATER TANK
ENGINE SHED
CARRIAGE SHED
COAL
STACK
W. COL.
MESS
W. COL.
STORE
SIGNAL BOX
to
Dover Marine
TUNNEL
HUT
GOODS SHED
10 T CRANE
Priory
Station
5 T CRANE
N
Feet
0
100

SOUTHERN
269

The shed in 1927.

H.C. Casserley

The shed stood on the west side of the station and was opened when the London and Chatham company reached Dover in 1861. It was a four road depot with workshops and a large carriage shed closely associated. A coal stage and a large water tank were provided by the turntable at the far end of the yard. A larger 50 ft. table was installed some distance to the north towards the end of the century.

Built in brick, with a pitched slated roof, Priory was a major depot of the LCDR and provided engines for the prestigious boat trains as well as numerous freight and local shunting turns.

It became increasingly important after 1899, when the ex-SER sheds at Dover were closed and the engines and duties transferred to Priory. However, in 1924, shortly after its formation, the Southern Railway decided to build a new depot at Dover Marine, part of a large scheme in which Priory station was to be enlarged and the Archcliffe Fort Tunnel removed. The shed was gradually abandoned and eventually demolished when the new depot opened in 1928, the site afterwards being occupied by a goods yard.

Epsom Town

1924

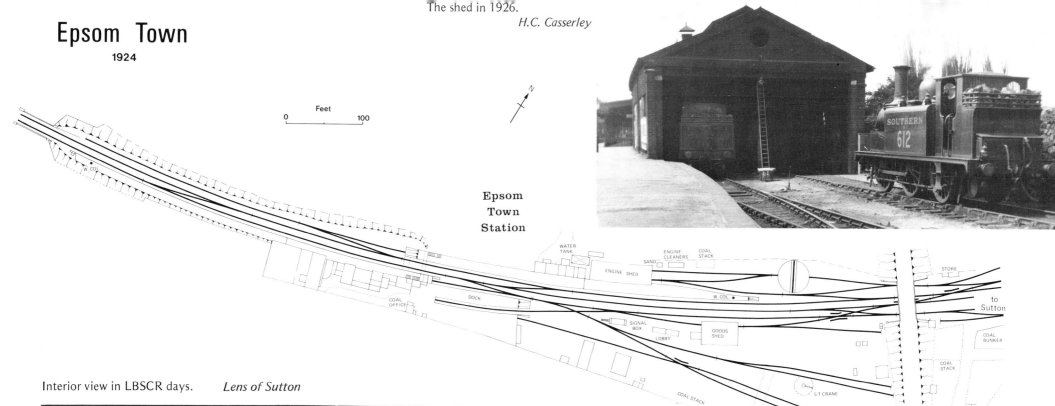

Epsom
Town
Station

Interior view in LBSCR days.   *Lens of Sutton*

Epsom Town shed was sited adjacent to the station and was opened by the LBSCR in 1857. It was constructed in brick with a slated pitched roof and one of the two roads led directly onto a 40 ft. turntable. In 1913 the shed was altered slightly, the two separate doors giving way to a larger, single entrance. In the years up to the grouping the shed was responsible for a variety of local goods and passenger services, as well as coping with regular influxes of locomotives on Race Days. Turntable and servicing facilities were also maintained by the LSWR at their station, the SECR at Tattenham Corner and the Brighton again at Epsom Downs.

The shed, like many others in and around London, owed its demise to electrification and was closed when electric services commenced from Victoria in 1929. A new station was built some distance to the south west but the shed and yard were sold off to a private concern and the turntable removed. The building survived in use as a 'goods depot' into the mid 'thirties but has now been demolished.

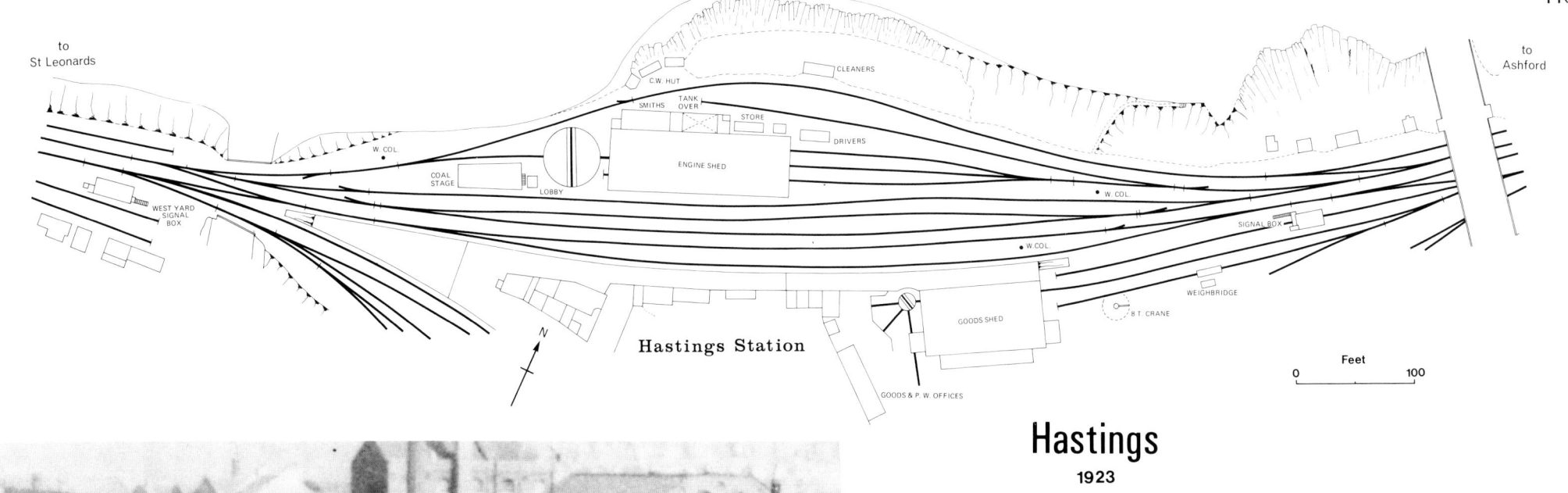

to St Leonards

to Ashford

C.W. HUT

CLEANERS

SMITHS · TANK OVER

STORE

W. COL

COAL STAGE

LOBBY

ENGINE SHED

DRIVERS

W. COL

WEST YARD SIGNAL BOX

W. COL

SIGNAL BOX

W. COL

WEIGHBRIDGE

GOODS SHED

8 T. CRANE

N

Hastings Station

GOODS & P. W. OFFICES

Feet
0   100

Hastings
1923

The original shed at Hastings stood on the north side of the old station and dated from 1852 when SER main line trains began running from Tunbridge Wells. The station at Hastings was worked jointly between the SER and LBSCR and the shed, although built by the South Eastern, was shared for a number of years. It was a brick built shed with a pitched slated roof and offices and a water tank were provided on the north side. The middle road ran through the building onto a 45 ft. turntable.

LBSC engines ceased to use the shed after the 1870s when St. Leonards was built, but it continued to be an important depot of the SER and its successor the SECR. It serviced engines for main line and local duties and after 1902 was responsible for a sub shed at Bexhill West.

The depot had a fairly short life under the Southern and was demolished, the engines being transferred, to make way for station improvements. Its decline had been heralded by the construction of entirely new servicing facilities at the west end of the station, a 55 ft. turntable and coal stage being approved in 1926 at a cost of £7,850. The entire allocation was moved to St. Leonards in 1929 and the buildings demolished in the same year. The subsequently enlarged station, opened in 1931, completely obscured the site, but a turntable and water tank were retained for some years on the north side. The replacement servicing facilities to the west remained in use until 1957.

The SER station and shed in 1893.

Author's collection

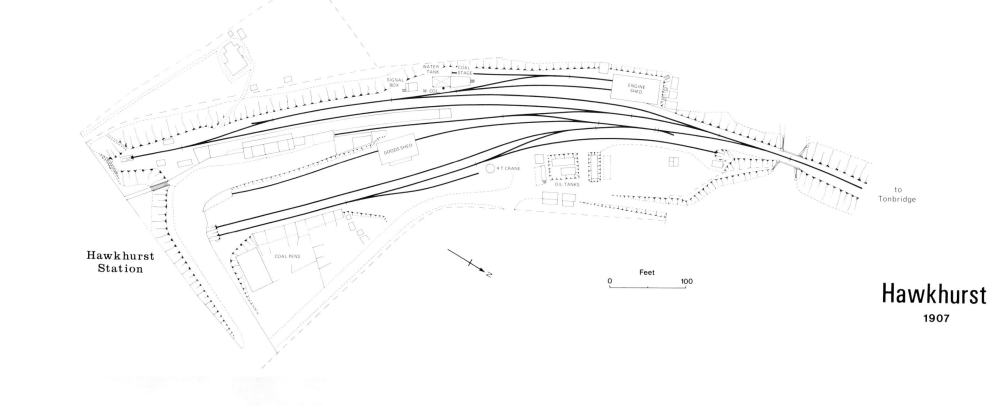

Hawkhurst
Station

Feet
0   100

Hawkurst
1907

This was a commodious brick built shed with two roads covered by a pitched slated roof. A water tank and coal stage were provided at the far end of the yard near to the signal box. It was opened by the SER in 1893 when the branch was completed from Tonbridge, but it never accommodated more than one engine, normally an ex-LCD 'Q' or 'R1' 0-4-4T, supplied from Tonbridge, the parent depot.

It never appears to have had an official status, being absent from SER and succeeding SECR and SR lists. It was closed about 1931 but along with water tank, remains today under private ownership, surviving even the closure of the branch in 1961.

No. 31543 passes the two road shed.
Collection of R. Randell

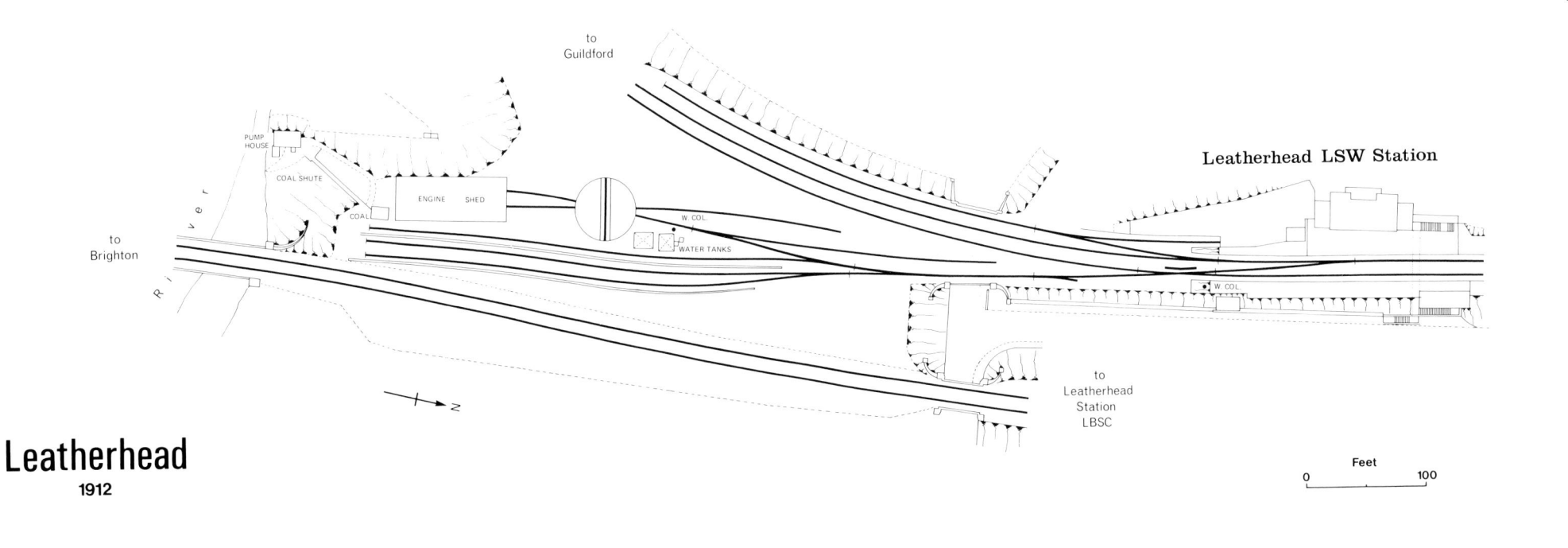

Leatherhead

1912

to Guildford

to Brighton

PUMP HOUSE

COAL SHUTE

ENGINE SHED

COAL

W. COL

WATER TANKS

Leatherhead LSW Station

W. COL

to Leatherhead Station LBSC

Feet
0   100

The LSWR approved the construction of a shed here in 1885 at a cost of £227. A turntable had been provided at Leatherhead for many years but the new arrangements included a water tank and small one road shed, to accommodate one loco, with access via a turntable. In 1903 a replacement shed was authorised, this time costing £1,600, and a new two road depot, intended to house four engines, was built in corrugated iron, again with access via the turntable. The new table at 55 ft. was much larger than its predecessor. There were still only four locos allocated in 1922, the last year of the LSWR, and it is probable that the small stud of engines for various minor local work never exceeded this number.

Once again, like many other small sheds near to London, Leatherhead did not long survive Southern Railway ownership, falling victim to electrification after only four years. The shed went out of use when the ex-LSW station closed and its lines reduced to sidings in July 1927. By 1932, the shed had completely disappeared.

0-4-4T No. 108 and 4-4-0 No. 386 on shed in 1925.
H.C. Casserley

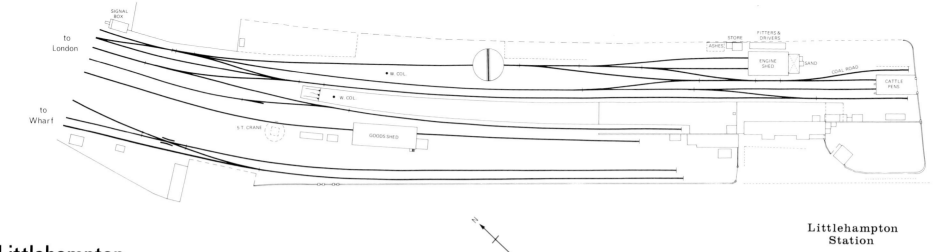

Littlehampton

1910

SIGNAL BOX

to London

to Wharf

5 T. CRANE

W. COL.

W. COL.

GOODS SHED

STORE

FITTERS & DRIVERS

ASHES

ENGINE SHED

SAND

COAL ROAD

CATTLE PENS

Littlehampton Station

Feet
0   100

The shed here was built by the LBSCR when the new Littlehampton station opened in 1863, and it replaced a much earlier shed sited by the original station at Lyminster Crossing. The two road shed stood at the north side of the station and was built in brick with a slated pitched roof. A water tank surmounted the rear part of the shed and the two roads led onto a turntable at the far end of the yard.

In the early years the depot was sub to Horsham but the increasing importance of the parent depot's various sub sheds led to Bognor gaining its independence in the 1920s, Littlehampton then becoming sub to its neighbour along the coast. Nine or ten engines were normally stationed at the depot including a number of 'Terriers', especially in the earlier years, and three or four 'D1' 0-4-2Ts.

The electrification of the branch brought about the closure of the shed and although the electric service, part of the 'Portsmouth No. 2 Project', did not begin until 1938 the remaining engines at Littlehampton were transferred away to Bognor and Brighton in 1937. The premature closure of the shed was to enable alterations to be made to the station but the building itself, minus the water tank, was converted for use as a store and can still be seen in that use today.

0-6-2T and 0-4-2Ts and a mixture of liveries at Littlehampton in 1927.

H.C. Casserley

Maidstone East

1920

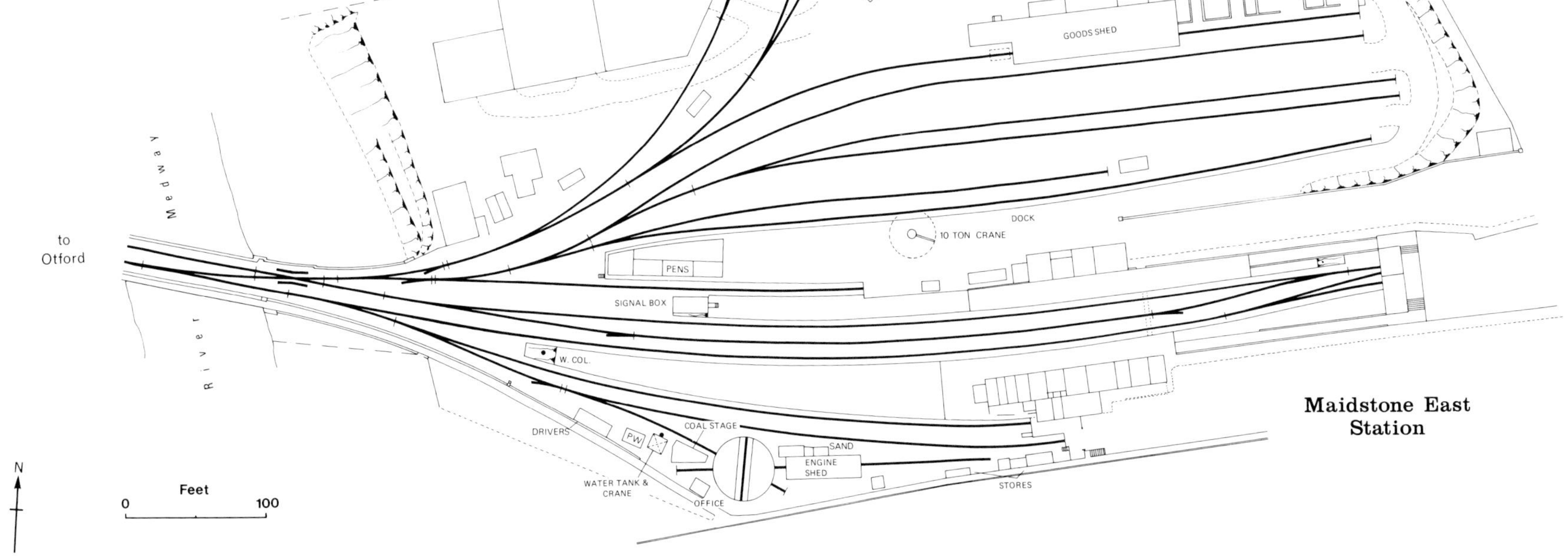

MIDLAND SIDING

GOODS SHED

to Otford

Medway

River

10 TON CRANE

DOCK

PENS

SIGNAL BOX

W. COL.

DRIVERS

PW

COAL STAGE

SAND

ENGINE SHED

STORES

WATER TANK & CRANE

OFFICE

Maidstone East Station

N

Feet

0   100

This single road through building was the LCDR shed in the town and seems to date from the opening of the station in 1874. Access to the shed was via a turntable sited immediately outside. It stood to the west of the station and was much smaller than its SER counterpart at Maidstone West.

Its physical remoteness from the ex-SER system probably saved it from the kind of rationalization carried out in many areas after the amalgamation of 1899. Under the SECR the shed, along with Maidstone West, maintained a separate coding, but the Southern downgraded the depots, placing them sub to Ashford. The shed housed the station pilots and turned visiting locomotives and also possessed a stud of eight 'F1' 4-4-0s for passenger work. It closed along with its neighbour in 1933, several years in advance of electrification and shortly afterwards was completely demolished, no trace now remaining of the shed.

This view of the engine siding at Maidstone East in 1932 just shows part of the small one road shed.

H.C. Casserley

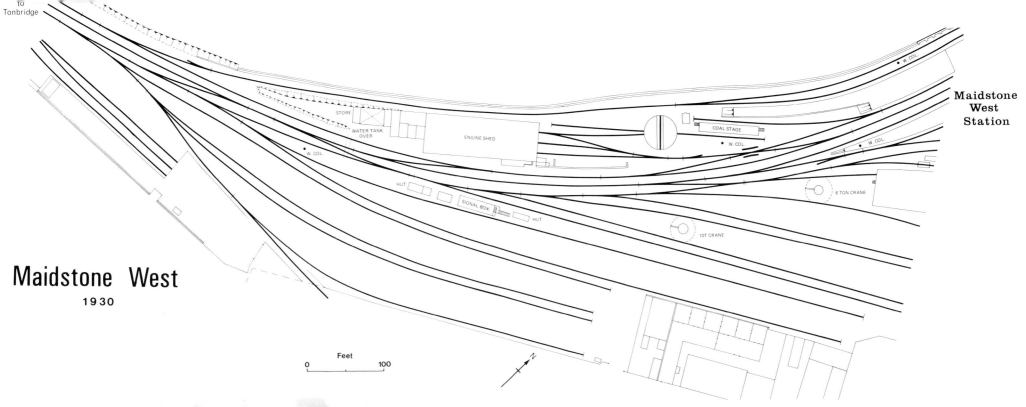

Maidstone West

1930

to
Tonbridge

Maidstone
West
Station

W. COL.

STORE

WATER TANK
OVER

ENGINE SHED

COAL STAGE

W. COL.

W. COL.

W. COL.

HUT

6 TON CRANE

SIGNAL BOX

HUT

10T CRANE

Feet
0   100

N

This was a fairly large three road shed built in brick with a slated pitched roof, and was sited just south of the station. It would seem to date from the opening of the station in 1844. One of the roads led directly onto a 45 ft. turntable and a coaling platform was provided nearby. The shed was of SER origin and it would doubtless have taken over the duties of its much smaller ex-LCD counterpart at Maidstone East if the two stations could have been integrated in 1899.

The sheds remained independent of each other under the SECR but after the grouping became sub to Ashford, until closure in the mid 1930s.

The allocation numbered seventeen locomotives at closure, mainly passenger tanks of the 0-4-4 and 0-4-2 type for local passenger work. Three 'O1' 0-6-0s were also allocated. It was closed in 1933 along with Maidstone East and afterwards partly demolished, but the coal stage and turntable were left intact, remaining in use till 1939 when electrification finally reached the town.

The shed in 1932.

H.C. Casserley

115

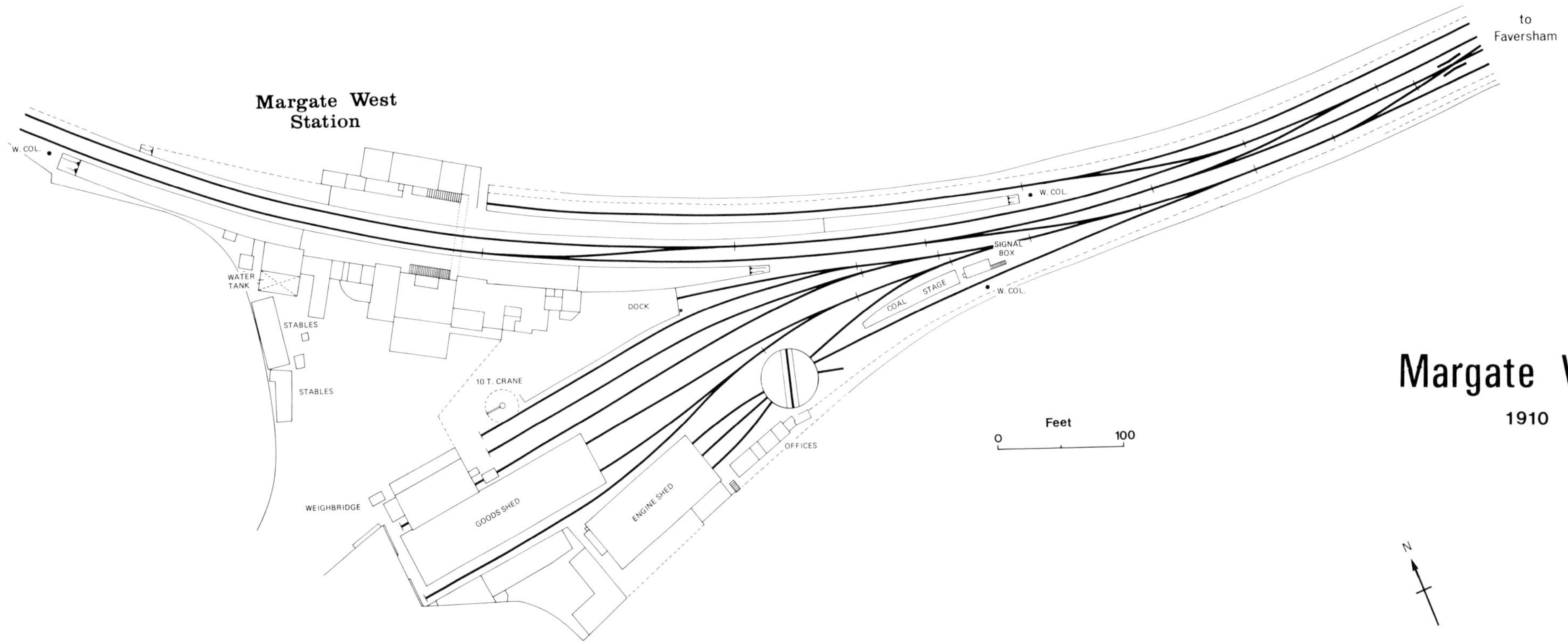

to
Faversham

W. COL.

**Margate West
Station**

W. COL.

W. COL.

WATER
TANK

SIGNAL
BOX

W. COL.

STABLES

COAL STAGE

STABLES

DOCK

10 T. CRANE

Margate West

1910

OFFICES

Feet

0   100

WEIGHBRIDGE

GOODS SHED

ENGINE SHED

N

This brick built shed stood on the north side of the line and dated from the opening of the LCDR station in the 1860s. It became known as Margate West, along with the station, after the fusion of 1899. The three roads led directly onto a turntable outside the shed and a coal platform was provided beside the approach roads.

The shed shared the duties in the Thanet area with Deal and Ramsgate depots but the reorganization of the lines in the area by the Southern resulted in its closure within a few years of the grouping. The scheme for the new station and depot at Ramsgate was approved in 1925 and Margate was gradually run down as the new facilities were brought into use. It was entirely redundant by 1928 and was demolished to make way for a new parcels depot, completed in the same year. Visiting engines, however, continued to be serviced at the turning and watering point established by the SR on the opposite side of the line to the original shed. This successor, though not classified as a depot, did not finally go out of use until the early 'sixties.

An early view of Margate West.

A.B. Macleod

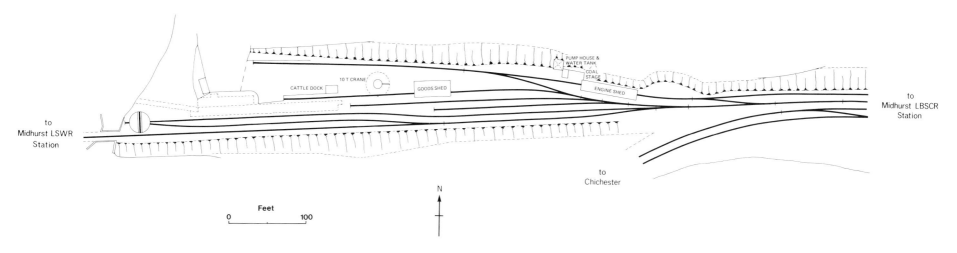

to
Midhurst LSWR
Station

to
Midhurst LBSCR
Station

to
Chichester

Feet
0   100

N

Midhurst LB & SCR
1885

This was a timber built through shed and opened with the LBSC line from Petworth in 1866. A coal stage and water tank were supplied outside the shed at the west end and originally a small turntable was also installed, although it was actually sited some distance to the west, near the road dividing the LBSC tracks from the LSW. The shed was lengthened and rebuilt, again in wood and with a pitched slated roof, in 1907. The new building occupied the same site and the water tank and coal stage were retained unaltered.

The shed was sub to Horsham, housing 0-4-2Ts with 'Terriers' appearing in the 1880s and these worked local trains to Pulborough and Chichester. The station was resited half a mile to the east in 1881 but the shed remained intact, although the turntable was removed after a few more years. It was closed by the Southern shortly after the grouping and the final three 'Terriers' were afterwards operated from Horsham. The building itself was demolished and no traces now remain.

The original Brighton shed in very poor condition, the reason for its replacement being obvious. The new shed was closely similar in style.

Lens of Sutton

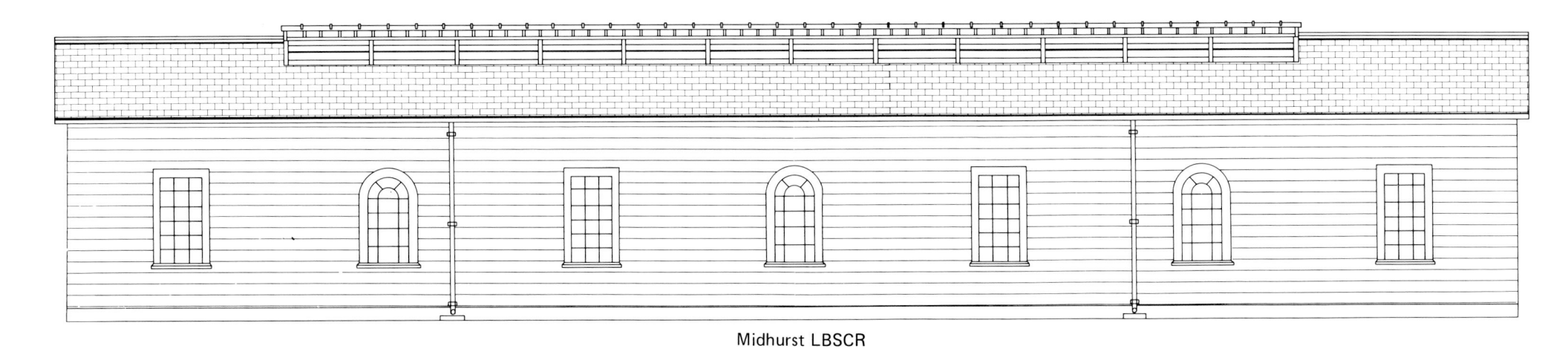

Midhurst LBSCR

Feet

0   10

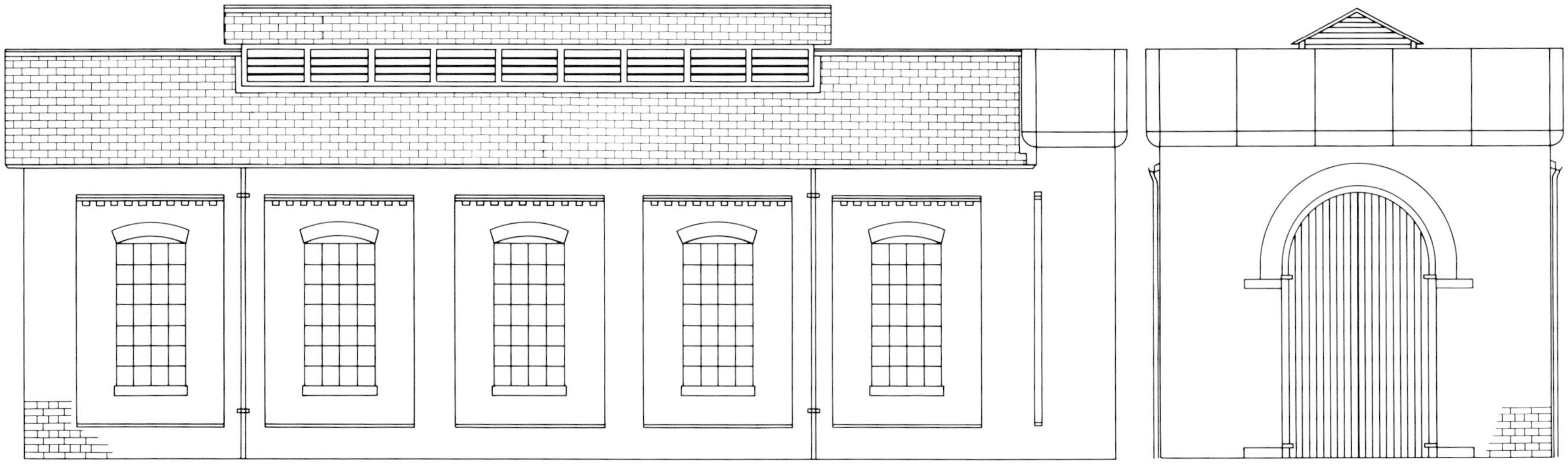

Midhurst LSWR

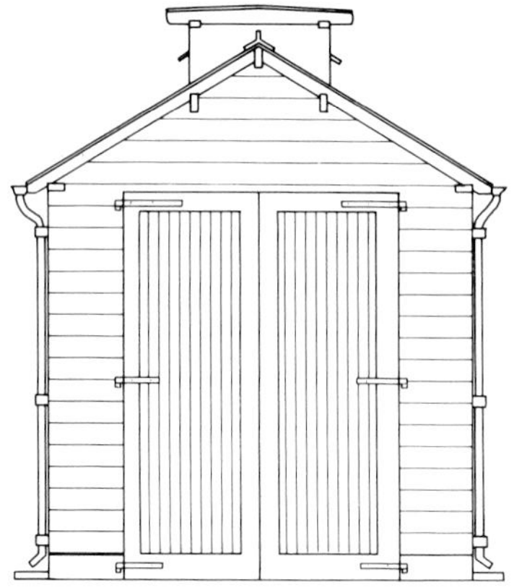

Midhurst
LBSCR
End Elevation

Midhurst LSWR

1912

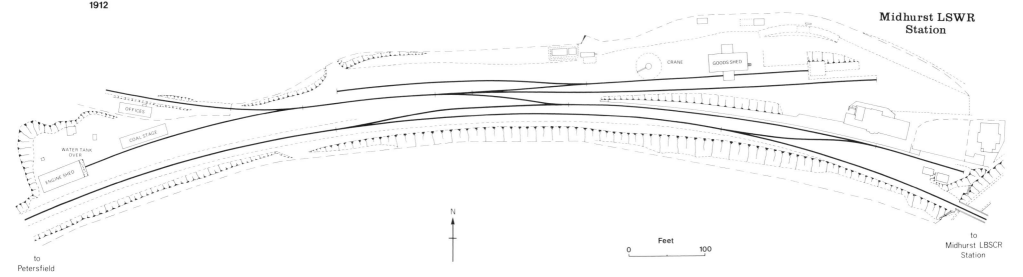

Midhurst LSWR
Station

OFFICES

COAL STAGE

WATER TANK
OVER

ENGINE SHED

CRANE

GOODS SHED

N

Feet
0   100

to
Petersfield

to
Midhurst LBSCR
Station

This brick built shed was of LSWR origin and opened with the line from Petersfield in 1864. It was a small single ended building with a water tank surmounting the entrance and when first built, a 45 ft. turntable was provided directly outside. Fratton was the parent depot and one or two engines were normally outstationed at Midhurst, at first Beattie tanks but for many years 'T1' 0-4-4Ts.

The shed became the only one in the town after 1923 and survived its ex-LBSC neighbour for a number of years. Nevertheless, closure was always likely and it saw less use under the Southern. The turntable was removed many years before the grouping and the shed itself closed completely in 1937, the branch engine afterwards being supplied by Guildford. The building has since been demolished.

The roofless shed in 1937 shortly after closure.

W.A. Camwell

Orpington

1909

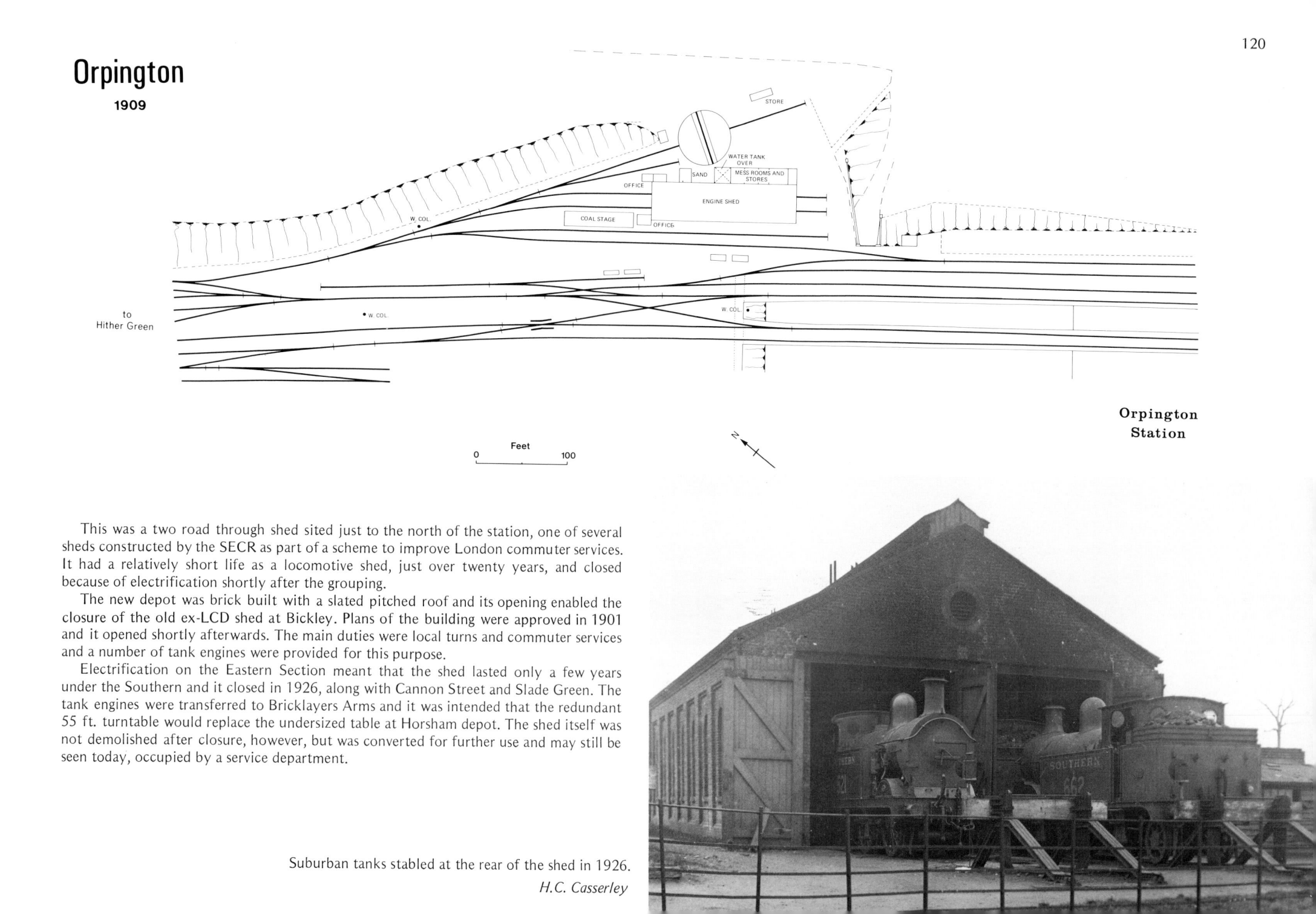

STORE

WATER TANK OVER

SAND · MESS ROOMS AND STORES

OFFICE

ENGINE SHED

COAL STAGE · OFFICE

W. COL.

W. COL.

W. COL.

to
Hither Green

Feet
0 · 100

N

**Orpington
Station**

This was a two road through shed sited just to the north of the station, one of several sheds constructed by the SECR as part of a scheme to improve London commuter services. It had a relatively short life as a locomotive shed, just over twenty years, and closed because of electrification shortly after the grouping.

The new depot was brick built with a slated pitched roof and its opening enabled the closure of the old ex-LCD shed at Bickley. Plans of the building were approved in 1901 and it opened shortly afterwards. The main duties were local turns and commuter services and a number of tank engines were provided for this purpose.

Electrification on the Eastern Section meant that the shed lasted only a few years under the Southern and it closed in 1926, along with Cannon Street and Slade Green. The tank engines were transferred to Bricklayers Arms and it was intended that the redundant 55 ft. turntable would replace the undersized table at Horsham depot. The shed itself was not demolished after closure, however, but was converted for further use and may still be seen today, occupied by a service department.

Suburban tanks stabled at the rear of the shed in 1926.

H.C. Casserley

Loco shed, carriage repair shop and carriage shed at Pilton Yard in 1926.
H.C. Casserley

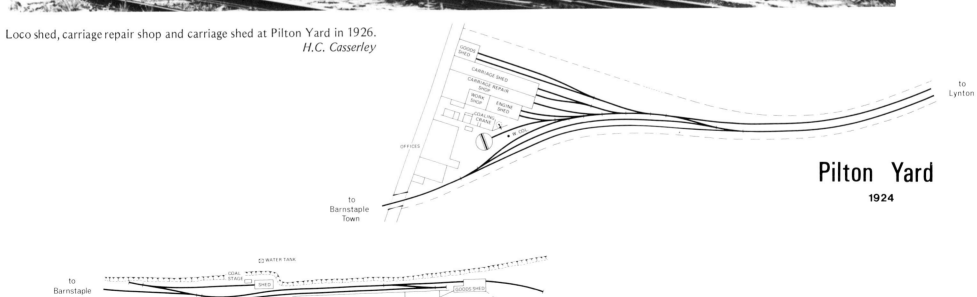

GOODS SHED

CARRIAGE SHED

CARRIAGE REPAIR SHOP

WORK SHOP   ENGINE SHED

COALING CRANE

OFFICES

W. COL.

to Lynton

Pilton Yard

1924

to Barnstaple Town

WATER TANK

COAL STAGE   SHED

SIGNAL BOX

GOODS SHED

W. COL.

to Barnstaple

Lynton Station

Lynton

1898

This unique 1' 11½" gauge line was absorbed at the grouping and ran from the LSW station at Barnstaple Town to the tiny station at Lynton, high up on Exmoor. Pilton Yard, at Barnstaple, was the largest of the two sheds on the line, the other being a small through shed at Lynton. Both opened with the line in 1898.

Pilton Yard was a two road building in corrugated sheeting, one road extending through to a workshop with a carriage and wagon shed alongside. This structure was later rebuilt, in wood, with a pitched tiled roof. A siding to the south of the shed served a coal stage and water column as well as a 30 ft. turntable. Three Manning Wardle 2-6-2Ts and a Baldwin 2-4-2T formed the engine stud working the variety of duties on the line. They were joined after 1923 when a fourth 2-6-2T, very similar to the originals, was supplied by the Southern.

The small shed at Lynton was designed to accommodate a single locomotive and was built in stone with a pitched roof. Access was originally from the Barnstaple end but shortly after opening this was reversed, the former approach road remaining with coal stage alongside.

Despite efforts by the Southern to improve the services, traffic steadily declined and the line eventually closed in 1935. Most of the buildings at Pilton Yard still survive under private ownership, although the turntable was purchased for use on the RHDR in Kent but the small shed at Lynton has now been demolished.

Lew outside the shed at Pilton Yard in 1935.

H.C. Casserley

Lynton station in 1935 with the shed in the left hand foreground.　　H.C. Casserley

Lynton shed.　　Lens of Sutton

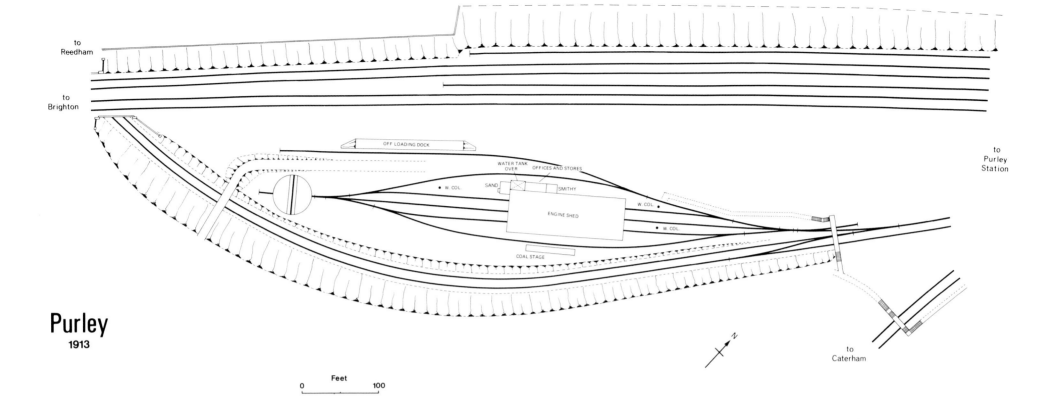

to
Reedham

to
Brighton

OFF LOADING DOCK

WATER TANK OVER   OFFICES AND STORES

W. COL.   SAND   SMITHY

W. COL.

ENGINE SHED

W. COL.

COAL STAGE

to
Purley
Station

Purley

1913

N

to
Caterham

Feet

0   100

Purley shed was opened by the SER in 1898, the last year of the company's existence and at the time was considered a modern well laid out depot. It was a through building constructed in brick with a northlight pattern roof, the three roads leading onto a 50 ft. turntable at the south western end of the yard. The opening of the depot enabled the closure of the shed at Caterham, and the single locomotive based there was transferred to Purley in the same year.

The shed was responsible for various local freight and passenger duties as well as commuter traffic, but was not destined to enjoy a very long life as a working depot. Electrification by 1927 resulted in its closure, and a proposal was considered to build an EMU shed on the site. This idea was abandoned and the building has survived to the present day, still surrounded by running lines. It was used to store freight vehicles for a number of years but the building has now been modified for private use and all the tracks removed.

The shed in 1928, shortly after closure.
H.C. Casserley

123

Sevenoaks Bat & Ball

1931

to
Otford

to
Sevenoaks Tubs Hill

Sevenoaks Bat & Ball Station

WATER
TANK

HUT

SIGNAL
BOX

W. COL.

ENGINE
SHED

GOODS
SHED

COAL WHARF

Feet

0   100

The small shed at Sevenoaks Bat and Ball Station was opened when the LCDR constructed the line from Swanley in 1862. It was at first a terminus, the connection to the SER Tubs Hill Station not opening until 1869, and for many years Maidstone trains reversed at Bat and Ball. This obviously provided the initial requirement for an engine shed and entrance to the one road building was via a 45 ft. turntable.

It was a wooden structure with a pitched slated roof and central raised vent and after 1882, when Maidstone trains began to run via Otford, a handful of passenger tanks were allocated for working the local trains. An 'R' 0-4-4T was provided by Stewarts Lane in 1913 for the Otford service, this being the only one of several engines using the shed to stable overnight. Electrification of the line in 1935 made the shed completely redundant and it was demolished by the following year. No trace now remains of the building.

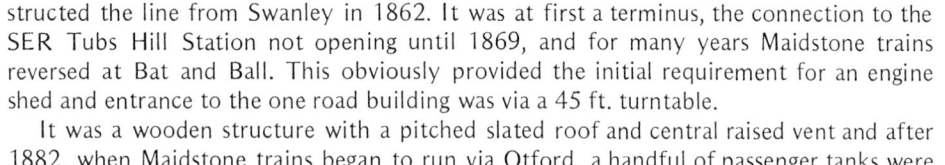

The wooden shed and turntable at Sevenoaks in 1930, shortly before demolition.

R. Kidner

Sidmouth

1905

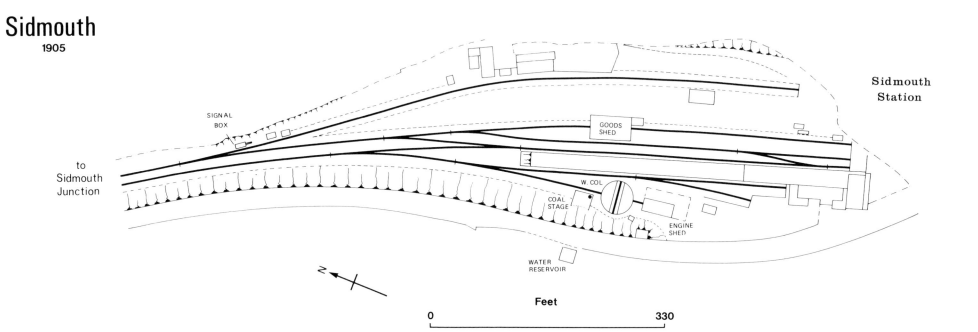

SIGNAL BOX

to
Sidmouth
Junction

GOODS SHED

Sidmouth Station

W. COL

COAL STAGE

ENGINE SHED

WATER RESERVOIR

N

Feet

0   330

The shed opened when the line was completed in 1874 and was a small brick built structure with a slated pitched roof. It was a single ended building with an arched entrance and at first a small turntable was provided immediately outside. The line was worked from the first by the LSWR, the shed eventually becoming sub to Exmouth Junction, which normally supplied an 'M7' or 'O2' 0-4-4T.

In 1900 a disastrous fire all but destroyed the shed but repairs costing £200 soon restored the building to working order. The turntable remained in place, even though as early as 1914 the branch services were worked exclusively by tank engines. The actual closure date of Sidmouth is not clear, but it seems to have lost all official status in the mid 'thirties. The turntable had been removed by 1933 and the shed had disappeared from Exmouth Junction's list of sub sheds. Nevertheless, engines continued to use the building as late as 1938 but it would seem to have been classed simply as an engine siding, the single road later being cut short of the shed by SR. The line itself closed in 1967 but the building is still intact, having been converted for private commercial use.

Sidmouth shed with turntable removed.
Lens of Sutton

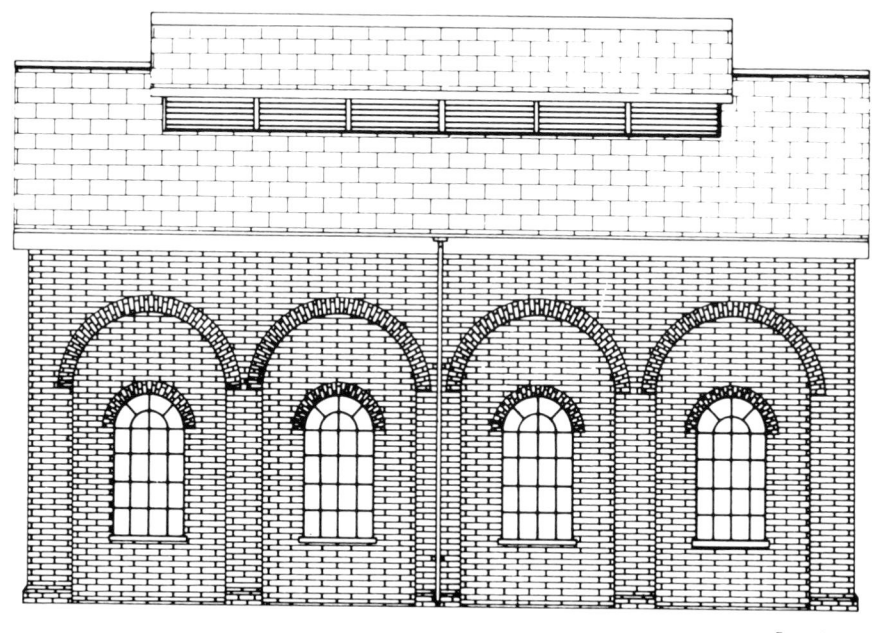

'M7' class 0-4-4T No. 253 outside Sidmouth shed.

W.A. Camwell

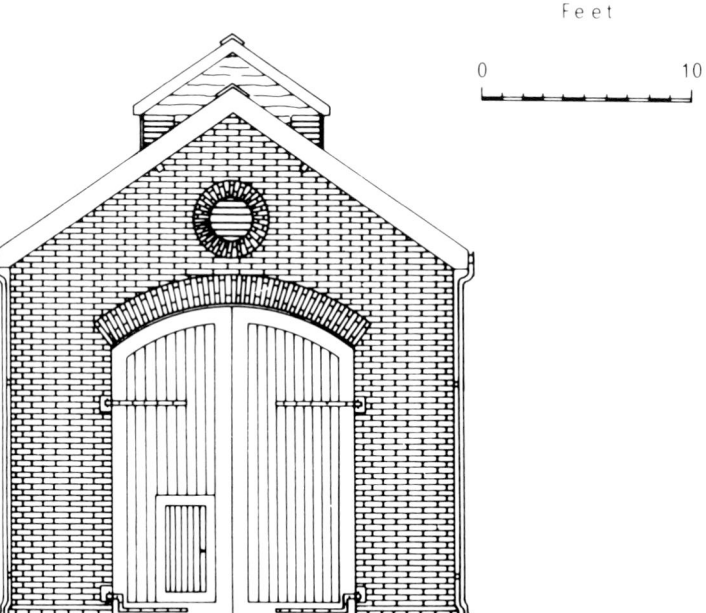

Feet

0   10

Slade Green

1922

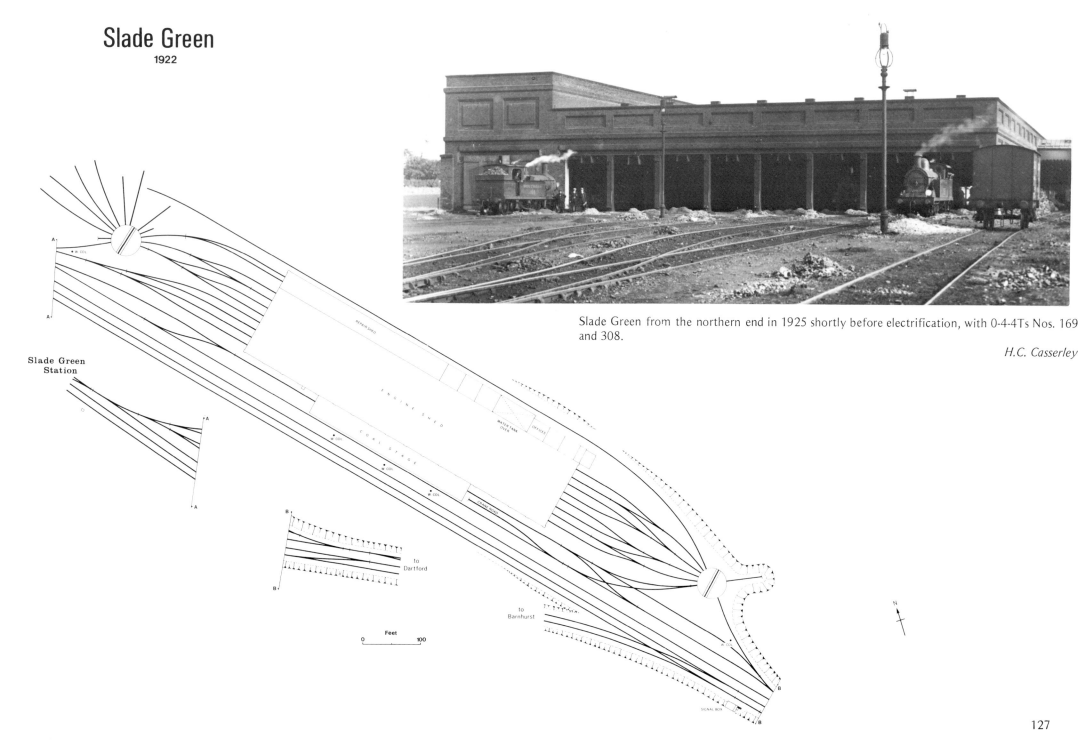

Slade Green from the northern end in 1925 shortly before electrification, with 0-4-4Ts Nos. 169 and 308.

H.C. Casserley

W COL

A

A

A

Slade Green
Station

A

A

REPAIR SHED

ENGINE SHED

WATER TANK
OVER

OFFICES

COAL STAGE

W COL

W COL

W COL

CRANE ROAD

B

B

to
Dartford

to
Barnhurst

W COL

Feet
0   100

N

SIGNAL BOX

B

B

The shed from the southern end, the concrete parapet concealing the northlight pattern roof.

Collection of W. Palmer

The first proposals for an engine shed at Slade Green came in 1898 as an alternative to enlarging the existing depot at Bricklayers Arms where space was required for expansion of the goods facilities. The new depot was at first referred to as 'Whitehall, Erith' but soon became known as the more familiar 'Slades Green', the 's' going out of use after a few years. Sited at Erith on the north Kent line, the shed came fully into use in 1901. Thus, although planned by the SER, it was not actually opened until after the amalgamation with the LCD. The shed building measured a huge 600 ft. long by 155 ft. wide, with a coal stage along the western side. A 150,000 gallon water tank stood on the opposite side, supplied with pre-softened water from a plant sited along with the electricity generator some quarter of a mile away. The brick built shed, with northlight pattern roof, had ten roads served by a 50 ft. turntable at each end of the yard. Two of the roads, on the eastern side, terminated in a repair shop served by a pair of 5 ton travelling cranes.

Designed to house a hundred and ten locomotives, the allocation at Slade Green comprised mainly tank engines for use on the network of commuter lines in south-east London. Many of them transferred from Bricklayers Arms on the opening of the new depot. Slade Green was one of the principal depots of the SECR after Battersea and Bricklayers Arms, but increasing electrification after the grouping soon led to the redundancy of much of the locomotive stud. The decision to convert the building to emu maintenance was taken in 1924 and in the following year the construction of a large repair depot near to the steam shed was authorised at a cost of over £30,000. The steam engines disappeared with the commencement of the electric services in 1926, but the shed building, apart from an extension at the northern end in 1959, remains in use as the inspection shed, much in its original condition.

This contrasting view shows the interior of the shed not long after opening, with some of the many suburban tanks on shed.

Collection of W. Palmer

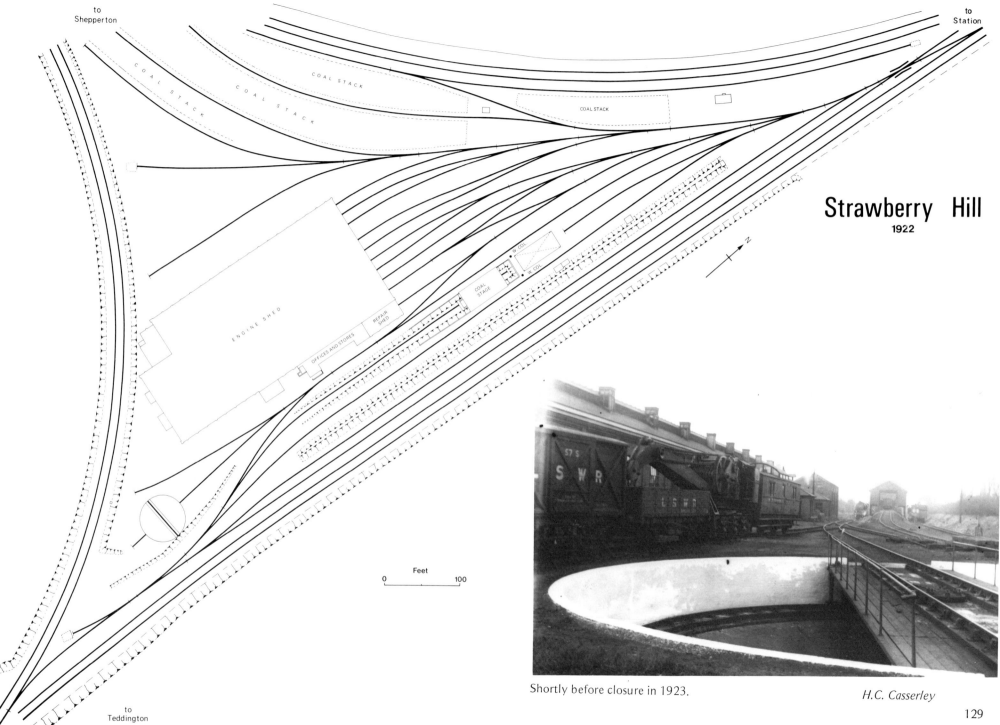

to Shepperton

to Station

COAL STACK

COAL STACK

COAL STACK

COAL STACK

Strawberry Hill

1922

W COL

W COL

ENGINE SHED

OFFICES AND STORES

REPAIR SHED

COAL STAGE

Feet

0   100

to Teddington

Shortly before closure in 1923.

H.C. Casserley

A view taken in April 1923, during the changeover, shows 3rd rail already installed in some of the yard.

H.C. Casserley

As explained in detail in the description and history of Feltham depot, Strawberry Hill was run-down and closed by the LSW/SR during 1922-23. It only just falls within the scope of this book and in the last few months of its existence as a steam depot, during 1923, its activities were doubtless severely reduced. Despite this it should be included in any comprehensive history of Southern engine sheds.

Sited in a triangle of lines, it was a large brick built shed, single ended with ten roads covered by a slated roof of four pitches. A coal stage and turntable stood on the eastern side, near the repair shop. At first known as Fulwell Junction, its opening in 1897 enabled the closure of small sheds at Kingston and Twickenham. Fifty-eight locomotives were allocated at first, and it was enlarged after 1906, when plans for an extension were first submitted, the shed at that time only being able to accommodate thirty engines. A new 50 ft. turntable was approved the following year. Strawberry Hill was the principal depot in the area, being responsible for a variety of turns, mainly freight, as well as those local turns previously worked by Kingston and Twickenham. Engines were also provided for the small depots at Chertsey and Ascot.

As previously explained, the LSWR decided to replace the shed with a new modern depot at Feltham and the running-down and transfer process took place during 1922-23. The recommendation that Strawberry Hill be converted to e.m.u. maintenance was approved in May 1922 and by the end of the following year work was well in hand. The building may still be seen in this use today, much in its original condition, although the turntable and coal stage have long since vanished.

Much of the original building, of typical LSWR construction, can still be seen in this view taken in 1973.

Author's collection

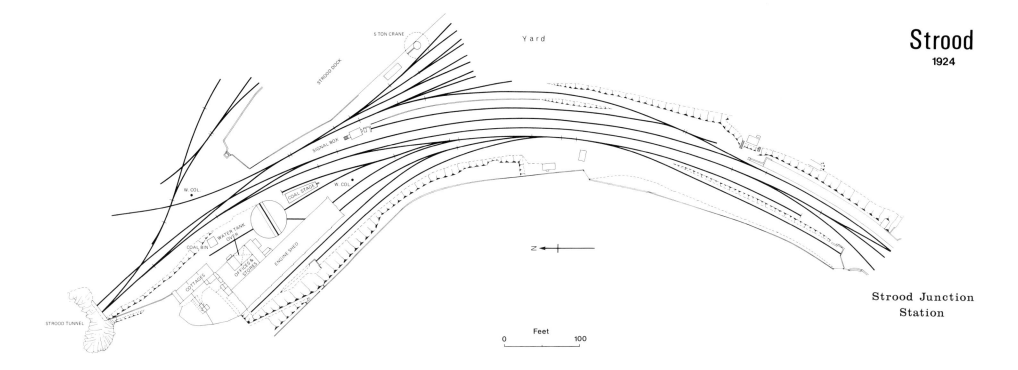

5 TON CRANE

Yard

STROOD DOCK

SIGNAL BOX

COAL STAGE

W. COL.

W. COL.

WATER TANK OVER

COAL BIN

COTTAGES

OFFICES & STORES

ENGINE SHED

STROOD TUNNEL

N

Strood Junction
Station

Feet
0   100

The shed at Strood probably dates from 1856 when the original terminus was rebuilt and the line extended by the SER through to Maidstone. It was an L-shaped building with only a single road at first and a 40 ft. turntable at the side. The building was constructed in brick with a slated pitched roof, a water tank surmounting the offices and stores on its eastern side. The SER later added a second road and installed a larger 45 ft. turntable, with a coal stage nearby.

The SER had stationed some eighteen locos at the depot and after 1899 the shed was, to a large extent, combined for operational purposes with the ex-LCD depot at Gillingham. In 1923 Strood was the busier of the two depots with steam operated services in north Kent. After electrification it became the 'poor relation' of Gillingham and its use and importance declined steadily over the years. It eventually went out of use with further electrification in 1939 and for many years was used as a goods shed, surviving demolition until 1970.

The disused shed with the water tank still prominent.

Edwin Course

West Croydon

1902

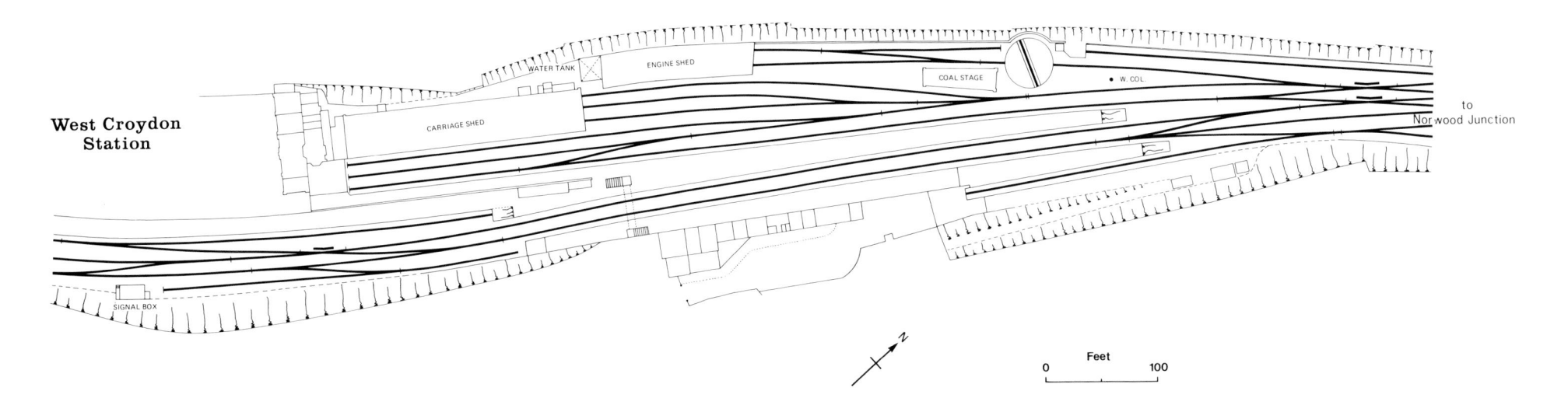

West Croydon
Station

WATER TANK ENGINE SHED

CARRIAGE SHED

COAL STAGE

W. COL.

to
Norwood Junction

SIGNAL BOX

Feet
0   100

The shed at West Croydon dates from the opening of the line to London Bridge in 1839 by the London and Croydon Railway, later of course passing into the ownership of the LBSCR. It was a brick built shed, single ended with a pitched slated roof and was increased in length prior to the 1870s. The building stood hard against the embankment at the west side of the station, a somewhat cramped site, with access to the two road shed via a 46 ft. turntable.

The shed was responsible for commuter passenger trains in its early years, a number of 'Terriers' being stationed there, but electrification had by the 'thirties reduced its duties to local freight and shunting turns. The allocation prior to closure consisted entirely of 0-6-2Ts, nine 'E4' and four 'E3' class and the turntable had been removed, presumably redundant with an all-tank locomotive stud. The Southern subsequently constructed a coal stage and shelter on one of the turntable approach roads. The shed eventually closed in 1935, when the Southern opened a new depot for freight engines at Norwood Junction. The locomotives and duties were divided between Bricklayers Arms and Norwood and the building was shortly afterwards demolished.

Freight train passing the shed in 1928.
H.C. Casserley

The site of the shed in 1960.

D. Loveday

The shed opened with the Westerham Valley Railway in 1881 and in that year passed into the ownership of the SER, becoming a sub shed of Tonbridge. It was a simple wooden structure mounted on a dwarf brick wall with a pitched slated roof. A water tank and single water column were provided, but no turntable was ever installed. Tonbridge normally supplied an 0-4-4 Tank, No. 366 being allocated in 1906.

The Southern closed and demolished the shed after only a short time, probably around 1925. Coal and water continued to be made available for many more years, however, the branch engine in fact stabling on the site of the shed until the late 'fifties.

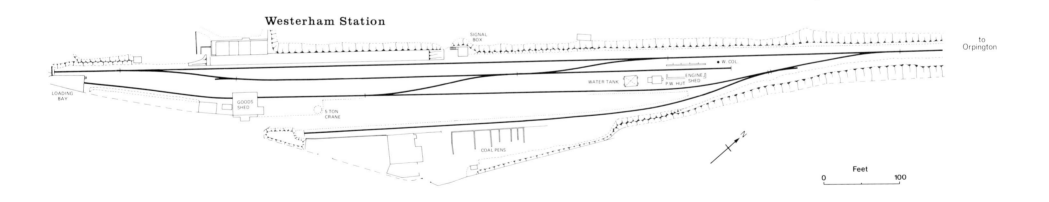

Westerham Station

SIGNAL BOX

W. COL.

WATER TANK

ENGINE SHED

P.W. HUT

to Orpington

LOADING BAY

GOODS SHED

5 TON CRANE

COAL PENS

N

Feet
0   100

Westerham
1954

to
Portland

to
Dorchester

JUNCT. SIGNAL
BOX

10 T. CRANE

GOODS SHED

STA. SIGNAL
BOX   • W. COL

OFFICE

COAL SHED

WATER
TANK

ENGINE SHED   COAL   • W. COL
STAGE

OFFICES &
STORES

Feet

0   100

**Weymouth
Station**

'H15' 4-6-0 No. 477 at Weymouth in 1936.
W.A. Camwell

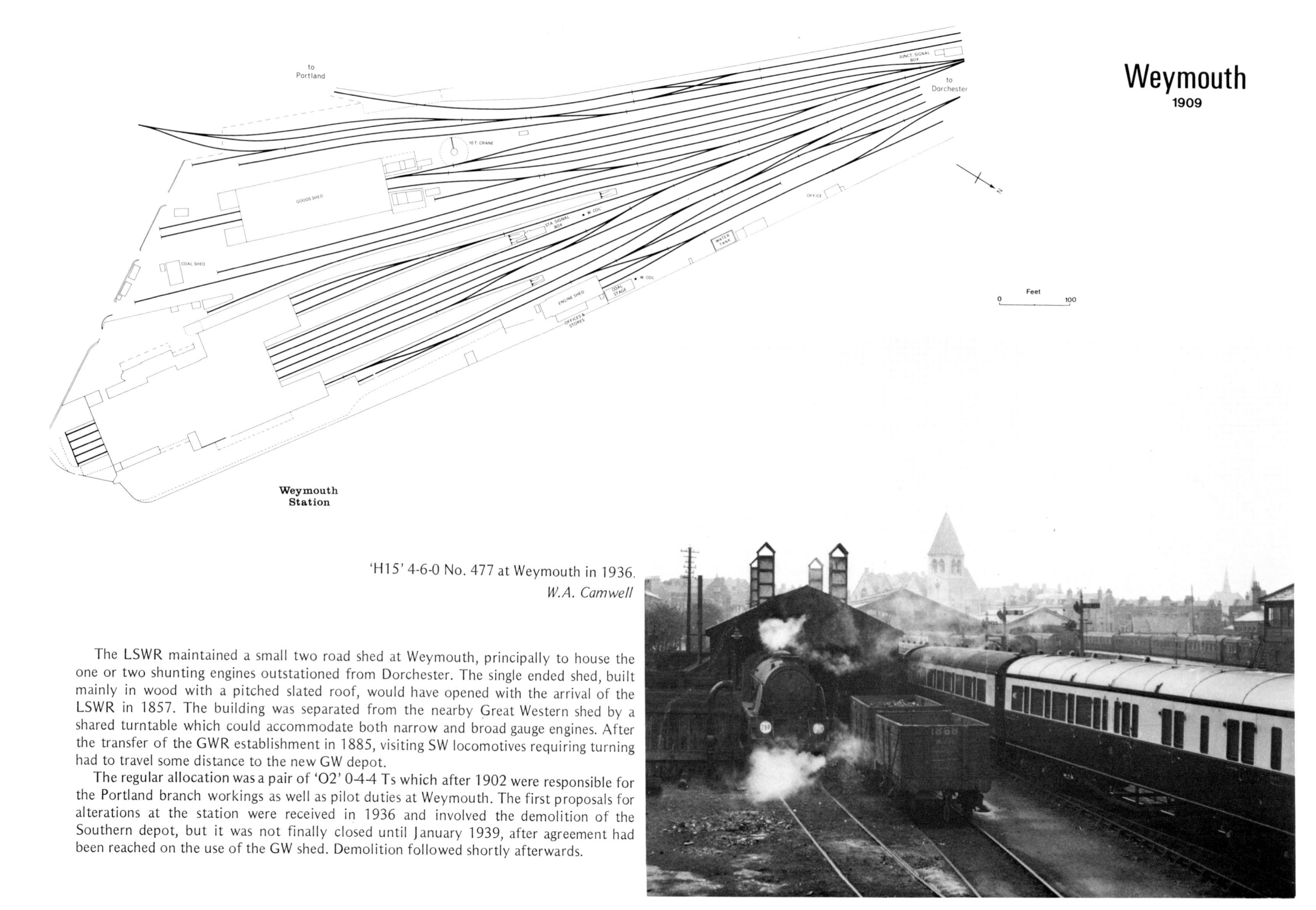

The LSWR maintained a small two road shed at Weymouth, principally to house the one or two shunting engines outstationed from Dorchester. The single ended shed, built mainly in wood with a pitched slated roof, would have opened with the arrival of the LSWR in 1857. The building was separated from the nearby Great Western shed by a shared turntable which could accommodate both narrow and broad gauge engines. After the transfer of the GWR establishment in 1885, visiting SW locomotives requiring turning had to travel some distance to the new GW depot.

The regular allocation was a pair of 'O2' 0-4-4 Ts which after 1902 were responsible for the Portland branch workings as well as pilot duties at Weymouth. The first proposals for alterations at the station were received in 1936 and involved the demolition of the Southern depot, but it was not finally closed until January 1939, after agreement had been reached on the use of the GW shed. Demolition followed shortly afterwards.

Windsor

1928

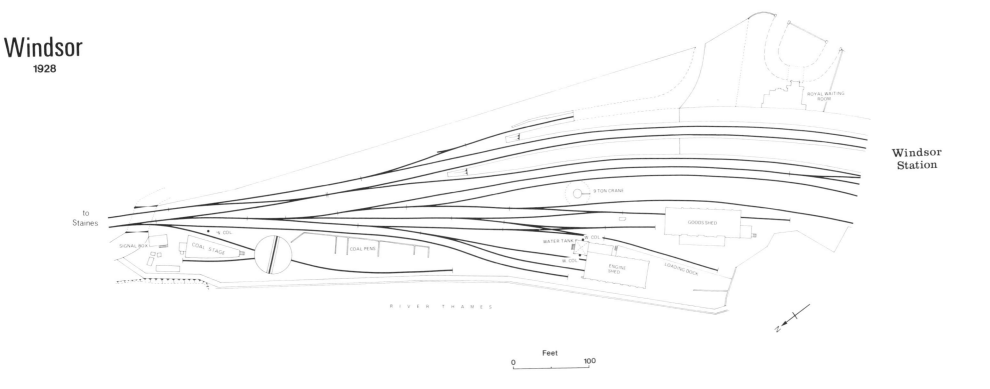

Windsor
Station

9 TON CRANE

GOODS SHED

WATER TANK

W. COL

W. COL

LOADING DOCK

ENGINE
SHED

COAL PENS

W. COL

COAL STAGE

SIGNAL BOX

to
Staines

RIVER THAMES

Feet

0   100

The small shed at Windsor stood to the north of the station near to the bank of the Thames. It was single ended and built in brick with a slated pitched roof. Water was originally supplied from a well near to the shed, and at first the turntable stood near the entrance. It would seem to have opened with the line in 1849.

The LSWR stationed seven locos there for various local workings and prior to the turn of the century installed a larger 50 ft. turntable, sited this time at the north end of the yard, together with the coal stage. A carriage body for locomen's self-help classes was approved in 1911 but no more improvements seem to have been made at the shed.

The line was electrified in 1930 but the shed appears to have been still in use as late as 1935. It did not survive the war and had fallen out of use prior to 1942. It has now been demolished.

Single engine on shed in 1930, the year of electrification.
H.C. Casserley

135

Appendix One

ADDITIONAL SHEDS

A number of buildings and sites have come to light during research and have been excluded for a variety of reasons.

The ex-Somerset and Dorset Joint Railway sheds have not been included as, although the railway was a joint MR/LSWR concern, the sheds and locomotives were Midland responsibility. A possible exception to this was the small depot at Wimborne, originally an important junction, where four LSW locos were outstationed in 1922. It is described as an S&D shed, however, and although there were two buildings it appears that LSW locos were merely housed at the shed in a similar arrangement with the S&D to that with the SER at Ash and Reading.

Another 'near miss' is the oft-mentioned Brighton shed at Dorking. This was a small two road affair with turntable, sited in the station yard. It was scheduled for closure before 1923 but apparently blew down in a storm and had to be demolished prior to the grouping. Engines continued to stable at the site, however, and coal and water were provided for a number of years. The authorities always seemed anxious to avoid officially recognising the depot and it has after much consideration been excluded from the main part of the book.

A third shed narrowly outside the scope of this work was the small South Western building at Hampton Court. It is fairly well documented, drawings for the two road brick structure being sent to the builders in 1894. It had a pitched slated roof and stood on specially raised ground near the station. It appears to have officially gone out of use with early electrification in 1916.

A large group difficult to classify were the turning and servicing points situated at many of the London termini and other places like Padstow and Brockenhurst. While providing similar facilities to officially recognised depots like Ewer Street and Southampton New Docks, the differences lay in the staffing levels or the near proximity of a large main depot, as at Nine Elms and Waterloo, Stewarts Lane and Victoria, etc. A further group comprised the various small depots operated by the service departments of the Southern. Perhaps the best known being the small single road sheds at Redbridge sleeper depot and Meldon Quarry, they were not classed along with the running sheds of the operating department and have been excluded for that reason.

Still more depots missed inclusion because of closure prior to 1923 but often turning and other facilities were retained for many years, even into Southern ownership. This was the case at Hayling Island where for decades after closure and demolition of the shed, a coal stage and other facilities were provided. Rosherville turntable, at Gravesend, was still in use in 1923, some years after the nearby ex-LCD shed had been put out of use. This occurred to a greater or lesser degree at a number of other places including Twickenham, Kingston, Ringwood, Haslemere, Alton, Woking, Budleigh Salterton and Chard, although the latter was an LSW/GWR joint shed. Two final oddities are the LBSC shed at East Grinstead and the LCD establishment at Sheerness. Various sources mention a small depot or deny the existence of a shed at East Grinstead but a single engine was stationed there by the Brighton, and this practice may have continued under the Southern. It was a small single road building with a water tank at the rear but by 1910 it had been demolished leaving only the water tank, water column, and engine pit.

The shed at Sheerness, Isle of Sheppey, was opened with the line in 1860 and was subsequently rebuilt as a two road structure with a 45 ft. turntable supplied outside. It stood to the south of the station and an 'H' or older ex-LCD 0-4-4T was normally supplied by Gillingham. It does not appear on any SER list and it is unlikely to have survived until the grouping, having been reported as closed in 1915 and completely demolished by 1930. Further information on this small depot would be very much welcomed.

In any work of this sort disagreement will result concerning individual, marginal sites. This is inevitable and the authors welcome any constructive comment and are always open to correction.

The departmental shed at Meldon Quarry in 1966, with 'USA' 0-6-0T DS234.

J.H. Meredith

Appendix Two
COALING FACILITIES

Coaling facilities at most of the sheds inherited by the Southern in 1923 took the form of some kind of raised stage from which coal could be pitched into the tender or bunker of the locomotive being fuelled. Variations on a theme, the facilities ranged from huge wagon ramps, with canopies to protect the men and handling equipment, capable of fuelling several engines simultaneously, to a simple brick or sleeper platform three or four feet high.

The LSWR appeared to be the most advanced of the pre-grouping companies in this field, with large modern ramps at its major depots, the coal being transferred from wagons to wheeled tubs inside the shelter before loading onto locomotives. The SW was also the first to plan modern mechanical coaling plants, at Feltham and Nine Elms, although the equipment was not actually installed until after 1923. The company had been a forerunner in providing mechanical aids to coaling, installing hydraulic cranes at several locations as early as 1904.

The other two main constituent companies, the SECR and LBSCR seemed less concerned with fuelling equipment, due in part to their generally smaller depot allocations, and often were content to provide a fairly low platform with a hand-worked crane to assist coaling operations. The 'Brighton' in particular favoured cranes, and even at fairly large depots like Brighton the coaling was by crane directly from wagons onto the locomotives. At the smaller sheds of all three companies coaling was often of the very crudest kind, hand shovelling from an unsheltered platform or even the ground being commonplace.

The Southern completed the mechanical plants planned by the LSW but afterwards chose mainly to install the cheaper coaling ramp type of structure. A roughly standard construction gradually evolved, of an earth ramp surmounted by a steel framed shelter clad in corrugated sheeting. Typical of these were the structures at Ashford and Redhill. Further coaling plants, however, were added at Exmouth Junction and Ramsgate and later another unit was built at Stewarts Lane, but other constructions at less busy depots were of the ramp type. The reasons for not continuing the installation of mechanical coaling plants, apart from cost, were problems caused by breakage of the soft Welsh coal supplied to most Southern sheds and the dust cloud occurring when bunkers were filled. Ramsgate, with nearby residential development, eventually had to be specially supplied with harder Yorkshire coal, and general instructions were issued to keep the bunkers as full as possible at all times, in order to reduce the dust problem.

Various other improvements were carried out by the Southern, usually involving the supply of more modern machinery or new shelters on existing sites, but apart from minor alterations, such as greater capacity equipment at places like Salisbury to cope with the Bulleid Pacifics, coaling facilities remained little changed till closure in the 'sixties.

The mechanical coaling plant at Stewarts Lane.
R.C. Riley

Coaling at its simplest! 'Terrier' at Havant in 1962.

J. Scrace

Typical Southern coal ramp shelter, but an untypical locomotive! Willesden '8F' No. 48544 at Redhill in 1965.

J. Scrace

Ex-works, 'M7' 0-4-4T No. 30026 by the huge LSW coaling ramp at Eastleigh in 1950.

Gresley Society

Nine Elms mechanical coaling plant in 1967.

J. Scrace

Appendix Three

WATER TANKS, COLUMNS AND SOFTENERS

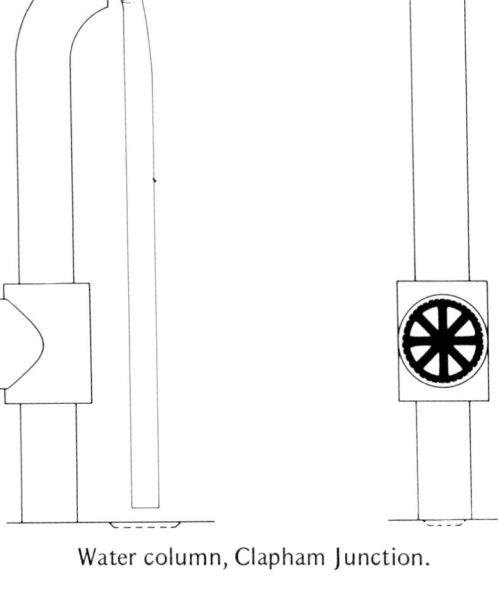

Water column, Clapham Junction.

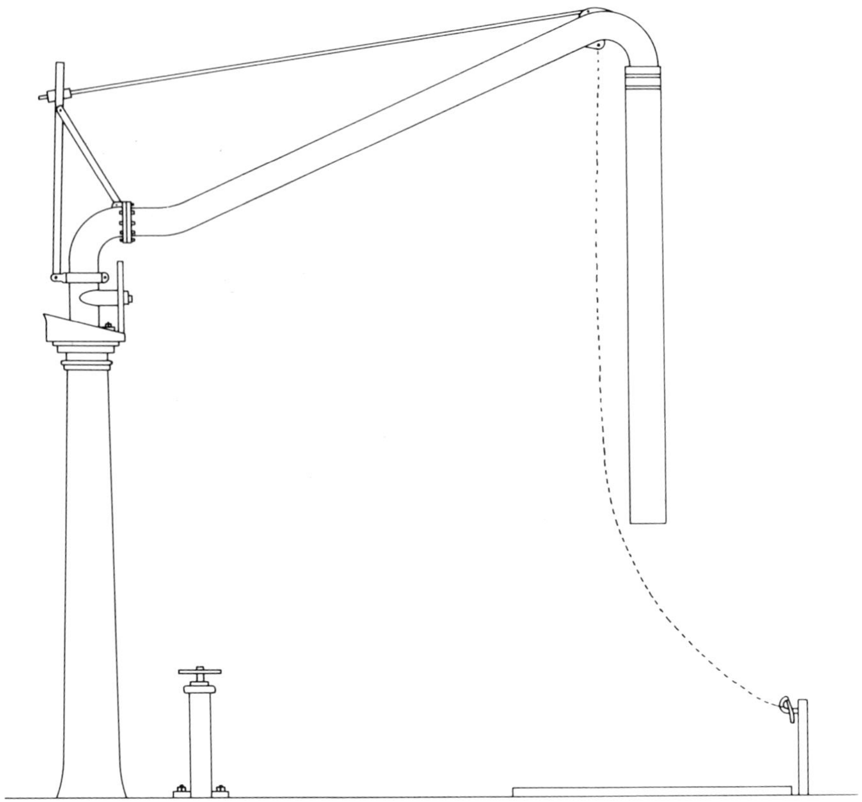

Feet
0   5

Later Southern 'Boom' water column, Stewarts Lane.

At most sheds elevated tanks were installed to provide a good 'head' of water for the column. Water was usually directed via a pump housed beneath the tank itself but occasionally at sheds like Slade Green and Bexhill West, the pump house was situated some distance away. It can certainly be said that there was no apparent standardization in the construction of water tanks within the three constituent companies but it is interesting to note the variety of sites chosen to build them. They were often located on towers within the vicinity of the shed yard, as at Exmouth Junction and Reading. Another popular site was the shed building itself. Midhurst LSW had a tank surmounting the shed entrance and the new SR sheds at Hither Green, Norwood Junction, Ashford and Ramsgate used similar forms of construction, obviating the need for separate towers, so considerably reducing building costs. A greater saving, however, was the use of the local relief, such as St. Leonards where the adjacent cliff was used to provide the required elevation for the tank.

Probably the greatest disadvantage to the Southern was the geology over which much of the system was constructed. The mainly chalky bed rock produced a very hard water which quickly caused scaling in locomotive boilers. The 'Brighton' seemed to be the pioneer of the constituent companies with water softening apparatus, installing such

equipment at many of its depots, at Brighton and Eastbourne in the 1900s and Coulsdon in 1911. The Southern continued this practice, supplying plants to not only the large sheds at Bournemouth, Ramsgate, Nine Elms, Stewarts Lane, etc. but to stations such as London Bridge and Dover. However, the plants were not without their fair share of maintenance chores; tanks had to be regularly wheeled under them to remove the lime sludge, a job not envied by many of the shed's personnel.

Water columns, like tanks, varied greatly from company to company, the Brighton having probably the most convenient, a 'boom' type that made filling easier. The Southern introduced a similar crane that became familiar at most of its depots, stations and yards.

The LSWR had preferred a simpler type of column, substituting a straightforward leather hose for the crane arm, while on the SECR rather more complex, double arm units were favoured. The SW variety was notorious for catching firemen unaware with a backlash of freezing cold water. Very little has been documented on water columns but it would appear that the maintenance of them was usually the responsibility of the area shed. Although steam traction disappeared from the Southern Region in 1967, a handful of water columns were retained for the use of diesels and may still be seen today.

Ancient LCD tank still surviving at Stewarts Lane in 1977.
Author's collection

LBSCR type of column, out of use at Horsted Keynes in 1977. Units installed at sheds were of course several feet taller.
Author's collection

The 1938 water softener at Bournemouth shortly after construction, with sludge tank beneath.
S.C. Townroe

Southern modification of old LSW type, at Clapham Junction in 1977.
Author's collection

Somewhat ornate Southern tank at Ramsgate, 1973.
Author's collection

Slightly later, more austere tank, Hither Green, 1977.
Author's collection

SR water column at Stewarts Lane after closure to steam.
Author's collection

An early Southern water softener surviving at Stewarts Lane in 1972.
Author's collection

Appendix Four

SOUTHERN RAILWAY TURNTABLES

Turntables were not only provided at locomotive depots but were also required at numerous terminal stations, junctions and freight yards. In the early years, 42 ft. and 45 ft. turntables were in general use on the constituent companies of the Southern but by the grouping these had mostly given way to large 50 ft. and 55 ft. tables, 60 ft. and 65 ft. examples also having appeared at the more important points. The majority were of the under-girder type, but over-girder units were occasionally installed, the longest surviving being the 55 ft. examples at Guildford and Eastleigh.

The Southern installed new 65 ft. tables at several locations; articulated and vacuum operated, these became the standard units until the introduction of power-operated 70 ft. tables for the Bulleid Pacifics during the war. Overleaf is a list of the turntables in 1934, providing a good picture of the distribution over the system, which changed surprisingly little between 1923 and 1947. The sizes given refer to the actual rail length. The pit diameter was of course slightly larger and this is the measurement normally quoted.

A STANDARD LSWR OVERGIRDER TURNTABLE

The articulated variety of turntable was in fairly common use over the Southern. This view of Redhill in 1960 shows the 65 ft. example installed there.

J. Scrace

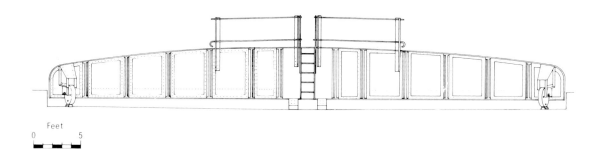

Feet
0   5

The 55 ft. turntable at Eastleigh in BR days. Of the over-girder pattern, the shallow pit required normally made construction cheaper than other types of turntable.

J. Scrace

The turntable at Bude.   *K.A. Stone*

TURNTABLES

Aldershot	49' 8"
Alton	41' 8"
Amesbury	54' 10"
Andover Junction	51' 0"
Ascot	49' 9"
Ashford	64' 10"
Barnstaple Junction	50' 0"
Basingstoke	54' 9"
Battersea Loco	64' 10"
Battersea Park Loco	49' 8"
Bexhill West	54' 9"
Bognor Regis	54' 10"
Bournemouth Central	49' 11"
Brighton	59' 10"
Brockenhurst	49' 11"
Bude	49' 10"
Charing Cross	50' 2"
Chatham	45' 5"
Chichester	44' 11" plus extension gear
Crystal Palace High Level	44' 10"
Dartford	54' 10"
Deal	50' 1"
Dorchester	49' 6"
Dover Marine	64' 10"
Eastbourne	59' 10"
Eastleigh	54' 10"
Ewer Street	54' 10"
Exmouth Junction	64' 10"
Faversham Loco	49' 11"
Feltham	64' 9"
Folkestone Junction	64' 10"
Fratton	50' 0"
Gillingham	50' 1"
Gravesend West Street	50' 0"
Guildford	54' 9"
Halwill Junction	49' 10"
Hastings	54' 8"
Hither Green Sidings	64' 9½"
Holborn Low Level	30' 0"
Ilfracombe	64' 10"
Launceston	49' 11"
Lewes	44' 9"
Littlehampton	41' 9"

London Bridge	46' 5"
Maidstone East	54' 8"
Maidstone West	44' 9"
Margate West	59' 9"
New Cross Gate	49' 9"
Newhaven	59' 10"
Nine Elms	64' 10"
Okehampton	50' 2"
Padstow	49' 9"
Pilton Yard	30' 0"
Plymouth Friary	51' 1"
Portsmouth Burnaby Road	54' 10"
Portsmouth Harbour	56' 0"
Portsmouth Southsea	50' 0"
Port Victoria	44' 10"
Pulborough	41' 9"
Ramsgate	64' 9"
Reading	64' 10"
Redhill	64' 10"
St. Leonards (West Marina)	49' 11"
Salisbury	64' 10"
Sevenoaks Bat & Ball	45' 2"
Sevenoaks Tubs Hill	44' 9"
Shepperton	49' 9"
Southampton Terminus	49' 8"
Strood	44' 9"
Swanage	50' 0"
Swanley	44' 8"
Tattenham Corner	54' 10"
Templecombe Lower (S&D)	42' 0"
Three Bridges	59' 9"
Tonbridge	54' 9"
Tunbridge Wells West	46' 1"
Victoria Central	60' 0"
Victoria Eastern	54' 10"
Wadebridge & Quay	49' 9"
Waterloo	49' 11" and 54' 9"
Windsor	49' 9"
Woking	50' 11"
Yeovil Junction	50' 1"

NOTE: Bricklayers Arms under reconstruction at this time 65' 0"

Final development. The new turntable at Okehampton ordered along with Basingstoke in 1943 was one of the first of the 70 ft. variety. It is shown here with Mogul No. 31628 in 1949.

J. Meredith

The Cocking derailment of 1904, with two breakdown cranes in attendance. The fifteen ton cranes, new in 1898, were both built by Cowans, Sheldon of Carlisle. 316S, on the left, was at this time stationed at New Cross, having been originally allocated to Battersea Park, while the crane on the right, 315S, had been stationed at Brighton since delivery. The pair eventually found themselves at Stewarts Lane and Ramsgate respectively. Both were withdrawn in 1963.

Collection of R.C. Riley

Appendix Five

BREAKDOWN CRANES

Many of the strategically important depots on the Southern included a breakdown crane among their equipment. The uses and importance of such cranes are obvious and generally they were stabled, often ready for use, on a specific road inside the shed. At a number of locations, however, the crane and its train of coach and wagons were parked in a siding mainly in the open.

Earlier cranes acquired from the constituent companies were built by a variety of manufacturers, but beginning in 1927 the Southern obtained a succession of heavy duty cranes from Ransoms and Rapier of Ipswich who also constructed many of the company's turntables. At thirty-six and later forty-five tons capacity, they were considerably larger than most pre-grouping units, which rarely exceeded twenty tons. At the end of the Southern's existence in 1947, some fourteen engine sheds housed a steam breakdown crane, and these are listed opposite.

Shed	Capacity	Number
Ashford	36 tons	80S
Bournemouth	20 tons	30S
Bricklayers Arms	36 tons	1197S
Brighton	36 tons	1196S
Eastleigh	36 tons	35S
Exmouth Junction	45 tons	1580S
Feltham	20 tons	34S
Fratton	36 tons	81S
Gillingham	15 tons	202S
Guildford	45 tons	1561S
Nine Elms	45 tons	1560S
Ramsgate	15 tons	315S
Salisbury	36 tons	37S
Stewarts Lane	15 tons	316S

Appendix Six

THE STAFF

The staff employed in the locomotive running department of the Southern Railway in November 1926 totalled 10,655, declining to around 8,000 some ten years later. This total included a large number of people stationed not at running depots but at places like Waterloo, divisional offices, stations, etc.

An average shed would include on its staff a loco shed foreman or superintendent, two or three clerks including a stores issuer, a dozen or so assorted boiler washers, coalmen, chargemen, labourers, a similar number of cleaners, a boilersmith and his mate, three or four fitters and their apprentices, and of course the largest single group, the engine crews. At our average shed these would probably total between thirty and forty pairs of men.

There were many other grades too numerous to list, employed in the running department at this time, but they ranged from 'sandmen' and 'glandpackers' to 'tubers' and 'toolmen' through to the more prosaic carpenters and painters. We have reproduced a condensed list of the staff in 1926 showing the numbers employed at each depot, excluding of course the various offices, etc. The figures in brackets refer to the number of pairs of drivers/firemen employed at each shed.

Andover Junction	29	(10)	Launceston	7	(3)
Ascot	7	(3)	Littlehampton	32	(11)
Ash	24	(10)	Lyme Regis	5	(2)
Ashford	236	(73)	Lymington	5	(2)
Barnstaple Junction	45	(13)	Maidstone East	60	(22)
Pilton Yard	11	(4)	Maidstone West	99	(31)
Basingstoke	86	(28)	Margate	91	(20)
Battersea (Stewarts Lane)	545	(150)	Midhurst (LSW)	5	(2)
Battersea Park	337	(103)	New Cross Gate	591	(171)
Bexhill West	5	(2)	Newhaven	72	(24)
Bognor	65	(18)	Newport	66	(22)
Bordon	5	(2)	Nine Elms	820	(234)
Bournemouth	235	(72)	Okehampton	17	(7)
Bricklayers Arms	824	(264)	Plymouth Friary	96	(31)
Brighton	648	(185)	Purley	79	(26)
Bude	10	(4)	Ramsgate Town	132	(41)
Callington	8	(3)	Reading	108	(36)
Canterbury West	19	(7)	Redhill	169	(55)
Chertsey	12	(5)	Ryde	39	(14)
Coulsdon	120	(39)	St. Leonards	62	(20)
Deal	50	(13)	Salisbury	310	(94)
Dorchester	86	(26)	Seaton	5	(2)
Dover Priory	219	(67)	Sevenoaks Bat and Ball	13	(6)
Eastbourne	169	(54)	Sidmouth	5	(2)
Eastleigh	565	(184)	Southampton	28	(9)
Epsom Town	29	(10)	Strood	2	(--)
Ewer Street	9	(--)	Swanage	7	(3)
Exmouth	19	(8)	Templecombe Upper	8	(4)
Exmouth Junction	430	(119)	Three Bridges	92	(33)
Faversham	140	(40)	Tonbridge	280	(95)
Feltham	350	(117)	Torrington	22	(8)
Folkestone	52	(20)	Tunbridge Wells West	97	(30)
Fratton	293	(101)	Wadebridge	38	(12)
Gillingham	300	(94)	West Croydon	117	(38)
Gosport	15	(6)	Westerham	4	(2)
Guildford	465	(164)	Weymouth	18	(6)
Hamworthy Junction	16	(6)	Windsor	43	(15)
Hastings	111	(33)	Woking	3	(1)
Horsham	121	(36)	Yeovil Town	105	(36)
Ilfracombe	10	(4)			

Smokebox cleaning at Lyme Regis in the '50s.

K.A. Stone

Appendix Seven

DUTY ROSTER FOR EXMOUTH JUNCTION M.P.D.

The following is the duty roster for Exmouth Junction shed for a summer weekday in 1961. It was issued daily to enable the shed staff to ensure engines were ready for their particular duties. MO and MX of course indicate 'Mondays Only' and 'Mondays Excepted' respectively, while the section at the end refers to spare engines in steam, locos booked for boiler inspection and washout, etc. The by-now familiar 24 hour clock has been used, but in 1961, of course, 'a.m.' and 'p.m.' would have been normal. Although the year is 1961, the system used at that time was similar in all respects to that previously used on the Southern Railway.

EXMOUTH JUNCTION M.P.D.

(Duty Roster)

Summer 1961   Wednesday 14th June, 1961

No.	Duty		Engine
590MO	00.20 Wadebridge	23.00	
MX	00.01 Wadebridge	22.40	1875
610MO	00.30 Exeter Shtg.	23.29	
MX	00.09 Exeter Shtg.	23.00	82017
547	01.20 Yeovil	00.01	34035
577MO	01.45 Yeoford	00.45	
505	02.00 Salisbury	00.34	796
557	02.06 Ilfracombe	00.57	34081
581MO	03.15 Friary	01.55	34024
MX	03.25 Friary	02.10	
589	03.30 Bude	02.15	1834
612	03.38 Exeter	02.53	82022
608	03.38 Carr. Shtg.	02.53 Sun.	24
619MO	01.21 Junc. Yard	23.16	
MX	03.40 Junc. Yard	02.55	957
545MO	01.40 St. Davids	00.40	
MX	04.04 Salisbury	02.44	846
578	04.30 Yeoford	03.30	1839
607	04.50 Seaton	03.45	82024
556	05.06 Ilfracombe	03.35	34023
573	05.12 Friary N.C. Thurs	03.35	34072
596	05.12 Okehampton	03.35	1856
614	05.10 Exeter and	04.25	41306
	06.00 Sidmouth	05.00	—
551MO	04.25 Exeter	02.23	
MX	05.21 Ilfracombe	03.25	34110
572	05.35 Friary	04.15	34075
622	05.40 Dept. Shtg.	04.40	952
559	06.00 Barnstaple	04.40	1849
615	06.05 Exmouth	05.05	82013
623	06.10 St. Davids and loco shunting	05.25	951
613	06.10 Exeter	05.25	41299
562	06.25 Barnstaple	05.25	691
523	06.30 Waterloo	04.55	35003
524	06.40 Waterloo	05.10	34097
574	06.50 Axminster	05.35	34096
667	06.55 Yeoford	05.55	34079
611	06.45 Exmouth	05.35	25
525	07.30 Waterloo	06.09	35026
592	07.32 Meldon	06.15	1842
568	07.35 Friary	06.21	34058
621	08.00 Banker	07.15	955
586	08.10 Pinhoe	06.55	1838
566	08.42 Friary	06.21	34066
575	09.00 Whimple	07.40	827
620	09.22 Banker	08.33	956
526	10.30 Waterloo	09.10	35025
617	10.45 Exmouth	09.50	82019
552	11.27 Ilfracombe	10.02	34086
574	11.47 Friary	10.19	34096
527	12.30 Waterloo	11.10	34036
616	12.35 B. Clyst	11.20	41307
570	13.16 Friary	11.41	34062
563	13.20 Riverside	12.15	667
615	13.25 Topsham	12.25	82013
557	13.28 Ilfracombe	23.41	34081
544	13.25 Salisbury	12.05	845
583	13.40 Okehampton & Wadebridge	12.40	34080
611	13.50 Honiton	12.55	25
582	14.11 Ilfracombe	12.40	34033
581	14.21 Padstow	12.40	34064
491	14.30 Waterloo	12.58	35006
561	14.40 Yeovil	13.25	35009
500	15.20 Salisbury	14.03	832
616	15.00 Sidmouth Jct.	14.15	41307
503	15.29 Sidmouth Jct.	14.03	34048
592	15.48 Okehampton	14.25	1832
595	16.30 Wadebridge	15.08	—
546	16.35 Yeovil	14.55	845
568	16.48 Friary	15.25	34058
547	17.51 Ilfracombe	15.25	34035
586	17.52 Okehampton	16.25	1857
528	17.54 Waterloo	16.22	35010

607	18.15 Chard	16.05	82024
21	18.37 Friary	17.06	—
6	18.48 Waterloo	17.23	—
552	18.52 Ilfracombe	17.06	34086
575/602	19.00 Yeoford	17.40	34079
566	19.38 Salisbury	17.56	35013
461	19.50 Salisbury	18.34	34003
573	20.07 Friary	19.45	—
563	20.12 Riverside	19.25	667
613	20.45 Exmouth	19.40	41299
594/506	20.50 Salisbury	19.30	34011
508	21.15 Sidmouth Jct.	20.15	827
576	21.20 Friary	20.00	1833
501	21.45 Salisbury	20.25	825
570	22.23 Friary	21.00	—
419	22.40 Waterloo	21.04	—
506	23.30 Salisbury	22.12	828

Steam 35013, 1831, 34080, 831, 827, 1853, 676, 1841, 1831

Boiler Inspection 34034, 34065, 841, 669

Washout 1901, 34034, 34065, 841, 669, 717, 41308

06.00 Steam test 34079

Servicing

Specials			
	05.45 Seaton	06.45	—
	07.05 Axminster	06.00	—
	08.55 Ascot	07.25	34109
	09.50 Seaton Jct. Brookwood	08.50	73114
	07.34 Sidmouth	06.30	41307
	09.40 Ilfracombe	08.25	34011

Each individual duty could vary greatly in complexity and a contrasting sample pair are given for Exmouth Junction in the summer of 1961.

EXMOUTH JC. DUTY No. 525

8 P. (M.N. Class)

—	Exmouth Jc.	...	...	...	...	...	07.09*
07.13	Exeter Ctl.	...	...	...	...	...	07.30P
11.08	Waterloo	...	...	...	...	...	11.26*
11.40	Nine Elms Loco	...	...	...	...	...	17.26*
17.49	Waterloo	...	...	...	...	...	18.00P
21.59	Exeter Ctl.	...	...	...	...	...	22.04*
22.08	Exmouth Jc.	...	...	...	...	...	—

EXMOUTH JC. DUTY No. 611

F.X.-2 P.T. (M.7. Class)
F.O.-2 P.T. (L.M.R. Class)

—	Exmouth Jc. Loco	...	...	...	...	...	06.20*
06.24	Exeter Ctl.	...	...	...	...	...	06.45P
07.10	Exmouth	...	...	...	...	...	07.16P
	(06.55 Budleigh S.)						
07.43	Exeter Ctl.	...	...	...	...	...	08.00P
08.35	Honiton	...	...	...	...	...	—
	F-Shunting 08.50 to 09.10						
	F-Shunting 09.45 to 11.15						
—	Honiton	...	...	...	...	...	11.15*
11.23	Sidmouth Jc.	...	...	...	...	...	11.25*
11.33	Ottery St. M.	...	...	...	...	...	11.48F
12.00	Sidmouth Jc.	...	...	...	...	...	12.02*
11.38	Exmouth Jc.	...	...	...	...	...	13.50*
14.21	Honiton	...	...	...	...	...	—
	F-Shunting 14.40 to 15.00						
—	Honiton	...	...	...	...	...	16.00P
16.32	Exeter Ctl.	...	...	...	...	...	17.35P
18.09	Honiton	...	...	...	...	...	18.38P
1912	Exeter Ctl.	...	...	...	...	...	—
	F-Shunting 19.30 to 21.00						
	Banking 21.00 to 02.45						
—	Exeter Ctl.	...	...	...	...	...	02.45*
02.48	Exmouth Jc.	...	...	...	...	...	—

P   Passenger
F   Freight
*   Light engine

Each depot on the Southern was allotted a sequence of numbers for its duties, but inevitably these duty numbers changed, with adjustment of timetables, etc. In many cases the number carried also indicated the locomotive's home shed, and the use of these numbers may be one reason why the Southern never found it necessary to use a shed coding system. Listed below are the duty numbers allotted to Southern engine sheds in November 1947. The numbers, 505, 621, etc. were carried on the smokebox, on the headcode discs.

EASTERN DIVISION WORKINGS

Stewarts Lane	1	(Commencing duty number)
Bricklayers Arms	81	
Hither Green	175	
Gillingham	220	
Faversham	260	
Tonbridge	290	
Ashford	340	
St. Leonards	400	
Folkestone Junct.	420	
Dover	425	
Ramsgate	465	

LONDON CENTRAL DIVISION WORKINGS

Stewarts Lane	501
Bricklayers Arms	530
Norwood Jct.	580
Redhill	620
Tunbridge Wells West	655
Three Bridges	675
Horsham	700
Brighton	735
Newhaven	780
Eastbourne	795
Fratton	810

LONDON SW DIVISION WORKINGS

Nine Elms	2
Feltham	101
Reading	181
Guildford	201
Basingstoke	251
Andover Jct.	271
Eastleigh	274
Lymington	358
Fratton	360
Gosport	377
Bournemouth	381
Swanage	420
Hamworthy	421
Dorchester	423
Weymouth	429
Salisbury	439

WESTERN DIVISION WORKINGS

Salisbury	471
Yeovil Town	487
Lyme Regis	502
Seaton	503
Exmouth Jct.	506
Exmouth	568
Barnstaple	572
Torrington	582
Ilfracombe	589
Okehampton	593
Launceston	598
Bude	600
Wadebridge	602
Callington	611
Plymouth Friary	614

Salisbury shed with a variety of locomotives in 1959.   *Photomatic*

Tunbridge Wells west shed.   *Ken Fairey*   149

CODINGS

Various shed coding systems were used by the Southern's various predecessors. The LBSCR favoured a two or three letter abbreviation code, in common with many other British Railways, while the SECR preferred the use of numbers to denote individual sheds. The code numbers used by the SECR were in the form of cast iron plates, bolted inside the engine cabs, while the LBSC abbreviations were painted on the front of the locomotive main framing. The LSWR does not seem to have been too concerned with any formal coding system and in the first years after the grouping, ex-SW depots were not given codes, although ex-LBSC and ex-SECR depots retained the old systems for a short while.

The Southern in its turn did not seriously consider using a code system, although various abbreviations were used for reporting purposes, etc.

LBSCR shed codes, 1910	SECR shed codes, 1916
B – *Battersea*	1 – *Battersea*
Bog – *Bognor*	2 – *Bricklayers Arms*
Bton – *Brighton*	3 – *Cannon Street*
Couls – *Coulsdon*	4 – *Slade Green*
Dor – *Dorking*	5 – *Tonbridge*
E – *Eastbourne*	6 – *Ashford*
Eps – *Epsom*	7 – *Orpington*
F – *Fratton*	8 – *Purley*
Hors – *Horsham*	9 – *Redhill*
Lton – *Littlehampton*	10 – *Gillingham ('New Brompton') and Strood*
Mid – *Midhurst*	11 – *Dover*
N+ – *New Cross*	12 – *Hastings*
N – *Newhaven*	13 – *Ramsgate Town*
St. L – *St. Leonards*	14 – *Margate West*
3B – *Three Bridges*	15 – *Maidstone East*
TW – *Tunbridge Wells*	16 – *Maidstone West*
WC – *West Croydon*	17 – *Faversham*
	18 – *Reading*
	19 – *Folkestone Junction*

British Railways, of course, adopted the familiar LMS system in 1950, of numbers with successive letters. These altered considerably over the years, with transfers to and from other regions and reorganization within the Southern Region itself. Some small sheds, like Launceston and Gosport, while remaining open for servicing were never officially coded, or were uncoded for many years. The re-classifications from 1950 to the end of steam are given below:

Andover	sub 71A
Ashford	74A, re-coded 73F Oct. 1958
*Barnstaple Junction	72E, re-coded 83F Dec. 1962
Basingstoke	70D
Bognor Regis	sub to 75D
Bournemouth	71B, re-coded 70F Sep. 1963
Bricklayers Arms	73B
Brighton	75A

*Bude	sub to 72A, re-coded 83D Dec. 1962
*Callington	sub to 72D, re-coded 83H Feb. 1958, transferred sub to 72A from 1960 re-coded 83D Dec. 1962
Dorchester	71C, sub to 71B Mar. 1955
Dover	74C, re-coded 73H Oct. 1958
Eastbourne	75G, re-coded sub to 75A Feb. 1958
Eastleigh	71A, re-coded 70D Sep. 1963
*Exmouth	sub to 72A, re-coded 83D Dec. 1962
*Exmouth Junction	72A, re-coded 83D Dec. 1962
Faversham	73E
Feltham	70B
Folkestone Junction	sub to 74C, re-coded sub to 73H Oct. 1958
Fratton	71D, re-coded 70F by 1956
Gillingham	73D, re-coded sub to 73J June 1959
Guildford	70C
Hither Green	73C
Horsham	75D, re-coded sub to 75E 1960/61
*Ilfracombe	sub to 72E, re-coded sub to 83F Dec. 1962
*Lyme Regis	sub to 72A, re-coded sub to 83D Dec. 1962
Lymington	sub to 71A, re-coded sub to 70D Sep. 1963
Newhaven	sub to 75A
Newport	71E, re-coded 70G by 1955
Nine Elms	70A
Norwood Junction	75C
*Okehampton	sub to 72A, re-coded 83D Dec. 1962
Plymouth Friary	72D, re-coded 83H Feb. 1958
Ramsgate	74B, re-coded 73G Oct. 1958 re-coded sub to 73F June 1959
Reading	70E, re-coded sub to 70C Dec. 1962
Ryde	71F, re-coded 70H by 1955
St. Leonards	74E
Salisbury	72B, re-coded 70E Dec. 1962
*Seaton	sub to 72A, re-coded sub to 83D Dec. 1962
Southampton Docks	71I, re-coded 70I Sep. 1963
Southampton New Docks	sub to 71I, re-coded sub to 70I Sep. 1963
Southampton Terminus	sub to 71A, re-coded sub to 70D Sept. 1963
Stewarts Lane	73A, re-coded 75D June 1962
Swanage	sub to 71B, re-coded sub to 70F Sep. 1963
Three Bridges	75E
Tonbridge	74D, re-coded 73J Oct. 1958, re-coded sub to 75D 1962
Tunbridge Wells West	75F
*Torrington	sub to 72E, re-coded sub to 83F Dec. 1962
*Wadebridge	72F, re-coded 84E Dec. 1962
Winchester	sub 71A, re-coded sub to 70D Sep. 1963
*Yeovil	72C, re-coded 83E Dec. 1962

*These depots were not officially designated their WR codes until September 1963, but transfers were effective on the dates given.

ALLOCATIONS

The following lists show the locomotives allocated to the various sheds of the Southern in January 1947. Locomotives outstationed at sub-depots were listed together with the main depot.

ASHFORD

0-6-0T	1010, 1069, 1147, 1174
0-4-4T	1158, 1239, 1261, 1269, 1274, 1305, 1306, 1307, 1322, 2357, 2363, 2364, 2365, 2380, 2388
0-6-4T	1595, 1596, 1597, 1598, 1599
0-6-0	1123, 1191, 1218, 1262, 1268, 1373, 1385, 1426, 1589, 1711, 1721
4-4-0	1477, 1549, 1577, 1726, 1748, 1770, 1771, 1772, 1773, 1774, 1775, 1776, 1777
2-6-0	1400, 1401, 1402, 1403, 1404, 1405, 1821, 1824
4-6-0	803, 804, 805, 806

Total 60

BARNSTAPLE JUNCTION

0-4-4T	23, 36, 42, 44, 247, 250, 321, 670
0-6-2T	2094, 2095, 2096, 2608, 2610, 2696

Total 14

BASINGSTOKE

0-6-0T	278, 348
0-4-4T	244, 248
0-6-0	368, 693
4-4-0	307, 407, 418, 426, 706, 708
2-6-0	1614, 1615, 1621, 1622, 1623, 1624, 1625, 1627, 1629, 1632, 1633, 1634

Total 24

BRICKLAYERS ARMS

0-6-0ST	1685
0-6-0T	2097, 2128, 2141, 2151
0-4-4T	1162, 1324, 1326, 1328, 1500, 1533, 1541, 1542, 1546, 1550
0-6-2T	2165, 2166, 2168, 2170, 2453, 2454, 2458, 2459, 2460, 2461, 2462, 2463, 2468, 2474, 2565
4-4-2T	2075, 2076, 2077, 2085
0-6-0	1033, 1071, 1093, 1102, 1223, 1277, 1280, 1287, 1294, 1297, 1388, 1389, 1395, 1397, 1398, 1425, 1428, 1429, 1460, 1584, 1687, 1693, 1723, 1724, 1725, 2442, 2446, 2448, 2524, 2525

4-4-0	920, 921, 922, 923, 931, 932, 933, 934, 935, 936, 937, 938, 939, 1036, 1159, 1166, 1175, 1176, 1275, 1315, 1491, 1547, 1758, 1759, 1782, 1783, 1784, 1785, 1786, 1787, 1788, 1789
2-8-0	77086, 77090, 77094, 77101, 77180, 77205, 77226, 77256, 77259, 77311, 77321, 77355, 77481, 77485, 78569

Total 111

BRIGHTON

0-6-0T	1178, 1557, 2122, 2127, 2153, 2606
0-4-2T	2235
0-4-4T	2368, 2372, 2376, 2385, 2386, 2397
0-6-2T	2470, 2471, 2480, 2486, 2491, 2496, 2505, 2513, 2566, 1567, 2576, 2583, 2587, 2592
4-4-2T	2079, 2080, 2084, 2086, 2088
4-4-2	2037, 2038, 2039
0-6-0	2437, 2438, 2443, 2523, 2528, 2539, 2543, 2546
4-4-0	423, 428, 430, 928, 929, 930, 2043, 2052, 2071, 2072, 2073
2-6-0	1406, 1817, 1843, 1851, 1854, 1858, 2337, 2338, 2339, 2340, 2341, 2342, 2343, 2344, 2345, 2346, 2347

Total 71

BOURNEMOUTH

0-4-0T	92, 99, 100
0-6-0T	239, 265
0-4-4T	21, 28, 40, 47, 50, 51, 52, 57, 59, 104, 106, 107, 111, 112, 131, 251, 318, 363, 379
0-6-0	548, 549, 696, 700
4-4-0	113, 136, 161, 168, 169, 173, 286, 337, 345, 398, 399, 415, 429, 719, 728
4-6-0	478, 736, 743, 772, 787, 789, 790, 850, 851, 852, 853, 854, 855, 862, 863, 864, 865

Total 60

DORCHESTER

0-6-0T	162
0-4-4T	177, 221, 223, 229, 233
0-6-0	695
4-4-0	146, 281, 284, 387, 410

Total 12

DOVER

0-6-0T	1027, 1325, 1555, 1556, 2108, 2109
0-4-2T	2359
0-4-4T	1161, 1276, 1512, 1517, 1520, 1530, 1531, 1532, 1548, 1673, 1705, 1708
0-6-0	1065, 1108, 1252, 1255, 1291
4-4-0	924, 925, 926, 927, 1441, 1443, 1450, 1545, 1727, 1735, 1753, 1754, 1755, 1756, 1757
2-6-0	1631, 1639, 1808, 1819, 1820
4-6-0	767, 768, 769, 770, 771

Total 49

EASTBOURNE

0-4-2T	2234, 2259, 2274, 2299, 2358, 2361, 2605, 2699
0-4-4T	2377, 2391, 2395
0-6-2T	2402, 2404, 2406, 2485, 2574, 2588
4-4-2T	2005, 2008, 2009, 2010, 2595, 2596
0-6-0	2538
4-4-0	2042, 2044, 2054, 2062, 2063, 2068, 2284
2-6-0	2348, 2349

Total 33

EASTLEIGH

0-4-0T	82, 83, 87, 88, 3741, 3744
0-4-4T	1, 2, 5, 6, 8, 29, 48, 53, 109, 120, 125, 198, 200, 213, 225, 231, 242, 357, 366, 367, 479, 674
0-6-0T	240, 261, 264, 267, 272, 274, 275, 277, 351, 2133, 2147, 2160, 2609
0-8-0T	952
0-4-2	597, 598, 609, 624, 625, 627, 629, 636, 642, 648
0-6-0	306, 316, 350, 530, 532, 535, 536, 3101, 3397, 3509, C11, C12, C13, C14, C15, C16, C17, C18
4-4-0	148, 150, 151, 154, 155, 157, 159, 170, 171, 175, 302, 313, 336, 341, 342, 393, 394, 395, 397, 420, 463, 464, 465, 466, 467, 468, 469, 470, 471, 472, 707
2-6-0	1827, 1829, 1865, 1866, 1867, 1870, 1874
4-6-0	473, 474, 521, 522, 523, 524, 737, 739, 740, 741, 742, 749, 750, 751, 752, 754, 784, 785

Total 126

EXMOUTH JUNCTION

0-4-4T	24, 30, 34, 37, 39, 46, 49, 55, 105, 124, 133, 192, 193, 199, 207, 224, 230, 232, 245, 252, 253, 255, 256, 320, 323, 356, 374, 375, 376, 377, 668, 669, 671
0-6-2T	2124, 2135, 2695, 2697
4-4-2T	3125, 3488, 3520
0-8-0T	954
0-6-0	C29
4-4-0	135, 137, 138, 156, 282, 283, 301, 329, 408, 409, 411, 436, 439, 722, 723, 724, 725, 730
2-6-0	1407, 1408, 1409, 1828, 1831, 1832, 1833, 1834, 1835, 1836, 1837, 1838, 1839, 1840, 1841, 1842, 1845, 1847, 1853, 1855, 1856, 1869, 1871, 1875
4-6-0	823, 824, 825, 826, 827, 844, 845, 846, 847
4-6-2	21C1, 21C2, 21C3, 21C4, 21C5, 21C101, 21C102, 21C103, 21C104, 21C105, 21C106, 21C107, 21C108, 21C109, 21C110, 21C111, 21C112, 21C113, 21C114, 21C115, 21C116, 21C117, 21C118, 21C119, 21C120, 21C141, 21C142, 21C143, 21C144, 21C145, 21C146, 21C147

Total 125

FAVERSHAM

0-4-4T	1279, 1309, 1310, 1667, 1674, 1699, 1709
0-6-0	1046, 1106, 1229, 1242, 1260, 1369, 1379, 1438, 1481, 1495, 1499, 1691, 1692
4-4-0	1231, 1246, 1440, 1448, 1470, 1487, 1489, 1493, 1496, 1501, 1502, 1505, 1509, 1739, 1741

Total 35

FELTHAM

0-4-4T	9, 25, 31, 32, 254, 352
4-6-2T	516, 517, 518, 519, 520
4-8-0T	492, 493, 494, 495
0-6-0	346, 687, 688, 689, 697, 698, 3154, 3163, 3167, 3400, 3433, 3496, C19, C20, C21, C22, C23, C24, C25, C26, C27, C28, C29, C30, C31, C32, C33, C34, C35, C36, C37, C38, C39, C40
4-4-0	139, 140, 144, 153, 158, 167, 174, 347, 383, 385
4-6-0	496, 497, 498, 499, 500, 501, 502, 503, 504, 505, 506, 507, 508, 509, 510, 511, 512, 513, 514, 515, 833, 834, 835, 836, 837, 838, 839, 840, 841, 842, 843
2-8-0	77052, 77056, 77059, 77062, 77359

Total 95

FOLKESTONE JUNCTION

0-6-0T	1047, 1107, 1127, 1128, 1154, 1323, 1337, 1340, 1558
0-6-0	1381

Total 10

FRATTON

0-6-0T	2139, 2644, 2655, 2659, 2661, 2662, 2690, 2691, 2694
0-4-2T	2269
0-4-4T	20, 27, 45, 54, 480, 2244
0-6-2T	2490, 2509, 2559, 2562
0-6-0	2537, 2548, 2554
4-4-0	114, 115, 118, 164, 166, 172, 287, 300, 304, 338, 384, 400, 401, 417, 424, 425, 441, 716
2-6-0	1796, 1797

Total 43

GILLINGHAM

0-4-4T	1278, 1308, 1658, 1659, 1660, 1662, 1663, 1665, 1666, 1697
0-6-0	1003, 1007, 1014, 1039, 1044, 1051, 1064, 1066, 1112, 1234, 1238, 1256, 1267, 1317, 1384, 1391, 1430, 1439, 1510, 1573, 1579, 1583, 1585, 1682, 1684, 1688, 1713
4-4-0	1002, 1013, 1092, 1105, 1215, 1449, 1574, 1746, 1750

Total 46

GUILDFORD

0-6-0T	262, 268, 269, 270, 349, 756
0-6-2T	2487, 2500, 2504
0-4-4T	22, 26, 43, 56, 60, 108, 110, 128, 246, 324, 328, 378, 481, 676
0-6-0	308, 309, 325, 326, 327, 545, 546, 3083, 3155, 3436, 3439, 3442, 3506, C1, C2, C3, C4, C5, C6, C7, C8, C9, C10
0-4-2	614, 618, 630, 634, 638, 643
4-4-0	121, 141, 165, 311, 343, 381, 416, 419, 422, 433, 434, 438, 704, 705, 726
2-6-0	1798, 1799, 1800, 1801, 1802, 1803, 1804, 1805, 1806, 1809, 1868

Total 78

HITHER GREEN

0-4-2T	2239
2-6-4T	1911, 1913, 1921, 1922, 1923, 1924, 1925

0-8-0T	950, 951, 953, 955, 956
0-6-0	1018, 1054, 1059, 1061, 1068, 1090, 1109, 1113, 1243, 1244, 1245, 1248, 1253, 1257, 1258, 1270, 1271, 1298, 1374, 1377, 1378, 1386, 1390, 1480, 1572, 1581, 1689, 1695
4-4-0	1021, 1028, 1031, 1205, 1455, 1457
2-6-0	1878, 1879, 1880
2-8-0	78688, 79203, 79210, 79262, 79281

Total 55

HORSHAM

0-4-2T	2252, 2283
0-4-4T	2373, 2384, 2387
0-6-2T	2399, 2401, 2464, 2501, 2511, 2514, 2515, 2556, 2557, 2570, 2571, 2573, 2584, 2594
0-6-0	540, 542, 543, 544, 2300, 2301, 2306, 2307, 2308, 2449, 2521, 2550
4-4-0	2045, 2050, 2055, 2067

Total 35

ISLE OF WIGHT

0-6-0T	W1, W2, W3, W4, W8, W11, W13
0-4-4T	W14, W15, W16, W17, W18, W19, W20, W21, W22, W23, W24, W25, W26, W27, W28, W29, W30, W31, W32, W33
0-6-2T	2510

Total 28

NEW CROSS GATE

0-6-0T	2142, 2164
0-4-2T	2253
0-6-2T	2407, 2408, 2409, 2410, 2411, 2412, 2413, 2414, 2415, 2416, 2417, 2418, 2564, 2568, 2575, 2578, 2586
4-4-2T	2087, 2089, 2601
0-6-0	2536, 2549, 2551
4-4-0	2051, 2056, 2060, 2070, 2074
4-4-2	2424, 2425
2-6-0	1823, 1825, 1826

Total 36

NEWHAVEN

0-6-0T	2636, 2647
0-6-2T	2475, 2482, 2492, 2494, 2499, 2508
0-6-0	2434, 2533, 2534
4-4-2	2421, 2422, 2423, 2426

Total 15

NINE ELMS

0-6-0T	160, 257, 259, 263, 266, 271, 273, 353, 354
0-4-2T	2286, 2289
0-4-4T	33, 38, 123, 130, 132, 179, 204, 212, 241, 249, 319, 322, 667, 672, 673, 1544, 1551, 1552, 1553, 1696, 1698
0-8-0T	949
0-6-0	339, 692, 694, 699, 701
4-4-0	119, 142, 149, 380, 386, 390, 391, 392, 406, 427, 431, 435, 437, 440, 442, 713, 718
2-6-0	1613, 1616, 1617, 1619
4-6-0	443, 444, 445, 446, 447, 459, 460, 461, 462, 477, 482, 483, 484, 485, 486, 487, 488, 489, 490, 491, 738, 753, 755, 766, 773, 774, 777, 779, 786, 788, 791, 792, 856, 857, 858, 859, 860, 861, 2327, 2328, 2329, 2330, 2331, 2332, 2333
4-6-2	21C11, 21C12, 21C13, 21C14, 21C15, 21C16, 21C17, 21C18, 21C19, 21C20

Total 114

NORWOOD JUNCTION

0-4-2T	2299
0-6-2T	2167, 2169, 2455, 2456, 2457, 2466, 2467, 2469, 2472, 2473, 2476, 2477, 2478, 2479, 2481, 2489, 2493, 2495, 2498, 2502, 2506, 2561, 2563, 2579
2-6-4T	1916, 1917, 1918, 1919, 1920
0-6-0	2302, 2309, 2440, 2444, 2447, 2526, 2535, 2540, 2544, 2547
2-6-0	1844, 2350, 2351
Diesels	1, 2, 3

Total 46

PLYMOUTH FRIARY

0-4-0T	84, 91, 94, 103
0-4-4T	3, 7, 35, 182, 183, 197, 201, 216, 236
0-6-2T	757, 758
4-4-0	116, 280, 289, 711

Total 19

RAMSGATE

0-4-4T	1016, 1164, 1182, 1265, 1521, 1522, 1523
0-6-0	1004, 1080, 1316, 1592
4-4-0	911, 912, 913, 914, 915, 916, 917, 918, 919, 1151, 1451, 1452, 1453, 1778, 1779, 1780, 1781
4-6-2	21C121, 21C122, 21C123, 21C124, 21C125, 21C126, 21C127, 21C128, 21C129, 21C130, 21C131, 21C132

Total 40

READING

0-6-0T	258, 260
0-4-4T	1183
4-4-0	1042, 1043, 1062, 1078, 1140, 1156, 1188, 1195
2-6-0	1610, 1611, 1620, 1628, 1807, 1850, 1857, 1860, 1861

Total 20

REDHILL

0-6-2T	2507, 2517, 2558, 2560
0-6-0	531, 533, 534, 537, 538, 539, 541, 547, 2435, 2441, 2450, 2522, 2541
4-4-0	1157, 1273, 1587, 1728, 1729, 1730
2-6-0	1814, 1815, 1816, 1818, 1849, 1852, 1863, 1864, 1890, 1891, 1892, 1893, 1894, 1895, 1896, 1897, 1898, 1899

Total 41

St. LEONARDS

0-4-4T	1135, 2371, 2379, 2383, 2394
0-6-0	1037, 1038, 1041, 1432, 1720
4-4-0	900, 901, 902, 903, 904, 905, 906, 907, 908, 909, 910, 1075, 1101, 1339, 1737, 1740, 1744, 1766, 1767, 1768

Total 30

SALISBURY

0-6-0T	237, 279
0-4-4T	10, 13, 41, 243, 361, 675
0-8-0T	957
0-6-0	315, 317, 355, 690, 691, 3441
4-4-0	117, 122, 127, 285, 288, 310, 312, 314, 382, 388, 389, 405, 421, 432, 709, 715, 721, 727, 729
0-4-2	652, 654
2-6-0	1612, 1618, 1626, 1630, 1636, 1846, 1848, 1872, 1873
4-6-0	330, 331, 332, 333, 334, 335, 448, 449, 450, 451, 452, 453, 454, 455, 456, 457, 475, 476, 744, 745, 746, 747, 748, 828, 829, 830, 831, 832
4-6-2	21C6, 21C7, 21C8, 21C9, 21C10, 21C148, 21C149, 21C150, 21C151, 21C152

Total 83

STEWARTS LANE

0-4-0ST	3458
0-4-0T	1302
0-4-4T	1005, 1177, 1184, 1259, 1263, 1266, 1295, 1311, 1319, 1321, 1329, 1554, 1661, 1706, 1710
0-6-0T	1602, 1604, 2100, 2101, 2102, 2103, 2104, 2105, 2106, 2107
4-4-2T	2081, 2082, 2090, 2091
2-6-4T	1912, 1914, 1915
0-6-0	1293, 1380, 1434, 1497, 1498, 1508, 1575, 1576, 1578, 1582, 1681, 1683, 1690, 1694, 1712, 1714, 1716, 1717, 1718, 1719, 1722
4-4-0	1019, 1067, 1145, 1160, 1163, 1165, 1179, 1217, 1247, 1445, 1446, 1454, 1459, 1492, 1494, 1504, 1506, 1507, 1511, 1514, 1515, 1516, 1736, 1743, 1745, 1749, 1760, 1764, 1765, 1769
2-6-0	1410, 1411, 1412, 1810, 1811, 1812, 1813, 1900, 1901, 1902, 1903, 1904, 1905, 1906, 1907, 1908, 1909, 1910
4-6-0	763, 764, 765, 775, 776, 778, 780, 781, 782, 783, 793, 794, 795, 796, 797, 798, 799, 800, 801, 802
4-6-2	21C133, 21C134, 21C135, 21C136, 21C137, 21C138, 21C139, 21C140

Total 131

SOUTHAMPTON DOCKS

0-4-0T	81, 85, 86, 89, 90, 93, 95, 96, 97, 98, 101, 102, 147, 176
0-6-0T	2122, 2156, 2162, 2689

Total 18

THREE BRIDGES

0-6-2T	2400, 2405, 2465, 2484, 2497, 2516, 2518, 2519, 2520, 2572, 2577, 2585, 2593
4-4-2T	2002, 2007, 2598, 2599, 2602, 2604
0-6-0	2303, 2436, 2445, 2451, 2527, 2529, 2532, 2545, 2552, 2553
2-6-0	2352, 2353

Total 31

TONBRIDGE

0-6-0T	2113, 2129, 2138, 2145
0-4-4T	1193, 1320, 1327, 1503, 1518, 1519, 1540, 1543, 1670, 1671, 1672, 1675, 1700, 1703, 1704, 1707, 2367, 2370, 2374, 2378
0-6-2T	2488, 2503, 2580
0-6-0	1048, 1063, 1086, 1150, 1219, 1221, 1225, 1227, 1272, 1370, 1396, 1437, 1461, 1486, 1513, 1580, 1588, 1590, 1593, 1686, 1715
4-4-0	1057, 1488, 1490, 1586, 1591, 1731, 1732, 1733, 1734, 1738, 1761, 1762, 1763
2-6-0	1822, 1876, 1877

Total 64

TUNBRIDGE WELLS WEST

0-4-2T	2215
0-4-4T	2366, 2389, 2390, 2393, 2398
0-6-2T	2512, 2581, 2582, 2589, 2590, 2591
4-4-2T	2001, 2003, 2004, 2006, 2021, 2022, 2023, 2025, 2026, 2027, 2028, 2029, 2030, 2078, 2083, 2603
4-6-2T	2325, 2326

Total 30

WADEBRIDGE

2-4-0T	3298, 3314, 3329
0-4-4T	181, 203
4-4-0	703, 717

Total 7

YEOVIL TOWN

0-6-0T	238, 276
0-4-4T	58, 129
4-4-0	134, 143, 145, 152, 163, 303, 340, 344, 412, 702, 710, 712, 714
2-6-0	1790, 1791, 1792, 1793, 1794, 1795

Total 23

LYNTON AND BARNSTAPLE (narrow gauge)

| 2-4-2T | 762 *Lyn*. |
| 2-6-2T | 759 *Yeo*, 760 *Exe*, 761 *Taw*, 188 *Lew*. |

Total 5

UNALLOCATED AWAITING CONVERSION TO OIL FUEL BURNING

At Fratton

| 4-4-0 | 396, 402, 403, 404, 413, 414, 731, 732, 733 |

Total 9

At Eastleigh

| 2-6-0 | 1830, 1859, 1862, 1635, 1637, 1638 |

Total 6

At Eastleigh Works

| 4-4-0 | 305 |

Total 1

ON LOAN TO THE KENT AND EAST SUSSEX RAILWAY

| 0-6-0T | 2678 |
| 0-6-0 | 3440 |

Total 2

Salisbury shed in 1947.
H.C. Casserley